The Pocket Book of

GREAT OPERAS

THE POCKET BOOK OF

GREAT OPERAS

by

Henry W. Simon

and

Abraham Veinus

Illustrated by LOUIS GLANZMAN

Collector's Edition

POCKET BOOKS, INC., NEW YORK

CONTENTS

FOREWORD

THERE IS AT LEAST one popular and totally erroneous myth which we hope may be partially buried in dishonor with the aid of this little book. That myth runs as follows: Grand opera, conceived as dramatic entertainment, consists largely of over-upholstered females complaining noisily in foreign languages to or about their scandalously unromantic-looking lovers. It is never possible to understand just why they are complaining or just what the answers to those complaints are. But that is a good thing. For if one were ever to try to unravel the stories behind these loud complaints by reading a translation of the words, one would encounter idiotic stories about impossible people whose unbridled passions (and passions are *never* bridled in opera) can bear no conceivable relationship to life as we know it—the Lord be praised.

The obvious fact is that all opera composers have to be highly trained men of considerably more than average intelligence. It takes many years of training and a peculiarly complex type of intelligence to be able to write *any* operatic score (let alone a good one) with the requisite understanding of what the many different voices and orchestral instruments can and cannot do and the mastery of harmony, counterpoint and all the other technicalities involved in preparing even a simple score.

Since the time of Gluck opera composers have considered their works primarily as vehicles for the dramatic stage—that is, as good stories revealed on a stage by singing actors with the assistance of an orchestra. Sometimes, of course, our composers made mistakes in judgment, just as the shrewdest of Broadway and Hollywood producers do. But that they tried their hardest to get good books for their music is revealed by the fact that Puccini took several times as long whipping the libretto of *La Bohème* into shape as he did composing the music, by Verdi's attention to every detail of the libretto of *Aïda* in his lengthy letters to the man who was writing it, by Wagner's and Leoncavallo's insisting on writing their own librettos in order to be sure to get worthy dramatic stories for their talents.

And the original sources to which these men went were often the most obvious sources for good stories —stories that had captured the imaginations of thousands before them. Wagner went mostly to the powerful ancient Norse myths; Gounod used the legend of Faust, which had appealed to dozens of authors before him; Puccini, in *Madame Butterfly* and *Tosca*, went to the popular dramatic hits of his day; Bizet went, for *Carmen*, to a thoroughly fascinating French novelette, and so on.

These fine stories had, for operatic stage purposes, to be altered—mostly made shorter and more compact; for singing speech is slower than any other, and an opera should not last longer than the hours between dinner and bedtime. The alterations were often an improvement over the original. *Carmen*, for instance, in Mérimée's tale, begins with a long and un-exciting account of how the author happened to be in Spain on a pseudo-scientific expedition when he happened to run across a particularly interesting fe-male criminal. This is all happily cut out in the operat-ic version, while an addition is made in the form of the simple village girl Micaëla, who provides an ex-cellent dramatic foil to Carmen herself. Most of Goethe's profoundest philosophy is cut out of the libretto of *Faust* because it would make long-winded, undramatic stuff set to music.

Sometimes, as I have said, the composer's judgment seems to have faltered. Verdi, for instance, went through a period when he suffered from an unac-countable admiration for second-rate Spanish trage-dies. *Il Trovatore* is one of the results, and there are few murkier bits of storytelling available anywhere than that. While it is almost impossible, without some guidance, to follow this story from the stage action alone, even here there is a power in each individual scene that has made the work one of the most popu-lar in all operatic literature.

For it is the peculiar power of music drama to pro-ject its passions more forcefully and more compel-lingly than any other form of art. All the stories we have to tell in this book have that quality—and most of them have also the advantage of being first-rate stories in their original form. To read our retellings of these tales is in no way a substitute for hearing them—and seeing them—on the stage. What we have tried to do is to describe what happens on the stage, to give the stories blow by blow as it were, and to give a hint as to the effect the music has in projecting them. We have never been technical in describing the music, and we have avoided interruption of the story itself as much as possible by placing all the direct musical quotations in the back of the book. Thus, the reader who is musically literate may please his memory and receive some enlightenment by turning to the Thematic Guide at the indicated places; while the reader who cannot or does not care to be bothered by musical quotations may read the tales simply for their dramatic values, which we hope we have in some measure preserved. The book may, of course, be used for study or to follow radio or phonographic performances, but it is our fondest hope that it may simply be enjoyed for itself.

A word of appreciation for our artist collaborator, Louis Glanzman. Mr. Glanzman read the stories, he listened to the music of the operas, he became enchanted (as every sensitive person must) with the art form, and he has drawn some of the finest illustrations for these works that there are. His pictures are not literal representations of what happens on operatic stages the world over. Rather, they are pictures of what would be seen on those stages if a fine, imaginative impresario were to engage the best-looking singers and the most gifted stage directors and scenic artists he could find. Strange as it may seem, some modern stage productions actually do approach this ideal.

H.W.S.

The Pocket Book
of Great Operas

AÏDA

AN OPERA IN FOUR ACTS

by Giuseppe Verdi

Cast

AÏDA	Soprano
RADAMES	Tenor
AMNERIS	Contralto
AMONASRO	Baritone
RAMPHIS	Bass
THE KING	Bass
MESSENGER	Tenor
VOICE OF A PRIESTESS	Soprano

PRIESTS, PRIESTESSES, SOLDIERS, SLAVES,
CAPTIVES, ATTENDANTS, CITIZENS

Libretto .... by Antonio Ghislanzoni
Time ... .Period of the Pharaohs' power
Place .. ..Memphis and Thebes

First Performance

Cairo, December 24, 1871

AÏDA

Prelude

T HE BRIEF PRELUDE begins softly in the violins with the theme usually played when
Aïda herself enters (No. 1).* This is followed by the ominous, magisterial theme
associated with the priests of Isis (No. 2), Aïda's un-
witting enemies. The Aïda theme is briefly developed,
and after a climax the Prelude fades to a quiet ending.

Act 1

The setting is the great hall of the palace of a king
of Memphis. In the back is a large gate, beyond which
can be seen the giant pyramids and Egyptian palaces
and temples. On one side of the hall are huge colon-
nades and the entrance to the temple of Isis. Ramphis,
the high priest, is in solemn conversation with
Radames, a young officer. He tells him that there is
a report that the Ethiopians are again attacking

---

*Thematic Guide, p. 308.

Thebes and the valley of the Nile. Isis, adds Ramphis, looking significantly at Radames, has already chosen the young and mighty soldier who is to lead the Egyptians in battle.

As the high priest solemnly leaves to make his report to the King, Radames begins the famous aria "Celeste Aïda" (No. 3), in which he expresses his love for the beautiful Ethiopian captive who is now the personal servant of the Princess Amneris, daughter of the King. The aria ends with the wish that he may be able to return Aïda to her own country and there build a throne for her near the sun itself.

A melody suggesting both the regal bearing and the intense femininity of the Princess announces the entrance of Amneris (No. 4). The young soldier is so completely lost in revery that he notices her only when she remarks on the joy that seems to transfigure his face. Then, in what is virtually an unashamed declaration of love, she adds that the woman who could call up such joy would certainly be an enviable person. Radames hastily assigns the emotion to the hope he has of being chosen general, but Amneris suspects a quite different motivation, and persists in asking him if some gentler desire has not prompted the look. Radames' expression tells her that if there is such a gentler desire, its cause is not Amneris.

Then the slave herself enters, announced by the gentle Aïda theme in the orchestra (No. 1). Amneris immediately senses that this is her rival. However, she turns at once to Aïda to welcome her—not as a slave, she says, but as a sister—and asks, with feigned concern, why she is weeping. Aïda replies that it is the prospect of war with her native land that has upset her. Amneris, however, sees through her just as easily as she had seen through Radames, while they, in turn, immediately sense her suspicions. Here an eloquent trio develops.

A fanfare now announces the entrance of Ramphis, accompanied by the King and a large portion of the army and the priesthood. As all assemble in the great hall, a messenger arrives and reports excitedly that the Ethiopians have invaded Egypt and have laid waste the crops; that Thebes is already resisting the invader; and that the Ethiopians are led by a fierce, indomitable warrior named Amonasro. Everyone recognizes his name—that of the King of the Ethiopians. As Aïda, in an aside, murmurs that it is her father, the crowd excitedly calls for battle. The King quiets them by announcing that Isis has chosen Radames to be Egypt's leader, and he orders the young warrior to go at once to the temple of Vulcan, god of weapons, to be armed for holy battle.

Led by the King, all join in a solemn, marchlike tune, calling on all Egyptians to defend the sacred Nile (No. 5). Aïda stands aside, her voice soaring above all the rest as she gives vent to her conflicting emotions. Whom is she to pray for? Her own countrymen? Or the man she loves, who is about to go to fight them? The music rises triumphantly to a series of shouts for battle, and then the Princess turns to Radames and sings proudly "Return as Conqueror!" *(Ritornà vincitor!)* (No. 6). The crowd marches off to the majestic measures of the King's call to battle.

Aïda is left alone in the great hall, and, with dramatic irony, she repeats Amneris' "Ritorna vincitor!" In a long, difficult aria, in which one magnificently appropriate melody follows another, she prays first for the safety of her father; then, recalling what his triumph would mean to Radames, finally ends with a pitiful, heartfelt prayer to the gods to have pity on her (No. 7).

(Scene 2) In the deep, dimly lighted temple of Vulcan, pillars stretch back into invisible distance. A high altar is in the middle, statues of various deities stand on the side, and golden tripods with incense smoking lend a dim, religious glow. The priests are gathered for the ceremony, while from the distance the voices of priestesses in prayer are heard (No. 8). As the priests chant solemnly, the dance of the priestesses takes place before the altar.

Now Radames enters. A silver veil is placed over his head, and the high priest presents him with an anointed sword, after which he begins a prayer to the gods for the protection of Egypt's sacred soil (No. 9). Radames and the priests repeat the prayer, the music reaching a dramatic climax. The ceremony ends with a solemn invocation to Ptah.

Act 2

On a terrace outside the apartments of Amneris, the Princess voluptuously reclines on a couch while female slaves prepare her for the ceremonies of triumph scheduled for the victorious return of Radames and his army. The women sing the praises of the warrior—in gentle rather than martial strains—and add that their songs are also about love. At the conclusion of each of the three stanzas, Amneris sings a slow, expressive descending phrase, like a great sigh of impatient love.

Seeing Aïda approaching, Amneris quickly dismisses her slaves, revealing in an aside that she means to find out whether her suspicions about Aïda's love are well founded. Then she greets her handmaiden compassionately, promising anything she wants to ease the sorrow she must feel. Nothing, says Aïda, can make her happy so far from her native land, ignorant of her father's and brothers' fate. Still, suggests Amneris, time may heal that sorrow should she fall in love. The suggestion has the expected effect. In an aside, Aïda sings of her love (No. 1), while the Princess, seeing the force of the emotion she has aroused, is surer than ever that her suspicions are correct.

Amneris invites her slave to confide in her: then she goes on to report that Radames has been killed by the Ethiopians. Aïda cries out sorrowfully, saying that she will weep for him forever. The passion with which she utters her cry completely convinces Amneris. She abandons her compassionate tone and accuses Aïda directly of being in love with Radames, and then tells her that he lives. The rapturous "Thank God" that greets this news forces Amneris to put their rivalry into words: she, the Pharaoh's daughter, is Aïda's rival.

Hopelessly, the handmaiden kneels before her mistress, begging for pity, but Amneris responds with threats of vengeance and hatred. Their voices rise together in a powerful duet which is suddenly interrupted by trumpets and the sound of voices singing triumphantly in the distance. The duet comes to a climax as Amneris commands her slave to follow her to the ceremonies and see whether she has any chance of being a successful rival. The Princess regally sweeps off, while Aïda remains behind long enough to utter once more her pitiful prayer to the gods (No. 7).

(*Scene 2*) The scene is a great avenue at an entrance to the city of Memphis, on one side of which is the Theban temple of Ammon, and on the other a throne with a purple canopy. Warriors, priests, dancers crowd the street. Finally the King himself appears, leading Amneris to the throne as the crowd sings a victorious welcome (No. 10). A dance of victory is performed, after which a brass band plays the familiar Triumphal March (No. 11).

The final part of the procession is headed by Radames drawn in a chariot. The King descends to greet the savior of the people, and Amneris places a crown upon his head. Anything Radames asks will be

9

granted, says the King, and the first request is to have the prisoners brought forth. Last among the captives, wearing a lionskin and two large horns on his head to show his rank of office, comes Amonasro. Aïda rushes to him with a cry, but in a quick aside he tells her not to betray his name or his real rank.

The King calls Amonasro to step forward, and Amonasro identifies himself simply as a man who has fought, and who in defeat sought vainly for death. Then, with a fierce, regal dignity, he begins what is perhaps the most overpowering ensemble in all grand opera (No. 12). He reports that the King of Ethiopia has been killed in the battle and swears angrily that if fighting for one's fatherland is a crime, they are all ready for death; yet, he adds softly, let the King now show mercy. His plea is echoed by the prisoners and Aïda, but Ramphis and the priests demand death for all of them. The prisoners cry for mercy, and finally the King and other Egyptians join in on the side of clemency. Meanwhile, Radames has eyes only for Aïda, and Amneris once more notes that her rival is being preferred. All these conflicting passions are expressed simultaneously, and the mounting music makes an unforgettable pattern of sound.

Now Radames steps forward and requests that all the Ethiopians be freed. Ramphis objects, the priests concurring. But the general population favors leniency, and Ramphis proposes a compromise: let the common prisoners be free, but let Aïda's father be held. The King agrees to this solution, and then turns to Radames and proclaims that he shall marry Amneris and rule after him. While Radames remains silent, the slaves and the people join in a chorus praising Egypt for its clemency and its victory (No. 10).

Radames and Aïda, recovering from the shock of the King's announcement, secretly express their consternation, while Amneris turns from her private triumph over her rival to express her joy in being promised to Radames. Amonasro, in the general rejoicing going on about him, tells Aïda that all hope for the fatherland is not lost, and the curtain comes down with a surge of stirring music.

Act 3

It is the night before Amneris and Radames are to be married. Palm trees line the banks of the Nile, which can be seen at a distance glistening in the moonlight. On one side on a hill of granite rocks stands the temple of Isis, from which can be heard the solemn chanting of priests and priestesses.

A boat glides up to the banks of the river, for Ramphis is leading Amneris to the temple to pray to Isis the night before her marriage. They are attended by veiled women and guards. As all disappear into the temple, Aïda, heavily veiled, arrives to keep a secret rendezvous with Radames. If he plans only to tell her goodbye, she says, she will drown herself in the Nile. In her second great aria *(O Patria Mia)* (No. 13), she gives voice to her other fierce longing —that for her native land.

Suddenly Amonasro appears. Knowing that Radames and his daughter are deeply in love, he has evolved a plan by which they may all escape. Together Aïda and her father sing warmly of their native land. Aïda prays that they may return home once more, and Radames now tells her that it may be possible—for the Ethiopians are ready to strike again. All they need to know is the path by which the enemy is prepared to march—and this Aïda must discover from Radames.

The young girl immediately recoils in horror at the suggestion that she betray her lover. Amonasro is enraged by her refusal. With great violence he repulses her and describes the attack of the Egyptians, the destruction and death that will come to the Ethiopian towns. Ignoring his daughter's pleas for mercy, he throws her to the ground, crying that she is not his daughter, but a slave of the Pharaohs.

Slowly Aïda drags herself to her feet, and quietly consents to do what he asks. Then her father, in a broad, noble melody (No. 14), takes her to his heart, bidding her think of the great service she is doing her people. Very, very softly Aïda sighs how dear her love of country costs her. Amonasro, hearing Radames approach, leaves her with a final word of encouragement.

Radames' first phrase is a burst of rapture on seeing Aïda once more. When she reminds him that he will be marrying Amneris the next day, Radames tells her that war is once more in the offing, and that he will again lead the Egyptians against their enemies; then, when he returns victorious, he will tell the King of his desire to marry Aïda. Once more Aïda reminds him of Amneris, who will most certainly give vent to revenge. However, if he really loves her, there is a way out. She sings him a ravishing description of the new country to which they could go together (No. 15). But Radames cannot visualize himself deserting his own country—the country he has fought for, the country that has given him his first taste of glory, the sky that has looked over their love.

Aïda is desperate, and she finally tells Radames to leave, to marry Amneris, to forget about her and her father. Radames' determination begins to weaken. Finally he agrees to run off with Aïda to her own land. As they are about to leave, she asks what way they will take to avoid the military. Radames falls into the trap and betrays the path by which the Egyptians are to attack the enemy. At this Amonasro jumps from his hiding place and triumphantly announces that he will place his men at the path—the gorges of Napata—and he reveals himself to the warrior as the king of the Ethiopians. Radames cries despairingly over his lost honor, while Aïda tries desperately to comfort him.

As Amonasro is trying to drag off the reluctant Radames, Amneris comes from the temple, followed by Ramphis and the guards. The Ethiopian king attacks Amneris with his dagger, but Radames stops him and urges him to flee with his daughter. Then, as Ramphis orders the soldiers to capture the fleeing pair, Radames turns to him and, with a despairing but heroic gesture, offers his sword in surrender.

Act 4

It is now the day on which Radames is to be tried for treason. In a passage near his cell, Amneris is waiting. Through this passage Radames and the priests who are to try him will pass, and from it Amneris can see into the hall of justice. In an attempt to make one final effort to save his life, Amneris commands the guards to bring the prisoner to her.

The Princess begs the doomed man to defend himself, but he replies coldly that he has no interest at all in living. She tells him that she can save him by pleading with her father, but she will do this only if he promises never to see Aïda again as long as he lives. Radames replies that he will gladly go to his death, knowing that he has given his life for Aïda's. He now learns for the first time that she has escaped, although Amonasro has been killed. Baffled by such strength of will, Amneris cries that heaven will see that she gets revenge for her suffering. Completely overcome by his obstinacy, she sinks to the ground, and Radames is led off by the guards.

The solemn, relentless theme of the priests is heard (No. 2), and Amneris, covering her face with her hands and choking with remorse, moans that by her jealousy, she herself has sealed the prisoner's doom. The priests file across the stage on their way to the judgment hall below. As they chant an unaccompanied prayer that the gods may kindle their hearts with the light of justice, Radames is led from the opposite side into the hall of justice to hear his fate.

The brief trial begins. The high priest accuses Radames first of deserting camp the day before battle, and second, of betraying his country, his king, and his honor. After each accusation, the priests call upon him to exonerate himself. Both times there is complete silence except for a low, ominous rumbling in the drums; both times Amneris despairingly calls on the gods to save him.

Then the priests, led by Ramphis, pronounce sentence: Radames, guilty of treason, is to be buried alive beneath the altar of the god he has failed to honor. Solemnly the priests come up from the judgment hall, their hands folded across their chests, and call out, "Traitor!" "Traitor!" "Traitor!" Amneris confronts them angrily, cursing them for condemning an innocent man, for violating all the laws of earth and heaven. Her rage has no effect on them, for even after they have filed off, they are heard repeating their condemnation of Radames, while Amneris works herself up to a wild fury with her vain curses upon them.

(*Scene 2*) The last scene shows two levels. Below is a small, dark crypt into which Radames has just been led to suffer his uncomfortable death, while above is the interior of the temple of Vulcan, with large statues of Osiris brightly lighted. Two priests are setting in place the stone that covers the crypt below.

Resignedly, Radames breathes a soft wish that Aïda may be happy wherever she is and never hear of his horrible end. Then he hears a sigh, and sees what he first takes to be a vision. But it is no vision: somehow Aïda has managed to creep into the tomb ahead of Radames. Passionately, but with great tenderness, Radames cries out against the horror that one so beautiful should die on account of him. Aïda, however, experiences none of this remorse. Above, the priests and priestesses chant their praise of Ptah—the same chant that had been used to bless Radames before he went to battle (No. 8). Using all his remaining strength, Radames tries to move the stone above him—but he cannot—and the chanting goes on.

Now Aïda sings her last, beautiful farewell to earth (No. 16). Radames joins her; and as their voices rise in this supremely moving ending, Amneris comes into the temple above, throws herself on the stone covering the crypt, and murmurs a final prayer for her beloved Radames. Below, her rival quietly dies in his arms as the priests relentlessly continue their chanting.

The Barber
of Seville

THE BARBER OF SEVILLE

(Il Barbiere di Siviglia)

AN OPERA IN TWO ACTS

by Gioacchino Antonio Rossini

Cast

COUNT ALMAVIVA	Tenor
BARTOLO	...Bass buffo
ROSINA	...... Soprano
FIGARO	...... Baritone
BASILIO	....Bass
FIORELLO	...... Baritone
AMBROGIO	... Bass
BERTA	Soprano

Libretto .... by Cesare Sterbini
(based on Pierre de Beaumarchais' play)

Time . ... Eighteenth century

Place . ... Seville

First Performance
Teatro di Torre Argentina, Rome,
February 20, 1816

THE BARBER
of
SEVILLE

Overture

A FAVORITE concert piece, the Overture is, after a slow introduction, so full of wit and high spirits that one may imagine it was written especially for this witty and high-spirited comic opera. Early critics, in fact, amused themselves by fancying they saw portrayals of the various characters of the opera in its Overture.

Actually, Rossini, a notoriously lazy fellow, had written this Overture seven years earlier for another comic opera entitled *L'Equivoco stravagante*. Subsequently he used it again for a couple of serious operas entitled *Aureliano in Palmira* and *Elisabetta, reghina d'Inghilterra*. For introducing the woes of Queen Elizabeth, this jolly piece could not have sounded very appropriate; but it serves admirably for *The Barber*, and its essential gaiety is both implicit and explicit in its two principal themes (Nos. 1 and 2).* The Overture, now lost, that Rossini wrote for the

---

*Thematic Guide, p. 311.

première, could scarcely have set the tone for the opera any better, even though it was based on Spanish songs.

Act 1

The curtain rises upon an open court in Seville. Old Dr. Bartolo's house, windows barred and blinds drawn, is on one side. Here Rosina, his lovely young ward whom he hopes to marry, is kept well secluded. It is near dawn and a group of musicians led by Fiorello, the Count Almaviva's servant, enter on tiptoe. While they are cautioning one another to be silent, Almaviva enters, confers with Fiorello concerning the arrangements, and then offers his beloved Rosina a florid serenade in praise of the dawn (No. 3).

Rosina fails to appear, however, and Almaviva, discouraged, hands his purse to Fiorello, who distributes money among the musicians. His liberality provokes an interminable chorus of thanks. Eager to be rid of them, and fearful that their uproar will awaken the neighborhood, Almaviva is finally compelled to drive them off. He glances up again toward the window, and then dismisses Fiorello; for he is determined to wait until Rosina appears as she has upon former mornings. When she does, there will be no need of a witness.

These predawn performances have been going on for some time now. The Count is convinced that Rosina has seen him and is aware of his love. He observes (for the audience's benefit, no doubt) that he fully intends to make her his Countess.

Someone is heard singing merrily off stage. Deeming it prudent to remain unobserved, Almaviva ducks under some arches and watches as the newcomer bounds onto the stage strumming his guitar and singing the boisterous *Largo al factotum* (No. 4).

It is Figaro, and the burden of his famous song is the wonderful life of a barber. He commands not only razors, lancets, combs, and scissors, but all the implements relating to the business he conducts privately for cavaliers and their young ladies. Day and night, both young and old crowd about him. One wants his beard trimmed, another, to be bled; this one needs a peruke, that one, a love letter made to order. He is, in short, the factotum of the town, always amused, and with a doubloon—the fruit of his reputation—always in his pocket. Not a girl in all Seville, he boasts, can find a husband without Figaro's help.

Almaviva and Figaro catch sight of each other. After a moment, during which each wonders apart who the other can be, mutual recognition results. The Count cautions that he must, for the while, remain incognito. A word to Figaro is sufficient. Almaviva observes that Figaro has prospered. "On starvation," replies the barber. "Rascal!" exclaims the Count. "Thank you, sir," counters Figaro politely.

The Count confides that he has fallen in love with the young lady who lives in yonder house, and whom he supposes to be the daughter of the dried-out old doctor. This is a situation made to order for Figaro. For in that house he is, among other things, barber, surgeon, herbalist, chemist, and confidential agent.

Moreover, he explains, Rosina is Bartolo's ward, not his daughter.

Rosina appears just then on the balcony, and the two retire under the portico to observe her. She has a letter for her persistent serenader, and is disappointed that she cannot see him anywhere about. Below, the Count mutters his ardent adorations into Figaro's sympathetic ear. Bartolo, who has stepped out on the balcony, instantly notices the paper; but Rosina puts him off with the assurance that it contains only the words of an aria from the latest comic opera, *Vain Precaution.*

While Figaro and the Count commend her wit in whispers, Bartolo delivers a musty tirade against the inanity, barbarousness, and degeneracy of modern music. Rosina has apparently spotted her worshiper, for she drops the letter, promptly sends Bartolo down to retrieve it, signals to the Count to pick it up (which he does), and then informs Bartolo, upon his arrival in the street below, that the wind has unfortunately carried it off. His suspicions aroused, Bartolo orders her in, muttering that the balcony had best be walled up.

Rosina's note, which Figaro now reads to the Count, runs as follows:

"Your assiduous attentions have excited my curiosity. My guardian is shortly going out; as soon as you see him quit the house, devise some ingenious method of acquainting me with your name, circumstances, and intentions. I can never appear on the balcony without being haunted by the inseparable attendance of my tyrant. Be therefore assured that everything is arranged on my part for breaking his chains. The unhappy Rosina."

The Count demands instantly to know more about this tyrant. And as Figaro is explaining the doctor's plan to marry Rosina and to secure her money, old Bartolo himself emerges from the house ordering Rosina, within, to admit no one but a certain Don Basilio. He locks the door and rushes off muttering that his marriage plans had best be concluded as quickly as possible.

His instructions have, of course, been overheard. In response to the Count's question, Figaro explains who Basilio is: a crafty scoundrel, a matchmaker, an accomplished hypocrite, a seedy character always short of cash, and at present Rosina's music teacher. The Count considers such information worth having. As for his immediate plans, he intends to keep Rosina ignorant of his true name and rank. Beyond this he does not know what to do and asks Figaro for his help. But the barber defers discussion of the point. He has just noticed Rosina standing behind the curtains, and thrusting his guitar at the Count, urges him to oblige with a ballad.

The Count is somewhat flustered by the suddenness of Figaro's tactic, but he complies with a verse (No. 5) informing Rosina that his name is Lindoro and that he adores her. Since she is obviously pleased with the effort, Figaro urges another stanza upon him. In this one the Count expands upon Lindoro's lack of treasure or high position. He has only his

devotion to offer. Whether or not this is sufficient
they do not find out, for Rosina's answer is broken
in mid-sentence, apparently by someone's unexpected
entry into the room.

The Count, beside himself with frustration, implores Figaro to arrange a speedy meeting for him
with Rosina; but the barber's customary powers of
invention seem dulled. He will do what he can. It
takes the Count a moment to see the point. He assures Figaro that an ample supply of gold will be
forthcoming, whereupon the irrepressible barber delivers a rollicking invocation to the inspirational
power of that magic metal (No. 6).

His wits suddenly aflame, Figaro whips up a master
plan in which the Count is to be disguised as a soldier. A regiment is due to arrive that day. No one
can refuse to put the Army up, and the Count can
be billeted on Bartolo. The plan seems feasible, especially since it occurs to the Count that the Colonel
is his cousin. One idea leads to another, gold (as
Figaro explains) having "wondrous powers to en-
large one's views." Almaviva will turn up as a drunken
soldier, the better to allay possible suspicion of his
being an agent for himself.

They congratulate each other on the sagacity of
their plan, and are about to go their separate ways
when the Count remembers to ask Figaro for his
address. This Figaro details at considerable length:
the number, the street, a full description of the house
and of his window display. They agree that Figaro
will manage all the details, and that the Count will
bring with him a well-lined pocket.

While the Count sings in joyous anticipation of his bliss (No. 7), Figaro amuses himself with jubilant interpolations concerning his expected reward. They recheck the address in duet, review once more their respective expectations of pleasure, and part—the Count leaving, Figaro entering the doctor's house.

* *

Blinds are drawn in a room in Bartolo's house. Rosina, holding a letter she has just composed to her Lindoro, sings of his voice enshrined in her heart *(Una voce poco fa)* (No. 8). It is a favorite coloratura display piece. With many a fanciful roulade Rosina looks forward to her marriage with Lindoro, and enumerates her various qualifications as a wife. She modestly evaluates herself as gentle, devoted, humble, obedient—in short, a most loving creature, easily manageable, except when her will is crossed; in which event, she serves notice that a viperish temperament provides her with a thousand and one tricks to get her way. At the moment such confidence and cunning stand her in good stead, for she is resolved to outwit the Argus-eyed old doctor. A trusty messenger is a prerequisite and, remembering that she saw Figaro with her beloved, she decides to get in touch with the barber.

Just then Figaro enters with a message for Rosina, but before the customary amenities between them are over (he inquires why so lively a lass should appear so dispirited, and she tells him her troubles), they hear Bartolo's footsteps approaching. Rosina retires, Figaro hides, and Bartolo enters fussing and fuming over Figaro's strange antics. It appears that the barber has been plying his household with narcotics, bleedings, and anesthetics. He demands of Rosina whether she has seen the scoundrel, but her saucy replies give him little information and less comfort. He calls his two servants; but Berta, as a result of Figaro's ministrations, keeps incessantly sneezing, while Ambrogio has been given a narcotic and can do nothing but yawn.

Bartolo's only remaining comfort is Don Basilio, who now enters bowing very low, and with important news to impart concerning Rosina's mysterious admirer. He has not only identified him as the Count Almaviva, but he has at hand a plan which will dispose of the Count in three days. It consists simply in discrediting him through slander, a technique at which Basilio is a past master.

The famous slander song which he now sings (No. 9) is a masterpiece of text setting, the music suggesting in graphic detail every stage of calumny's progress from a gentle zephyr to a roaring tempest. However, even slander's swift progress seems slow to Bartolo. Under the circumstances he must have action immediately, and a quick drawing up of the marriage contract seems the only way out. Once safely married, Bartolo feels that Rosina will be more manageable—an opinion with which Basilio, in an aside, disrespectfully disagrees.

They leave, and Figaro emerges imparting to Rosina, who promptly joins him, the plan he has overheard. They both agree that Bartolo would cut an imbecilic figure as her husband. She inquires about the young man she saw Figaro talking to underneath her window. Figaro passes him off as his cousin, an excellent young man in every respect who will, unfortunately, never make his fortune because he is distracted with love. This interests Rosina. Does his cousin's young lady live far from here? No, rather close by. And is she beautiful? Very, declares Figaro, describing her as sixteen, round, dimpled, dark, and rosy cheeked. And her name? That seems to have slipped his mind, but recalling the syllables one by one he finally manages to remember that her name is Rosina. It has the desired effect. With many coloratura embellishments Rosina breathlessly wonders if this can really be true, although, she adds parenthetically, she really knew it all the time.

Figaro promises that Lindoro will be with her shortly, and suggests that a letter from her indicating that she is expecting him would help a good deal. However, the ceremony of maidenly modesty must be gone through first. After a series of ritual observations to the effect that it would be too forward on her part, and that she really could not do such a thing, she extracts the letter already written and hands it to Figaro. The barber shrugs, and while Rosina spins rapturous coloraturas about nothing in particular, Figaro observes that he ought to take lessons from her in cunning.

He leaves just before Bartolo enters, still upset over Figaro's peculiar doings. Has she seen the barber this morning? Yes, they talked about Parisian fashions and his daughter's illness. "And didn't he bring an answer to the letter you mailed through the window?" asks Bartolo. He points to the inkstain on her finger. Ink, she explains, is a recommended cure for a burned finger. He observes that there are only five sheets of paper now when there were six before. The extra sheet, she tells him, was used as wrapping for some sweets she sent along to Figaro's ailing daughter. And the recently used pen, which he now calls attention to, she employed to draw a flower on her embroidery.

Losing patience, Bartolo informs her in a pompous aria (No. 10) that such excuses cannot be accepted by a man of his distinction. He declares himself willing to hear an admission of deceit. But receiving no answer from Rosina, switches from pomposity to a comic, rapid-patter rage. He, Bartolo, in defense of her reputation, decrees perforce that she be locked in; lamentations are henceforth useless; not even a fly will squeeze through to visit her.

Rosina, replying with defiance, follows Bartolo out of the room. Now Berta, the servant, enters, still sneezing, and curious about the rumpus she could not help overhearing. There is a knocking at the door, which Berta opens admitting Almaviva, blustering in the disguise of a cavalry soldier. Bartolo bounces back annoyed with this intruder who, with drunken persistence, methodically reads every conceivable comic variant of Bartolo's name from the paper he is holding. When they straighten it out between them that the name is *Bartolo*, Almaviva falls on the doctor's neck and announces that he has been billeted upon him.

Rosina reappears, and in the ensuing trio all three characters talk simultaneously to themselves. Rosina tells herself that something is up. The Count wonders how long this will have to go on. And Bartolo makes himself increasingly miserable by reiterating that he really doesn't know what to do. Amid the confusion, the Count manages to let Rosina know that he is Lindoro. She is properly entranced and terrified. Bartolo catches sight of her and orders her back to her room, and the Count obligingly offers to go along.

Bartolo, now sure he has a madman on his hands, remembers his order of exemption and hurriedly produces it. It has no effect. With a drunken grandiloquence of gesture, Almaviva tosses the paper aside, and when Bartolo orders him to leave the house, solemnly declares himself challenged and prepares to fight with the doctor. Under cover of an elaborate designation of imaginary trenches, the Count whispers to Rosina to drop her handkerchief over a letter which he lets fall. She complies, and affecting to catch sight of the letter for the first time, Almaviva picks it up and hands both it and the handkerchief to her ceremoniously. Bartolo, of course, seizes the letter which Rosina insists is merely a washing list, and discovers to his amazement that what she says is true.

Almaviva has, in the meanwhile, continued shouting "Shoulder arms!" Berta enters, from one side, to announce that Figaro has arrived with a mob at his heels; while, from the other, Basilio appears placidly practicing his *do, re, me, fa, sol* amid the confusion. Determined to make the most of the trap into which Bartolo has been led, Rosina is now in tears. The doctor, properly contrite, trails after her offering apologies. But he is distracted by the Count, who persists in threatening him with drawn sword.

Figaro's entrance temporarily restores relative quiet, if not order. The whole neighborhood is outside, aroused by the din. But the announcement has no effect upon the Count, who continues to brandish his sword at Bartolo. The two are soon busy hurling insults at each other, and in the uproar which starts anew upon attempts to quiet the Count, soldiers enter, led by an officer of the Guard who demands to know what is going on. Everybody explains at once.

Since Almaviva appears to be a drunken soldier, the officer orders his arrest. But when the Count takes him aside and produces his insignia of nobility, the officer and his Guard promptly draw away. General bewilderment and confused protestations bring no explanation from the Guard. As the curtain falls, everybody on stage has joined in a brilliant nine-part chorus in which each, for his or her own private reasons, foresees only madness as the outcome of this impossible situation.

Act 2

Bartolo, seated in his own library (equipped with a harpsichord with some music on it), is voicing his conviction that the intoxicated soldier was one of Almaviva's agents. The Count re-enters, this time disguised as Don Alonzo, a pupil of Basilio. He wears the distinguishing habiliments of the learned—a black cloak and shovel hat. His master, he explains, is too ill to attend to Rosina's music lesson himself and has instructed Don Alonzo to substitute for him. This doesn't please Bartolo at all. Suspecting another of

Almaviva's maneuvers, he announces that they will both pay Basilio an immediate visit.

The Count pretends to fall into a rage and starts to leave, shouting something about the Count Almaviva. This is just the right bait and Bartolo swallows it eagerly. Detaining and placating the new music teacher, he worms from him some story about one of Rosina's letters, which Almaviva supposedly left behind in his lodgings and which the music teacher picked up. With genuine embarrassment (for this improvisation is turning out not at all to his liking) the music teacher suggests that the letter be shown to Rosina as proof of the Count's infidelity. The letter is, of course, genuine enough.

Bartolo recognizes Rosina's handwriting, and he also recognizes the newcomer as an authentic product of Basilio's famous school of slander. The Count is aware that there is grief in store for him with Rosina on account of this ill-conceived fabrication, but he hopes eventually to straighten matters out.

Bartolo fetches Rosina in for her music lesson. She exclaims upon seeing her Lindoro, but covers it up by saying that she has just sprained her ankle. The Count seats himself at the harpsichord and accompanies Rosina in an aria which she informs Bartolo is from *Vain Precaution.** Interpolated between verses are appeals from Rosina for help, and promises from the Count to rescue her. They congratulate Rosina upon her performance, but Bartolo finds this

---

*It has long been customary for sopranos to substitute, for Rossini's original music in this Lesson Scene, anything from *Home Sweet Home* to the most elaborate coloratura arias.

modern music rather tiresome, and performs for their edification one of the songs of his day. He turns and finds that Figaro, who has entered during his song, has been mimicking him behind his back.

Figaro has his basin under his arm all prepared to shave the doctor, but Bartolo is too busy today. Unfortunately, says Figaro, he cannot manage it on any other. Consulting his appointment book, Figaro checks off the Marchesa Andronica whose wig needs dressing, the Count Bombe whose hair must be curled, the lawyer Barnardone who must be ministered to for indigestion, and many many others. When Bartolo seems unimpressed with these commitments, Figaro draws himself up and with outraged dignity gives him to understand that he cannot thus trifle with so important a personage as a barber.

Bartolo submits. He hands Figaro the keys to go fetch the soap and towel, but immediately takes them back and decides to go himself. He is gone but a moment—time enough for Figaro to find out from Rosina which is the key to the balcony—but returns muttering that it is not safe to leave the barber with Rosina. He gives Figaro the keys again, and the barber is off, delighted with the readiness with which old Bartolo has played into his hands.

While Bartolo is smugly informing the Count that Figaro cannot outwit him, a crash of crockery is heard off stage. Bartolo rushes out, leaving Rosina and the Count to exchange expressions of mutual affection. Bartolo re-enters, cursing Figaro for the wreck of his dishes. He settles himself in his chair to be shaved. And the barber (after indicating to the

Count that he has obtained the key) just begins to work on the doctor when Don Basilio enters to give Rosina her music lesson.

Amid a confusion of questions, exclamations, and cross-questions, nothing emerges clearly except Basilio's increasing disorientation. Everyone except Bartolo assures him he looks ghastly, and demands to know why he ventured out of bed. The poor fellow feels fine, but Figaro quickly diagnoses a case of scarlet fever, and the Count, observing that he could do with a strong tonic, hurriedly slips him a purse. During these persuasions they manage to keep Bartolo distracted: Figaro by shaving him whenever he can, and the Count by enjoining him not to press Basilio for intelligent answers since he knows nothing of the letter. In a most amusing quintet (No. 11), Basilio allows himself to be trundled off to bed by the other four.

Figaro resumes shaving the doctor, standing over him so as to shield the lovers from view. Under pretense of studying some music, Almaviva arranges with Rosina to be ready to elope with him at midnight. But just as he has begun to explain about the use to which he had put her letter, Bartolo overhears them. The deception uncovered, the best they can do is to attempt to quiet the doctor's ravings as they leave the stage.

Bartolo hastily summons Berta and Ambrogio, his servants. The latter he sends to fetch Basilio, and Berta he orders to watch the door. But he decides that he cannot trust her either, and goes off himself to see that no other intruder enters, leaving Berta alone on stage to sing a pretty aria (No. 12) about the foolishness that possesses people who are determined to get married.

She leaves as Bartolo re-enters with Basilio, who is sure that Alonzo was Almaviva himself, and not merely one of his emissaries. Bartolo wants the lawyer here tonight to draw up the marriage contract, but Basilio tells him that the lawyer has already been engaged for tonight to draw up a contract for Figaro's niece. Since Figaro has no relatives, Bartolo is more than ever insistent that Basilio arrange matters immediately.

Basilio leaves, and Bartolo, remembering the letter the Count has given him, calls Rosina. Using the letter as evidence—it is hers and was found in Almaviva's lodging—he convinces her that Figaro and Alonzo (her Lindoro) are in league to betray her to the vile Count Almaviva. This is the first Rosina has heard of any Count. Swearing vengeance upon Lindoro for his treachery, she promises to marry Bartolo forthwith and reveals to him the plans afoot for her elopement.

An orchestral interlude covers the passage of time and depicts the storm that is raging outside. Figaro and the Count enter through the balcony window just before Rosina appears and halts the Count's transports by denouncing him as a betrayer. The Count casts aside his cloak to reveal to her that Lindoro and Almaviva are one and the same person. She is properly enraptured, but Figaro, remarking that they are all three "almost dead with rapture," glances out of the window and sees two persons approaching with a lantern. A charming trio follows (No. 13), in which they caution one another to be quiet and decide to leave via the ladder outside the balcony.

The ladder has disappeared, however. Basilio now enters with the lawyer, expecting, of course, that Bartolo will be waiting for him. But the Count draws him aside, gives him a ring as a token of his protection, and informs him that there will be a bullet in his brain unless he co-operates. Basilio has no choice but to act with Figaro as a witness to the marriage which is immediately arranged.

Bartolo enters a moment too late, accompanied by an officer and a patrol of soldiers. He orders Figaro and the Count arrested as thieves, but Almaviva reveals himself and announces that he and Rosina are married. The Count obliges Bartolo with a richly ornamented aria in which he tells the old doctor that his power over Rosina is forever ended.

Bartolo admits defeat. He berates Basilio for betraying him, but Basilio assures him that the Count had a most persuasive implement in his pocket. The old doctor is especially aggrieved that it was through his own plotting (he removed the ladder) that he was undone. This, Figaro reminds him, is what comes of taking vain precautions. The Count generously tells Bartolo that he can keep Rosina's dowry, and the doctor, somewhat mollified, hopes that Heaven may see fit to bless their union. Figaro considers this well spoken and offers to embrace the old fellow. Then as the curtain falls, everybody joins in a general chorus of rejoicing.

La Bohème

LA BOHÈME

(The Bohemians)

AN OPERA IN FOUR ACTS

by Giacomo Puccini

Cast

RUDOLPH, A POET	Tenor
MARCEL, A PAINTER	Baritone
SCHAUNARD, A MUSICIAN	Baritone
COLLINE, A PHILOSOPHER	Bass
MIMI	Soprano
MUSETTA	Soprano
ALCINDORO	Bass
BENOIT, A LANDLORD	Bass
PARPIGNOL	Tenor
CUSTOM HOUSE SERGEANT	Bass

STUDENTS, WORKING GIRLS, CITIZENS, SHOP-
KEEPERS, STREET VENDORS, SOLDIERS, RESTAU-
RANT WAITERS, BOYS AND GIRLS

Libretto by Giuseppe Giacosa and Luigi Illica
(adapted from *La Vie de Bohème*
by Henri Murger)

Time	About 1830
Place	Paris

First Performance
Teatro Reggio, Turin, February 1, 1896

LA BOHÈME

Act 1

(*In the Attic*)

THE SETTING for the first act is a sparsely furnished attic in the Latin Quarter of Paris
on Christmas Eve. It is shared by four
friends: Rudolph, a poet; Marcel, a painter;
Schaunard, a musician; and Colline, a philosopher.
At the moment, only Rudolph and Marcel are on
stage, the former looking pensively out of a spacious
window at an expanse of snow-covered rooftops, the
latter at work on a masterpiece of sorts entitled "The
Passage of the Red Sea." It is a chilly subject and
Marcel, blowing on his fingers to keep them warm
enough to paint with, considers adding to the canvas
a drowning Pharaoh, by way of revenge.

Rudolph, watching smoke busily rising from other
people's chimneys, deplores the fact that their own
idle stove seems "content to live in ease like a lord"
(No. 1).* "It's a good long while," points out Marcel,
"since we paid his lawful wages." Out of the goodness of his heart, the painter offers to share with his
friend a profound thought which he has been mull-

---

*Thematic Guide, p. 314.

ing over for some time: to wit, that he is frozen. In point of fact, he adds, his fingers feel as if "they had been touching that iceberg . . . the heart of false Musetta." They exchange several prettily turned conceits on the nature of love, from which it is evident—although her name is mentioned no further—that the "false Musetta" is much on the painter's mind.

A fire must be started, at all costs, and in place of the rickety chair which Marcel proposes sacrificing, Rudolph pounces on the manuscript of his five-act tragedy. Marcel is willing to commit his "Red Sea" painting, but is overruled on the grounds of the stench its cremation would occasion. Reassuring Marcel that he does not mean to read it (for that, argues the painter, would only chill them), Rudolph declaims with tragic emphasis upon the great loss the world is about to sustain—and sets fire to the first act.

As they draw their chairs close to the fireplace, the door is thrown violently open and Colline enters, frozen and furious, with a heap of books which he dumps angrily upon the table. The pawnshops, it turns out, are all closed on Christmas Eve. A literary discussion ensues in which Colline praises the "sparkling" character of Rudolph's drama, but finds fault with its brevity. The second act, now added to the fire, is deemed colorful and ardent; but when the five acts have been consumed, the fickle critics turn on Rudolph with cries of "Down with the author!"

Just then two boys enter with food and fuel—of which they are promptly relieved, Colline carrying the wood to the fireplace, and the others taking over the provisions. Schaunard enters, triumphantly scattering on the floor a heap of coins which Marcel suspects are tin medals. But when Rudolph identifies and bows low before the portrait of Louis Philippe stamped upon them, the others, deeming it unbecoming for their king to lie thus humbly beneath their feet, pick up the money and then busy themselves arranging the table.

There is a story behind this stroke of good fortune, but Schaunard has no luck in getting his friends' attention. Amid a sustained crossfire of conversation and activity relating to the roast beef, the patty, and the conversion of a newspaper into a tablecloth so that food and news can be consumed simultaneously, Schaunard manages to let at least the audience know how he came by his wealth.

An English lord, it seems, required the services of a musician to provide an obnoxious parrot with such musical entertainment as would cause that dismal creature to lie down and die. For three days, relates Schaunard, his playing and singing proved vain. Then turning his charms upon the servant girl, he beguiled her out of a sprig of parsley which he fed to the parrot—who obligingly fell dead.

By now, the others are deep in the cold pastry which, however, Schaunard rescues for tomorrow's meal, exhorting them in the name of "a little religion" to celebrate Christmas Eve by drinking indoors, but dining out. Their landlord, Benoit, chooses this moment to come knocking on their door. There is no one home, calls Colline, and besides, adds Schaunard, the door is locked. Benoit pleads for a word and, when the door is opened for him, he pronounces it: "the rent."

Succumbing to their conviviality, old Benoit accepts a glass of wine and then another and another, until, considerably mellowed and thoroughly impressed by the money on the table, he allows himself to be complimented on the auburn-haired beauty he was seen with the other evening at the Mabille. It is not long before Benoit, acting the perfect old goat, is discoursing upon his taste in women. "I do not ask for a whale," he informs them, nor even for a world map or a full moon. But downright thin women he cannot abide. Neither their claws nor their tempers are reliable, and furthermore thin women are full of aches and grievances, in proof of which he cites his wife.

Immediately the four rise up in puritanical righteousness, one denouncing him for a reprobate, another declaring the attic polluted by his presence, a third advising fumigation with perfume, and all united in wishing the bewildered old fellow a Merry Christmas as they push him outside the door.

They now divide the money and make ready to leave for the Café Momus. But Rudolph must stay behind to finish an article for his new journal, the *Beaver*. He is enjoined to "cut short the Beaver's growing tale," which he promises to do. Holding a light for them as they descend the unreliable stairs, he calls after Colline, who has stumbled, to find out if he is still alive. Back in the attic he clears a space for himself at the table, but finds that he is in no humor to work.

A timid knock is heard, and a quiet voice from without asks pardon for the disturbance. Rudolph hurriedly opens the door and finds a slight, graceful girl standing pale and shy before him, her candle extinguished and a key in her hand. She has paused on her way to her room on the floor above to ask if her candle may be relighted. Breathless from the long climb, she is seized by a spasm of coughing, and Rudolph is just able to catch her as she falls into a faint. Somewhat embarrassed, he places her in a chair, sprinkles water on her face, and pours a glass of wine for her when she comes to. Neither her prettiness nor her pallor escapes him; and with reluctance and anxiety he relights her candle and escorts her to the door.

But the key dropped during her fainting spell is now missing (No. 2). As the draught from the open door soon extinguishes both their candles, they are presently on their knees in the dark, groping along the floor for the lost key. The conversation is desultory, charged with trivial exclamations and fragmentary remarks that reveal their growing attraction to each other.

Rudolph has managed to fasten the door, and to suppress an exclamation as he finds and surreptitiously pockets the key. Ultimately his hand touches hers in the dark and noting that it is frozen, he suggests that they discontinue their search for awhile. She remains silent, and when Rudolph releases her hand, she rises, finds a chair and sinks into it, obviously overcome with emotion.

Rudolph proceeds now to introduce himself. He is a poet, lacking in wealth but deeply appreciative of beauty, especially in women, and hence richer than all others on earth. At the moment, her bright eyes have driven his fancies from him (Nos. 3 and 3-a). With exquisite sweetness and simplicity she replies that she is called Mimi, although her name is really Lucia (No. 4). She earns a meager living by embroidering flowers on silks and satins, and the flowers give her pleasure, for they mean springtime and love (No. 5). Her song, grown for the moment rhapsodic, now relapses, and she makes once again a shy apology for having been so tiresome.

They are interrupted by shouts from the courtyard below. Rudolph's friends are growing impatient and they urge him not to delay. He opens the window, calls down that he is no longer alone, and urges them to go on ahead to the Café Momus and keep two places for them. He turns toward Mimi and, entranced by her appearance in the moonlight that now streams from the window, begins ecstatically to sing of her beauty. Her voice merges with his (Nos. 3 and 3-a)—the text now the power of love—and the duet concludes with a kiss. Rudolph suggests that they stay, but Mimi insists that his friends must not be kept waiting. They leave arm in arm. As the curtain falls, their voices are heard off stage raised in a mutual declaration of love.

Act 2

(*In the Latin Quarter*)

The curtain rises upon a crowded square in the Latin Quarter. Vendors are noisily shouting their wares, and gay crowds as noisily appraise and haggle over them. Street Arabs and young girls in groups wind through the festive mob, and waiters scurry in and out of the Café Momus, ministering both to the townsfolk seated at outside tables and to the boisterous customers within.

The four friends are separated for the moment, each pursuing his own amusement. Schaunard blows a horn he has just purchased and laments its execrable tone. Colline has his coat mended, extols its merits to the tailor, and then consigns to its vast and apparently innumerable pockets the books he has just acquired. Marcel goes from one group of girls to another declaring himself available. Rudolph admires the bonnet he has just bought for Mimi and promises that when the good God elects to take his millionaire aunt, Mimi will have a necklace far finer than the one which now catches her fancy. The two wander off in the crowd.

Schaunard, Marcel, and Colline, finding no room at the outside tables, glare furiously at the seated townsfolk and enter the café. Eventually they re-emerge carrying a table, followed by a waiter who supplies chairs. It is evident that the townsfolk find the trio somewhat too boisterous, for they soon vacate their places. Rudolph and Mimi wander back, and she is introduced by the poet to his friends, who receive her with a droll dignity compounded out of low bows and ceremonious Latin phrases.

A hawker named Parpignol crosses the stage, and while a group of distracted mothers try to disengage their children from the mob that assails the hawker and his wares, Mimi and the four friends proceed with the ordering of food and drink. Parpignol departs, followed by the urchin horde; the small talk at table continues pleasantly enough until a toast is proposed and Marcel grimly orders a phial of poison.

This abrupt change in mood is promptly explained by the appearance of Musetta, a pretty coquette, followed by her escort for the evening, a fussy, overdressed, pompous old gentleman named Alcindoro. The shop women gape while she orders Alcindoro about like a puppy. A vacant table, adjacent to the one at which the friends are seated, attracts her attention. Taking possession of it, she flounces around a bit, her annoyance growing more visible and articulate as Marcel, sitting with his back to her, studiously refuses to notice her. Mimi is impressed by her sumptuous attire.

In reply to her questions, Marcel finally grumbles that her name is Musetta, her surname Temptation. As for her vocation, like the rose, she has countless admirers. Musetta, overhearing this, remarks in an aside that if she could, she would scratch. By the time Marcel has come to comparing her with a screech owl, a most rapacious bird that feeds only upon the heart (as a case in point, his own has been devoured), Musetta's patience is at an end. A smashed plate relieves her feelings somewhat, but Marcel still refuses to turn around. This, plus Alcindoro's fussy remonstrances about her manners in public places, goads her into a fresh fury.

When the farce is at its height, Musetta switches her tactics and breaks into a waltzlike aria, obviously addressed to Marcel, in which she enlarges upon the general recognition of her charms (No. 6). Towards the end she addresses herself quite pointedly to him and taunts him with missing her more than he is willing to confess. Visibly affected by her aria he attempts to leave, but finds himself spellbound by her voice. Rudolph explains to Mimi that Marcel had once been Musetta's lover, but that she had forsaken him for wealthier victims.

In the ensuing quintet (Marcel alone is silent), Alcindoro tries to quiet Musetta who tells him to hold his tongue; Mimi expresses her sympathy for Musetta; Rudolph declares that dead love cannot be revived; while Schaunard assures Colline that if someone like Musetta should make eyes at him, he (Colline) would soon forget his moldy classics. Colline replies that as pretty as Musetta undoubtedly is, he would rather have his old pipe and a page of Homer.

Realizing that Marcel is ripe for reconciliation, and that Alcindoro had now best be dispensed with, Musetta pretends a violent pain in her foot which she coyly displays to the company. Her tight shoe, she exclaims hysterically, is killing her. Alcindoro unties it for her, and at her insistence rushes off to get another pair. It is plain to Mimi that Musetta still loves Marcel; although Rudolph, Schaunard, and

Colline are cynically agreed that this is a comedy, and truly a "stupendous" one. Inevitably Marcel and Musetta fling themselves passionately into each other's arms, and just as inevitably the waiter arrives with the bill.

Amid the general consternation—no one has any money, and Schaunard's purse has mysteriously disappeared—the sound of drums is heard off stage. While the stage fills with citizens, hawkers, shop girls, and street urchins eagerly awaiting the approaching soldiers' patrol, Musetta calls for Alcindoro's bill and blithely tells the waiter to present the two of them to the old man when he returns.

The patrol, when it appears, is greeted enthusiastically. Marcel and Colline, carrying Musetta who cannot walk without her shoe, fall in behind the patrol. After them come Rudolph and Mimi, arm in arm, then Schaunard blowing his horn, and finally the crowd, all marching in time to the music. Alcindoro arrives upon an emptied stage with the pair of shoes carefully packaged, only to be greeted by the double bill left him by Musetta. He looks at the amount and sinks into a chair, weary and dumfounded.

Act 3

(At the Tollgate)

The scene at the tollgate in one of the customs barriers in Paris is as bleak and dismal as the relationship that now exists among the lovers. Over a tavern (standing to the left) hangs Marcel's "Red Sea" masterpiece, now entitled in large letters "At the Port of Marseilles." Frescoes of a Zouave and a Turk adorn either side of the tavern door. Sounds of conviviality within contrast with the gray, gaunt trees which flank the tollgate square. Sundry custom house officials are seated snoring in front of a brazier. Several street scavengers, blowing desperately upon their frostbitten fingers, call loudly for admittance. It is the grimmest part of the Parisian winter (the end of February), and the officials are loath to bestir themselves away from the brazier. Eventually, to quiet the racket, one of the officials opens the gate for the scavengers and closes it again after they have passed into the rue d'Enfer.

Musetta's voice is heard from within the tavern, her waltz song (No. 6) rising above the chorus of male merrymakers. Groups of carters, peasant women, milkwomen come and go on stage, and shortly after Mimi appears, seemingly unsure of her whereabouts. (The orchestra, upon her entrance, sounds the initial phrase from No. 4). Recovering from a brief, though violent, coughing spell, she approaches the sergeant and inquires for the tavern where the painter is working. He points it out. And to the serving woman who now emerges, Mimi addresses an urgent plea to find Marcel for her.

When the painter appears, commenting dourly to Mimi upon the Zouave and the Turk which he paints these days for his and Musetta's keep, Mimi inquires after Rudolph. Upon learning that he is within, she pours out to Marcel the disquieting story of Rudolph's impossible jealousy. While she feels that he still loves her, he has lately taken to avoiding her.

Marcel advises a separation, to which Mimi agrees, imploring the painter's intercession to bring it about. Only the bond of gaiety, adds Marcel, keeps him and Musetta united. Motioning Mimi to the tavern window, he points to Rudolph who arrived before dawn exhausted and distraught, and who now lies sleeping on a bench. Another coughing spell assails her, and when Rudolph awakens, Mimi hastily conceals herself behind a tree.

Rudolph comes out on stage, greets Marcel, and announces bluntly that he wants to separate from Mimi. An avowal of love for her follows, and gives way to excited resentment over her flirtations. An occasional sarcasm from Marcel, to the effect that Rudolph can be tryingly jealous, choleric, and stubborn, scarcely breaks the flow of Rudolph's narrative. Poor Mimi is dying, he continues, and he feels a commingled grief and guilt for her failing health and for his inability, in his poverty, to provide for her properly. A violent coughing spell and her doleful exclamations ("Mimi must die") reveal her presence. But she refuses to allow Rudolph, now most solicitous and affectionate, to lead her into the tavern.

Musetta's brazen laughter from within reminds Marcel that he has a flirtatious woman of his own to watch over, and after he leaves, Mimi declares to Rudolph that she must leave him (No. 7). Her love and her life have not long to endure. The few possessions she values—a prayer book, a bracelet—she will send for. As for her little bonnet, perhaps he would care to keep it as a remembrance.

Their affecting duet is interrupted by the sound of plate-smashing in the tavern, Marcel's voice rising in accusation and Musetta's in denial. Both emerge to carry on their quarrel on stage, Marcel's recriminations provoking from Musetta assertions of her right to do as she pleases. Above this agitated dialogue, Rudolph and Mimi, grown gentle towards each other now that their parting is imminent, continue their enraptured duet. Ultimately Marcel and Musetta reach the stage of embittered name-calling. She flounces off, Marcel re-enters the tavern, and Rudolph and Mimi slowly move off, bidding each other farewell.

Act 4

(*In the Attic*)

In the interim between acts, the friends have been living lonely lives, and as the curtain rises to reveal the bleak attic of Act 1, both Marcel and Rudolph are seen presumably hard at work. Neither has much success in convincing the other of his absorption. The conversation is sporadic, although every remark is taken as an excuse to stop working.

Rudolph mentions a chance encounter with Musetta and a brief conversation he had with her. "How's your heart?" he reports asking the coquette. "It beats not," she replied, "or I don't feel it, thanks to this velvet I'm wearing." In his turn, Marcel tells of seeing Mimi in a carriage attired like a duchess. Both pretend to rejoice over the good fortune of their former sweethearts, although the one soon discovers that his pen is impossible to write with, and the other finds that his paint brush is no good.

As Rudolph sits lost in thought, and Marcel takes a bunch of ribbons and kisses it, the orchestra sounds the melody (No. 3) in which Rudolph first declared to Mimi his love. In the duet that follows (No. 8), each confesses that the features of his beloved still haunt him, however deeply he tries to absorb himself in his work. The old bonnet Mimi left him as a remembrance Rudolph now takes from the table drawer and clasps to his heart. In an endeavor to conceal his emotion he turns the conversation to such trivial subjects as a request for the time and an inquiry after Schaunard.

Both Colline and Schaunard now appear, the latter carrying four rolls and the former a paper bag from which he extracts a salted herring—"a dish," he assures his friends "that's worthy of Demosthenes." The dinner is conducted with ceremonial magnificence. They address one another as "duke" and "my lord marquis." A bottle of water is placed in Colline's hat (the icing of the champagne). Rudolph offers Marcel a crust of bread as his choice of salmon or turbot, while Marcel proffers Schaunard another crust, inviting him to sample some delectable *vol-au-vent* with mushrooms. Schaunard must politely decline, however, for tonight he is dancing; whereupon Colline, after voraciously devouring his roll, pompously announces that both the King and Guizot look forward to conferences with him this evening.

Dinner over, Schaunard proposes some dancing. Gavotte, minuet, pavanella, fandango are all proposed; but quadrilles take the company's fancy. After chairs and table have been moved aside, Rudolph bows low to Marcel who, in a simulated woman's voice, begs the gentleman to respect her modesty. While Marcel and Rudolph are dancing, Schaunard and Colline fall into an absurd quarrel which starts with grandiloquent challenges and ends in a mock duel, one armed with a poker and the other with tongs.

Suddenly Musetta bursts in upon the wild scene, declaring that Mimi is outside exhausted from climbing the staircase. Through the open door Rudolph sees her seated on the top stair, and while he and Marcel help her in, Colline and Schaunard drag forward a bed upon which Rudolph then gently lowers her. (A reminiscence of No. 4, Mimi's theme, is heard in the orchestra.)

While Mimi and Rudolph embrace, Musetta whispers to the others that she had heard that Mimi had left the rich old Viscount with whom she was living. Her account of her search for Mimi continues over an affecting recollection in the orchestra of the melody (No. 5) in which Mimi had first spoken to Rudolph of her flowers and their promise of love and springtime. Finally, relates Musetta, she found Mimi almost dead with exhaustion, and with rising excitement tells how Mimi begged to be brought here to die near her beloved.

Mimi is in raptures, but Schaunard, after looking closely at her, remarks quietly that in an hour she will be dead. The fact that their larder is empty, and that they can do nothing to help her, casts a pall over the group. Rudolph gently chafes Mimi's hands, for she complains that they are frozen, and he attempts to quiet her as she notices his assembled friends and cheerfully calls them by name. She is much concerned over Marcel and Musetta, and attempts needlessly to patch things up between them.

Taking Marcel aside, Musetta gives him her earrings to sell, instructing him to get medicine and a doctor, while she fetches a muff to keep Mimi's hands warm. As they leave, Mimi grows drowsy and Rudolph draws up a chair to keep watch by her bedside.

In this hushed and mournful atmosphere, Colline is moved to make the ultimate sacrifice. Addressing to his old, battered coat a genuinely moving farewell (No. 9), he folds it carefully under his arm and goes off to sell it, reminding Schaunard on his way out that it would be a kindness at this moment to leave Rudolph alone with Mimi. As justification for his departure, Schaunard looks about, picks up a water bottle, and then follows Colline.

Now they are gone, Mimi opens her eyes (the orchestra plays the melody of No. 3) and tells Rudolph that she had merely feigned sleep for she had wanted to be alone with him. (The melody in which she tells that she merely "feigned sleep," No. 10, recurs later in a most significant fashion.)

There is so much to ask and to tell, and time is so short. Does he still find her pretty? she asks. As lovely as the dawn, he replies. But she corrects him: the "sunset" would be a more fitting simile. And then, falling back into recollections of the happy past, she poignantly repeats a phrase from their first meeting: "They call me Mimi" (No. 4). In reply, he gives her the bonnet he had treasured all during their separation. She takes it, gaily reminding him (to the melody of No. 2) how they had gone shopping together, when first they were in love. During the exchange of reminiscences, Mimi tells him she had known all along that he had found and pocketed the key that night in the attic.

A coughing spell abruptly disrupts the warm, gentle tone of the duet. Schaunard, who at this moment returns, rushes to the bedside where Rudolph is distractedly trying to bring Mimi out of her seizure. They lower her gently back into bed, when with a smile she assures them that she is better and sweetly asks forgiveness for the trouble.

Musetta and Marcel now return, Marcel with a phial and news that a doctor has been summoned, and Musetta with a muff which Mimi accepts with childish glee. Turning to Rudolph, she begs him not to weep for her, since her hands are now much warmer and she can sleep. Reassured at seeing Mimi fall asleep, Rudolph quietly moves away from the bedside, cautioning the others in pantomime not to make any noise.

Meanwhile Musetta, busily heating the medicine Marcel brought, mutters a prayer to the Madonna for Mimi's recovery. Schaunard advances to the bedside. Realizing that Mimi is dead, he imparts the information to Marcel, just as Rudolph is hopefully remarking to Musetta that perhaps the illness is not really serious. A ray of sunshine falls upon Mimi's face, and, afraid that it will disturb her, Rudolph forms a screen by stretching Musetta's cloak across the windowpane.

Colline enters almost unnoticed, quietly puts some money on the table near Musetta, and asks Rudolph how Mimi is. Tranquil, replies Rudolph, and turning to take the medicine from Musetta, he suddenly notices the strange manner of Schaunard and Marcel. Barely able to speak, Rudolph demands to know the meaning of their anguished glances, and Marcel, unable any longer to keep up the pretense, hastily embraces him, stammering his sympathy.

Crying "Mimi . . . Mimi . . . ," Rudolph falls sobbing upon her body, while Musetta kneels weeping at the foot of the bed. Schaunard sinks into a chair, Colline stands as if dazed, and Marcel turns his back to the footlights, crying silently. As the curtain comes down, the melody (No. 10) which Mimi had sung a moment ago when she told Rudolph she had been only feigning sleep, thunders out of the orchestra and then dies away.

CARMEN

AN OPERA IN FOUR ACTS

by Georges Bizet

Cast

DON JOSÉ	Tenor
ESCAMILLO	Baritone
ZUNIGA	Bass
MORALES	Baritone
CARMEN	Mezzo-soprano
MICAËLA	Soprano
FRASQUITA	Soprano
MERCEDES	Mezzo-soprano
DANCAIRO	Tenor
REMENDADO	Tenor

DRAGOONS, GYPSIES, SMUGGLERS, CIGARETTE GIRLS, STREET URCHINS, OFFICIALS

Libretto
by Henri Meilhac and Ludovic Halévy
(based on a novel by Prosper Mérimée)

Time . About 1820
Place . In and near Seville

First Performance
Opéra-Comique, Paris, March 3, 1875

CARMEN

Prelude

THE HAPPY, vigorous, bustling tune (No. 1)*
with which the Prelude begins effectively
sets the sunny, Spanish background for the
tale of love and violence that is to follow.
A softer theme, used to accompany the change of
guard in Act 1 (No. 2), is heard briefly and, after a
quick *crescendo*, No. 1 returns.

Suddenly the martial tune of the "Toreador Song"
(No. 9) comes quietly from the strings and is repeated *fortissimo* by the whole orchestra. After a
dramatic pause, the fateful theme which is used to
suggest the irresistible but sinister attraction Carmen
has for **Don José** is played (No. 3). A quick climax,
another dramatic, suspenseful pause, and the curtain
rises.

Act 1

On one side of a bright square in Seville is a cigarette factory; on the other, a guardhouse; in the back,
a bridge. It is noonday. And soldiers, in the bright

---

*Thematic Guide, p. 317.

yellow and red uniforms which the Spanish army wore in the early nineteenth century, are idly grouped around the guardhouse, smoking and watching the passers-by.

As their leader, Corporal Morales, comments on the lively scene before them, he is suddenly attracted by a blonde, innocent-looking country maid who stands hesitatingly in the background. It is Micaëla; and when Morales asks her what she is looking for, she comes forward timidly and asks to see a corporal of the guard. Morales replies gallantly that he is a corporal, but Micaëla says that she is looking for a particular guardsman named Don José. Do they know him? They all do, but he is not of their company. He will be coming shortly with the changing of the guard.

Morales suggests that the lovely young girl wait for José in the guardhouse, but Micaëla hastily declines. The soldiers surround her, entreating her to stay. Shyly she insists that she will return later when the new guard has arrived, and then manages to escape. Reluctantly, the men settle back to watch the gay crowd.

The bright, marching music of the changing of the guard sounds in the distance. A bugler and two fifers come in, leading a crowd of street urchins in ragged military formation, and Captain Zuniga, Corporal Don José, and their troop of dragoons follow them. While they go through the rather complicated formalities of changing the guard, the boys amusingly enact their own formations, singing about their youthful military drill and its proud masculinity (No. 2).

Just before he and his company are about to leave, Morales informs Don José of the charming young girl who had been looking for him. "It must be Micaëla," muses José, as trumpets sound and the relieved guard marches off, the street boys behind them, singing their marching song.

Corporal Don José is second in command to Captain Zuniga in the freshly mounted guard; and as the two are left alone in the square, the corporal points to the cigarette factory and remarks that the girls who work there have interesting reputations. However, he adds hastily, he doesn't pay much attention to such things. The officer suspects that the blonde young girl who came looking for the corporal is holding all of his attention, and José admits that he is in love with her.

As the factory bell sounds, the men of the town gather about the entrance and frankly announce their intention of making the most of their noonday opportunities with the smoking *impudentes*. The cigarette girls now fill the square to sing a sinuous melody (No. 4), comparing the evanescent smoke of a cigarette and the evanescent vows of love made by their gallants. José, meanwhile, has busied himself with repairing the links of a small chain which has broken and tries to appear completely unaware of the girls.

"But where is Carmen?" all the men inquire. Suddenly she is announced in the orchestra by a quick, twisty version of the theme that suggests her fatal attractions (No. 3). The men immediately surround her, imploring her to tell them when she will love them. Carmen flirts with them all, and responds characteristically with "When shall I be in love? I don't know. Maybe never—and perhaps tomorrow—but certainly not today." Then, with the co-operation of her fellow workers, she sings the familiar "Habanera," (Nos. 5-a and 5-b) throughout which she attempts to attract the aloof corporal, with no visible success. The song over, the young men renew their pleas; but Carmen is interested only in the soldier who refuses to pay any attention to her.

To the accompaniment of the fateful theme that again and again is to suggest the irresistible but sinister attraction Carmen has for Don José (No. 3), she strolls saucily up to the corporal, takes a flower from her bodice, and tosses it in his face. Everyone laughs at his obvious embarrassment. As the factory bell sounds again, Carmen and the others leave him alone to pick up the flower.

At this moment Micaëla appears. Don José greets her eagerly, and the two engage in a melodious duet in which the young girl tells him of his home and his mother (No. 6). Micaëla has brought him a letter from his mother and something even more precious —a kiss, which she is to give him. She kisses him tenderly on the forehead, and José, genuinely moved, recalls the threat to his peace of mind that Carmen had presented. He thanks Heaven that the kiss his mother has sent him has averted that danger. But now Micaëla insists that she will leave him alone to read the letter. He reads to a melody from the recently completed duet, promising that he will marry Micaëla.

José is about to throw away the flower Carmen had tossed him when there is a great commotion in the factory. The girls stream out in confusion, as the guards, headed by Zuniga, rush from the guard-house. There has been a fight between Carmen and another worker, and, as the girls take sides, for and against Carmen, Zuniga sends José and two guards in to discover the cause of the trouble. Presently the corporal returns, leading the black-haired beauty who is in high spirits. She gaily refuses to answer Zuniga's questions, repeatedly singing a dancy phrase with *la plus grande impertinence*, as Bizet put it in the score. The captain, while attracted to Carmen, decides that he must order her to jail. He commands the corporal to take her there and he retires to the guardhouse.

As José seats Carmen in a chair and is tying her hands behind her back, she confidently informs him that he isn't going to take her to jail, but, on the contrary, is going to help her to escape. The corporal ignores her remark. And, still seated in the chair, Carmen sings the "Seguidilla" (No. 7), inviting a certain young officer who is neither a captain nor a lieutenant, but only a corporal, to come to her friend Lillas Pastia's inn and take the place of her recently dismissed lover.

José demands that she cease the singing at once; but Carmen nonchalantly replies that she was merely thinking aloud—and he certainly cannot forbid her thinking. She continues her song, and the corporal's emotions finally overrule his sense of duty. Earnestly he asks if she means what she says. Will she love him? Will she be faithful? Yes, says Carmen—and Don José loosens the cords.

As Zuniga returns from the guardhouse, Carmen hastily whispers instructions to the corporal. After tauntingly singing a phrase or two from the "Habanera" (No. 5-b) to Zuniga, she saunters to the bridge with José. Suddenly she gives her captor a shove, and gaily swinging the ties that bind her no longer, she runs off. As the curtain comes down, José ruefully picks himself up and surrenders to Zuniga.

Act 2

After an orchestral Entr'acte, based on José's soldier song (No. 10), the curtain rises on Lillas Pastia's inn on the outskirts of Seville—the inn which serves as a rendezvous for a gang of smugglers. A lively drinking and dancing party is in progress, dominated by gypsies who include Carmen and her two intimates, Frasquita and Mercedes. Captain Zuniga is a prominent member of the group. Carmen begins a fiery gypsy song (No. 8) in which her friends Frasquita and Mercedes and finally the whole group join her. As the music reaches a stirring tempo, the girls burst into a wild gypsy dance.

But the gaiety is soon interrupted by an announcement that it is time to close up the inn. Zuniga gallantly suggests that Carmen and her friends come with him, but they refuse. As one last effort to win a smile from Carmen, the captain then tells her that her soldier boy friend has now been released from prison.

"Fine," says Carmen, caustically, "and now, good night."

At this moment the sound of singing in the distance announces the coming of Escamillo, a popular matador. He swaggers into the inn, followed by a crowd of admirers, and immediately begins the "Toreador Song" (No. 9) in which he describes first the bullfight in detail, and then the dark eyes that await the hero. The dark eyes which attract him now are those of Carmen, and at the end of the song he goes over to her and makes a quick offer of his love. It is rejected with inviting finality: Carmen is thinking of a certain soldier.

As the toreador leaves, everyone follows except Carmen, Frasquita, Mercedes, and a pair of young gypsy smugglers named El Remendado and El Dancairo. A skillful and colorful quintet follows. Remendado and Dancairo have plans for a proposed smuggling raid, but they need the co-operation of women and would like the three girls to join them. Frasquita and Mercedes are delighted, but Carmen refuses. The others are amazed and press her for a reason. She replies that she is in love—one of the most astonishing bits of unreason, the two men say, they have ever heard. This isn't the first time she has been in love, they remind her. Besides, she is a past master at combining love and duty. But Carmen is firm.

At this moment Don José is heard approaching, singing a lighthearted soldier song (No. 10). Carmen, managing to get rid of her friends by promising that she will try to persuade the soldier to join their band, greets her new lover eagerly. José, in turn, assures her of his love, and shows his first signs of jealousy when he learns that some of the officers have been at Lillas Pastia's, making the girls dance for them. Carmen soothes him by promising to dance entirely for his benefit. Thereupon she seats him comfortably in a chair and begins a slow, provocative dance to a sinuous melody without words (No. 11), accompanying herself on castanets.

Before long the faint sound of bugles is heard, and when Don José notices them, he stops Carmen and tells her that retreat is being sounded. Carmen, pretending that she doesn't see what bugles have to do with it, proceeds to sing and dance more vigorously than ever. Again José stops her: he must return to camp. Now Carmen is furious. She derides and insults him bitterly, finally hurling his soldier's cap and sword across the floor at him. Don José pleads with her pitcously, reiterating his love for her, but Carmen only grows angrier.

The soldier insists that she must listen to him and finally succeeds in seating Carmen in a chair. Then he takes from his coat the flower she had thrown to him and sings the "Flower Song" (No. 12), describing how the flower, always suggestive of her, kept its fragrance through all the time he was in prison.

Although Carmen is obviously moved by this declaration, she insists that he does not really love her. For if he did, she says, he would follow her up to the free mountains where there are no officers to be obeyed, where their own will would be their law, and where they would be free. Don José, frantically torn between her invitation and his sense of duty, almost capitulates. He takes her in his arms and is about to kiss her, when he realizes the cowardice of what he contemplates, and suddenly pushes her away. Carmen shouts furiously after him as he is about to leave.

But there is a knock on the door, and Captain Zuniga suddenly enters. He orders the corporal out; and when José proudly refuses, Zuniga draws his sword and the two begin to fight. Carmen calls for help, and the gypsies pour in from every side. Remendado and Dancairo disarm the captain, and with exquisite politeness, but at the points of two pistols, Zuniga is invited to leave the inn. He submits, remarking that their arguments are irresistible.

Now José has no choice left but to join the gypsies, and the act ends with a joyous chorus in praise of liberty.

Act 3

Following an Entr'acte that features a lovely solo for the flute, the curtain rises on the smugglers, who have gathered their goods at a wild spot in the mountains preparatory to crossing some unspecified border. They sing a quiet, weird little march, encouraging each other in the dangers that their business presents. As they put down their loads, a short dialogue between Carmen and Don José reveals that their affair has not been going too well.

José thinks regretfully of how he has disappointed his mother in this new life of his. Carmen, of course, is thoroughly contemptuous of any such softness, and she tells him that he had better return to his mother at once. Angered by her suggestion that they part, José warns her that she had better not say such a thing again. "Then perhaps you will kill me," says Carmen, sensing the intensity of his anger. "What does it matter? It is all a matter of destiny."

Meantime, on one side of the stage Frasquita and Mercedes have seated themselves before a bale and are busy laying out cards to tell their own fortunes. In a gay, lighthearted duet Frasquita reports that the cards promise her a fine young lover; but Mercedes has what she apparently thinks an even finer fate predicted: she is to be wooed by a very rich old man who will marry her, and then, luckily, will die and leave everything to her.

Presently Carmen joins the two, spreading out her own pack of cards. Her mood and her music are quite different from those of her friends. She lays out a diamond, then a spade, and reads them to mean that she is to die first, then Don José—and she sings a slow, ominous melody (No. 13) concerning the futility of trying to avoid death. Mercedes and Frasquita take up their happier tune again, while Carmen continues to sing of her dark forebodings.

Now Dancairo appears and reports that it is time for them to cross the border. José is to stay behind to guard what they cannot carry on their first trip. All shoulder bales and sing another marchlike song as they carry off the contraband.

A moment after the group has left, Micaëla appears, looking for Don José. She sings an affecting aria (No. 14) in which she attempts to overcome her intense fear of this desolate place. Desperately she tries to support her own spirits, but all she can do is to pray to God to protect her. Nor is her courage helped by seeing Don José, who has mounted a hill so that he might have a view of the road, aiming his gun in her direction. As he fires, she runs away as quickly as possible.

However, it is not Micaëla but Escamillo whom Don José has seen climbing up to the smugglers' rendezvous. The Toreador arrives and José challenges him at once, for he knows of him by name only. When Escamillo identifies himself, José welcomes him but tells him that he has risked his life by coming to this wild spot. Escamillo reports that love has made him bold, and it does not take long for José to find out that it is Carmen whom the Toreador has come to see. He asks angrily if Escamillo is aware that to take a gypsy girl away a man must be willing to pay in knife thrusts.

The Toreador now understands that his companion is Carmen's lover. He announces that he will be glad to exchange blows, and each wraps his cloak about his left arm, draws his knife, and prepares to fight. Escamillo trips, his knife snaps, and José is about to strike when Carmen, who has heard the noise, grabs his arm. The other gypsies follow and separate the fighters.

Dancairo now demands that the Toreador leave. But before he goes, Escamillo pauses long enough to invite everyone to his next bullfight in Seville, where he promises to perform brilliantly. "Anyone who loves me," he adds, looking meaningly at Carmen, "will be there." At this Don José lunges toward him, but Dancairo and Remendado restrain him. Escamillo makes an effective exit to a slow, quiet version of the refrain from the "Toreador Song" (No. 9).

The smugglers are about to return to their work when one discovers Micaëla hiding among the rocks. José greets her with surprise and asks what could possibly have brought her here. She tells him that his mother asks him to take pity on her and return home, and Carmen sarcastically advises that he go. This suggestion infuriates José, who insists that he will not leave her now.

Micaëla then tells him that his mother is dying. This news gives him a change of heart, and he prepares to leave immediately with Micaëla. From the distance the voice of Escamillo is heard, and Carmen starts to run to him. But José turns back, throws her violently to the ground, and rushes off once more as the curtain descends.

Act 4

The Entr'acte before Act 4 boasts a theme taken from an old Andalusian song. The day of the bull-fight has arrived, and as the curtain rises, fan girls, orange girls, and program, cigarette, and water peddlers mix in among the soldiers and the citizens who are waiting outside the amphitheater to watch the expected procession of performers. Holiday bustle, noisy, rhythmic Spanish music, and dancing fill the square. Then the procession starts. First come the various functionaries and assistants, and finally the

Matador himself—Escamillo—with Carmen on his arm. The crowd greets him with a vigorous chorus from the "Toreador Song" (No. 9). Just before he goes into the ring he tells Carmen, in a tender duet, that if she loves him she can now be proud of him (No. 15). She replies that she certainly does love him—may she die if she has ever loved anyone so much!

After Escamillo has left, Frasquita and Mercedes rush up to Carmen, warning her that Don José is hiding in the crowd. Carmen replies that she is not afraid of him—in fact, she will wait and talk to him right here. The two girls follow the crowd into the amphitheater, and suddenly a rumbling *crescendo* and a loud chord usher in Don José.

Carmen greets José coldly and remarks that her friends have warned her that he means to kill her, but she is not afraid. José insists that he has come only to plead with her to go away with him. But Carmen tells him impatiently that all is over between them. Passionately Don José pleads with her; but the more he pleads, the more she scorns him. When the *vivas* hailing Escamillo are heard, Carmen tries to enter the amphitheater, but José blocks the way and demands to know whether she loves the Toreador. She shouts defiantly that she does.

The fate theme is heard in the orchestra (No. 3) as the frenzied José once more demands that she come with him, but Carmen cries angrily that he must kill her now or let her pass. Again a shout of "Victory!" comes from the arena, and Carmen tears from her finger a ring which José had once given her, hurling it away.

Then, while the crowd inside is spiritedly singing the chorus of the "Toreador Song" (No. 9) in praise of the victorious Escamillo, Carmen tries desperately to elude Don José and to rush into the amphitheater. Quickly he draws his knife, grasps hold of her, and plunges in the blade. The crowd, coming from the arena, finds him on his knees beside the body. Then, as the fate theme comes ominously from the orchestra, José cries out brokenly that they may arrest him, for it was he who killed his beloved Carmen. The curtain falls.

CAVALLERIA RUSTICANA

(Rustic Chivalry)

AN OPERA IN ONE ACT

by Pietro Mascagni

Cast

SANTUZZA	Soprano
LOLA	Mezzo-soprano
TURIDDU	Tenor
ALFIO	Baritone
LUCIA	Contralto

CHORUS OF VILLAGERS

Libretto

by G. Targioni-Tozzetti and G. Menasci
(based on the story by Giovanni Verga)

Time.... Nineteenth century; Easter Day

Place. .... A village in Sicily

First Performance

Teatro Costanzi, Rome, May 17, 1890

CAVALLERIA RUSTICANA

Prelude

BEGINNING with a quiet religiosity, suggestive of the Easter Sunday on which the
action of the play takes place (No. 1),* the
Prelude works up to a noisy climax and,
with dramatic suddenness, drops to a soft, pleading
melody—the one that Santuzza, the heroine, is to use
later when begging her lover not to desert her (No.
10). Suddenly the Prelude is interrupted by the voice
of the lover himself, Turiddu, singing a tender love
song to his mistress, Lola. This is the famous *Siciliana*
(No. 2), which finally dies away as the orchestra
again picks up more of the music that is later to express Santuzza's pleadings (Nos. 9 and 10). Gradually
the Prelude fades out softly on a religious note, like
the amen of a prayer.

Act 1

The curtain rises on the deserted square of a tiny
village in Sicily. On the right stands a church, and

---

*Thematic Guide, p. 320.

on the left, the inn belonging to Mamma Lucia, mother of the young soldier Turiddu. The quiet of dawn on this Easter Sunday is broken by the ringing of bells from the church steeple. In answer to them, peasants, villagers, and children appear, some entering the church, and others going about their individual errands, as the orchestra plays music at once strongly melodic and pastoral.

For a while the square is deserted again, but from a distance the voices of the women are heard singing the praises of this fine Easter morning. Soon they are joined in song by the men, who extol the many charms of women. As the villagers gradually return to the square, they weave their melodies and sentiments into a fine, effective climax.

Slowly the people wander off, and Santuzza hurries across the square. Nervously clutching her shawl about her, she knocks on the door of the inn and calls for Lucia, Turiddu's aged mother.

Lucia comes out, and Santuzza anxiously demands to know where Turiddu is. Although Mamma Lucia tries to evade answering, for she has no desire to get mixed up in her son's quarrels, she finally yields to Santuzza's frantic insistency and tells her that her son went off to Francofonte to get wine. Excitedly, Santuzza tells the old woman that he couldn't have gone to Francofonte, for he was seen in the village only last night. "Well, he hasn't been home," says Lucia impatiently. "Come to church." But Santuzza sadly reminds the old woman that she dare not enter the church, for she has been excommunicated.

Santuzza would like to go on discussing her

wretchedness with Mamma Lucia, but she is interrupted by the sounds of gaily jingling bells and the cracking of a whip, announcing the arrival of Alfio, the carter and the husband of her rival, Lola. The carefree fellow is accompanied by a happy crowd of villagers, who join him in a lusty song in praise of his trade and his loving wife (No. 3).

Then, spying Mamma Lucia, Alfio asks if she still has some of that fine old wine. "I don't know," says Lucia, "Turiddu is off trying to pick some up." Alfio is surprised at this, for he had seen Turiddu that very morning lingering near his house. Before Mamma Lucia can question the carter further, Santuzza, who knows full well why Turiddu would be lingering near Alfio's house, silences her, and the happy carter, still quite unsuspicious, goes off as sounds of organ music begin to issue from the church.

A group of villagers, hearing the music, gathers outside the church, while from within the choir begins the "Regina Coeli" (No. 4). The crowd in the square joins in with hallelujahs, and Santuzza, kneeling, leads them in singing the beautiful Resurrection hymn, her voice soaring passionately over all of them (No. 5).

As the villagers go into the church for the service, Lucia remains behind to ask Santuzza why she had silenced her when Alfio spoke of seeing Turiddu in the village. In the expressive aria "Voi lo sapete" (No. 6), Santuzza reminds the old woman that before her son had gone off to serve as a soldier, he had been engaged to Lola. But when he returned he found Lola married to Alfio. To console himself he turned to

Santuzza, who became his mistress and loved him passionately. But Lola was jealous and, disregarding her husband, lured Turiddu back again. With frenzied despair, Santuzza ends by saying that now there is nothing left for her but to weep while Lola and Turiddu make love to each other.

Mamma Lucia is shocked by this sordid tale on so holy a morning, but when Santuzza piteously begs her to pray for her, the old woman goes into the church muttering a hope that the Virgin Mary will help the distraught girl.

Now Turiddu appears. And when Santuzza stops him, he tries to avoid talking to her. She insists on knowing where he has been, and when he tells her that he has just come from Francofonte, she angrily accuses him of lying. Even Alfio, she goes on, knows where he has been. Menacingly, Turiddu warns her that he will not stand for her jealous possessiveness (No. 7), but Santuzza persists in berating him. Their voices rise higher and higher as their quarrel becomes more heated, and suddenly, with dramatic contrast, the voice of Lola is heard singing a happy ditty to her "King of Roses" (No. 8).

As Lola herself saunters in, twirling a rose in her hand, she nonchalantly asks Turiddu if he has seen her husband. Then, turning to Santuzza, she maliciously inquires whether she is making her devotions outside the church or whether she intends to go in to Mass. Santuzza replies pointedly that only those who are free of sin ought to go to church. Unperturbed, Lola, turning down Turiddu's offer to accompany her, tosses the rose at his feet and goes into the church alone.

Now the quarrel is renewed. Angrily Turiddu accuses Santuzza of spying on him. Disregarding his accusations, she passionately begs him not to leave her, expressing first desperation and then grief (Nos. 9 and 10). But the more she pleads with him, the more furious he becomes, until finally, in a terrific rage, he throws her to the ground and strides defiantly into the church. White with anger, Santuzza curses him bitterly.

Alfio now enters, also bound for church, and asks Santuzza how far they have gone with the Mass. "Almost over," says Santuzza—and adds significantly that Lola went in with Turiddu. Surprised by her agitated tone, Alfio asks what she means by that remark, and Santuzza, too angry to think about the consequences, blurts out the whole bitter story. At first he refuses to believe it, and then threatens to tear out her heart if she is lying. But there is something too desperately earnest about Santuzza for Alfio not to be convinced.

There is an ominous pause, and finally Alfio thanks Santuzza and swears a savage revenge. As he leaves, Santuzza, horror stricken by the realization of what she has done, is filled with shame and remorse. Sobbing, she follows him.

Again the square is deserted, and the orchestra softly begins the *Intermezzo*, which starts with the "Regina Coeli" melody of the prayer (No. 4) and continues with the most familiar melody of the opera (No. 11). The calm religiosity of the opening bars lends a striking contrast to the stormy passions which preceded it.

The steeple bells sound again, and the villagers emerge from the church singing happily. Everyone is in high spirits, and when Turiddu invites the crowd to have a drink on the house at his mother's tavern, they readily accept. Led by Turiddu, they sing the jolly "Brindisi," or drinking song, (No. 12), Turiddu and Lola rather ostentatiously drinking each other's health.

The gay scene is interrupted by the arrival of Alfio, who angrily refuses Turiddu's offer of a drink by saying that he would be afraid the wine would contain poison. Turiddu responds by throwing the wine at Alfio's feet, and the women, realizing what is coming, hurry the frightened Lola away. The two men now confront each other, and Turiddu quickly challenges Alfio according to Sicilian custom—by biting his opponent's right ear. Alfio calmly accepts the challenge.

The formalities over, Turiddu admits to Alfio that he is in the wrong and that he deserves to die like a dog. Then sorrow overcomes him as he thinks of his poor Santuzza. What will become of her if he should be killed? A moment later, his mood changes and he vows he will plunge his dagger into Alfio's heart. Unimpressed, Alfio replies that he will be waiting for Turiddu in the orchard, and he leaves with the other men.

Now Turiddu pathetically calls for his mother and, when Lucia comes, tells her that he has been drinking too much wine and is going for a walk to clear his head. He asks for her blessing before he goes and begs her to take care of Santuzza if, for some reason, he should not return (No. 13). Mystified, Mamma Lucia asks what he means. To quiet her fears, Turiddu tells her it is only the wine that makes him talk this way. Kissing his mother passionately, he dashes off. Lucia's fears mount, especially when the terror-stricken Santuzza rushes in and frightened neighbors fill the square.

Suddenly the shrill voice of a woman is heard shouting that Turiddu has been murdered. The villagers rush in, horrified—and both Santuzza and Lucia faint, as the curtain falls.

Don Giovanni

DON GIOVANNI

AN OPERA IN TWO ACTS

by Wolfgang Amadeus Mozart

Cast

DON GIOVANNI	Baritone
DON OTTAVIO	Tenor
LEPORELLO	Bass
THE COMMANDANT	Bass
MASETTO	Baritone
DONNA ANNA	Soprano
DONNA ELVIRA	Soprano
ZERLINA	Soprano

PEASANTS, MUSICIANS, DANCERS, CHORUS OF DEMONS

Libretto ....by Lorenzo da Ponte
Time . ...Seventeenth century
Place . ... In and about Seville

First Performance
National Theater, Prague, October 29, 1787

DON GIOVANNI

Overture

RHYTHMICALLY and dramatically, the first thirty bars of the Overture are closely based on the opera's most dramatic scene. This occurs at the end of the work, when the statue of the Commandant of Seville appears at the Don's house and orders him to repent. The Don merely scoffs, and, to the accompaniment of a series of scales that can be really terrifying when performed with great *crescendo*, the Commandant consigns him to hell.

After this solemn opening passage, the music runs along in a chattery, bubbling fashion (No. 1),* quite in keeping with the light comedy that is the main business of the evening, and then goes at once into the lumbering introduction to Leporello's opening words.

Act 1

In the garden outside the lavish house of the Commandant of Seville, Leporello, the lackey of the amorous Don Giovanni, is waiting impatiently for his

---

*Thematic Guide, p. 323.

master, who has secretly entered the house in an attempt to seduce Donna Anna, the Commandant's daughter. This business of standing guard outside while the Don enjoys himself within is not at all to Leporello's liking, and he complains bitterly about his thankless job (No. 2). One of these days, he threatens, he will quit. But as soon as he hears Giovanni coming from the house, he swallows his brave words and quickly hides himself.

The Don apparently has not been enjoying himself, as Leporello had supposed, for he comes rushing from the house, the furious Donna Anna pursuing him and demanding to know his name. Giovanni, covering his face with his cloak, attempts to quiet her, but she continues to scream for help. Her cries bring her father storming from the house, brandishing a sword. He immediately challenges the Don, who is at first unwilling to engage in a duel with so old an adversary. But the Commandant insists, and after a brief exchange, the agile Don runs him through.

Now Leporello emerges from his hiding place and indulges in a bit of sarcastic wit. The Don angrily silences him, and the two run off just as Donna Anna, who had rushed into the house to seek aid, appears with Don Ottavio, her fiancé. But she has come too late, for her father is already dead. Grief stricken, she kneels at his body and swears that she will seek vengeance on his murderer. Don Ottavio joins her in an oath of revenge.

A square just outside Seville. It is early morning. Leporello, having secured his master's promise that

he may speak freely without being punished, tells the
Don that this life he is leading is disgraceful. He
would go into greater detail, but Giovanni's threats
silence him. At this moment a veiled woman comes
along the road. The two withdraw a distance and
listen as she sings sadly of the man who had seduced
her and then deserted her (No. 3).

Gallantly Giovanni announces that he must comfort this lovely lady and perhaps, he thinks, in the
process of comforting her he may also make another
conquest. But as he steps forward he finds to his
dismay that the woman is none other than Donna
Elvira, whom he had loved briefly years before in
Burgos and had deserted. Recognizing him, Elvira
immediately begins to upbraid him. The Don attempts to make excuses, but she refuses to believe
anything he says, and in desperation he calls on
Leporello to help him. While the servant diverts the
lady's attention, Giovanni makes his escape.

Cynically, Leporello attempts to comfort Elvira
by telling her that she is only one of many—hundreds,
in fact—whom the Don has betrayed. Taking out a
book from which a long stretch of paper coils across
the stage, he begins the famous comic aria *Madamina*
(No. 4), in which he lists the Don's conquests: 640
in Italy, 231 in Germany, 100 in France, only 91 in
Turkey, but in Spain, 1,003! And, he points out, as
Elvira herself knows, the Don is quite a successful
lover. With this last bit of tactlessness, Leporello
runs off, leaving Elvira so infuriated that she determines to seek revenge.

In a rural spot near Don Giovanni's castle on

the outskirts of Seville, a group of villagers are gaily celebrating the engagement of Zerlina, a pretty peasant girl, to Masetto, her village swain. Into this pleasant scene come the Don and Leporello, and, following his usual instinct, Giovanni almost immediately picks out the attractive Zerlina as his next conquest. Feigning friendship, he invites the entire company to come to his castle for a celebration, but then, ordering Leporello to take the group on ahead, he cleverly manages to remain behind with Zerlina. When Masetto bitterly protests, Giovanni impatiently taps the hilt of his sword in warning, and Leporello hurries the grumbling lover off.

Left alone with Zerlina, the Don artfully flatters and cajoles her. The young village girl at first shyly resists him, but, in a charming duet (No. 5), she succumbs to his suave coaxing. Just as Giovanni is about to take Zerlina to the castle, Elvira, who has been watching this tête-à-tête from a distance, intercepts them. She denounces the Don bitterly, and, though Giovanni makes frantic excuses for what he calls a jealous outburst, manages to rescue Zerlina.

As soon as the two women have left, Donna Anna and her dutiful Don Ottavio appear. Not knowing, of course, that Giovanni is the murderer of the Commandant, they appeal to him for help with unconscious irony, and the Don—with conscious irony—replies that he would be delighted to be of any assistance. But the accusations of Elvira, who now returns, begin to arouse the suspicions of Donna Anna and Ottavio, and Giovanni hurries Elvira away.

When they have left, Donna Anna reveals that she

has recognized the voice of the Don as that of her father's murderer. Dramatically she recounts the whole bitter story of the seduction and the duel, and, in an aria of great strength and nobility, calls on Ottavio to renew his oath of vengeance (No. 6).

As she leaves, Ottavio, finding it difficult to believe that a nobleman could behave so badly, ponders over the state of affairs. In the beautifully serene aria "Dalla Sua Pace" (No. 7), he sings of his love for Donna Anna and declares that his happiness depends entirely on the happiness of his loved one. Finally he resolves that he will help her avenge her father's murder.

When Ottavio has left, Leporello returns, complaining as usual that he will one day quit this thankless employ of his. But as Giovanni joins him he changes his tone, and proceeds to inform the Don that he has handled everything quite ingeniously, even the troublesome Masetto. And when Zerlina came in with—of all people—Elvira, Leporello continues, he managed to lock Elvira out of the house.

Delighted, Giovanni bursts into the gay "Champagne" aria (No. 8), in which he instructs Leporello to round up all the pretty girls he can find and invite them to a party. By morning, he announces, he will have several more names to add to his list of conquests.

The garden outside of Giovanni's castle. It is the same evening and Masetto and Zerlina are still quarreling about the Don's presumptuous attentions. Zerlina pleads that she is not to blame, and, in a tender aria, "Batti, Batti" (No. 9), she manages to soothe Masetto.

When they hear the Don approaching, Masetto deliberately hides himself and leaves his fiancée in the dangerous Don's path. Zerlina tries to hide, too, but Giovanni catches her by the hand and renews his amorous advances. As he draws her into the privacy of the arbor, he is suddenly confronted by a belligerent Masetto. Losing his composure only momentarily, the suave Giovanni takes both lovers by the arm and invites them into the castle to join in the dancing.

When they have left, three masked figures enter the garden. They are the Donnas Elvira and Anna with Don Ottavio. The music of the famous minuet (No. 10) drifts from the house, and Giovanni and the ever-present Leporello appear on a balcony. Seeing the masked figures, the Don instructs his servant to invite them in to join in the frivolity. Just before the three enter the house, they pause for a moment to pray for heaven's aid in carrying out their plans for vengeance.

The main hall of Giovanni's castle. The brilliantly gay party is in full swing. Three orchestras are playing, and off the main hall two separate rooms for dancing can be seen, while to the back, doors open onto the colorfully lighted garden. Giovanni swings Zerlina into the dance as Leporello grabs Masetto and forces him to be his partner.

Giovanni skillfully contrives to lead Zerlina into the next room. A moment later a cry from her interrupts the dancing and everyone turns to the door of the room. It is locked. They are about to break it down when the Don comes out holding Leporello at sword's point. Treacherously he tries to blame the servant for his own actions, but no one is fooled. The crowd angrily attacks Giovanni, but in the general confusion he manages to slip away.

Act 2

A square near Donna Elvira's house. Don Giovanni and Leporello are arguing their pet theme: Leporello wants to quit but Giovanni will not let him. This time, however, the lackey is so insistent that the Don has to resort to bribing him with a purse of money in order to appease him.

But now Giovanni is anxious to get to the business of the hour. He is interested in Donna Elvira's pretty little maid and decides that the best way to woo her is to pretend that he is a servant too. He proceeds to exchange clothes with Leporello, whose protests go unheeded.

Now Elvira herself appears on the balcony. The Don takes cruel advantage of the situation, and, standing behind Leporello and moving the servant's arms in appropriately romantic gestures, he sings of his love for her and begs forgiveness. Elvira, succumbing to the false entreaties, comes down to join him. Meanwhile, Giovanni instructs his lackey to make love to her, for in the dark she will surely mistake him for the Don himself.

Although Leporello has doubts about the part he is to play, he carries out his master's commands and finds the job not at all disagreeable. As he is tenderly swearing eternal fidelity to the deceived Elvira, Giovanni, pretending to be a holdup man, jumps out and frightens the two away.

Now Giovanni may safely woo Elvira's maid, and he begins a serenade to the young girl (No. 11). But before she has time to respond, a group of armed peasants arrive. They are seeking the Don, whom they fully intend to murder. Safe in his disguise as Leporello, Giovanni instructs them how to find the villain, even describing the clothes which the unfortunate Leporello is now wearing. As the peasants leave, the Don detains Masetto. Cleverly he manages to get the unsuspecting Masetto to hand over his musket and pistol and proceeds to beat the unfortunate peasant with his own weapons. Then he runs off.

Zerlina arrives and rushes over to her lover. Realizing that Masetto's groans far exceed his actual injuries, she sings a lovely aria in which she says that her love will heal his wounds (No. 12). Tenderly she helps him to his feet and leads him off.

The garden of the Commandant's house. Leporello has been so successful in his role as the Don that he cannot escape from the amorous Elvira. As he tries to elude her, Donna Anna and Ottavio enter. Seeing them, Leporello redoubles his efforts to slip away. Just as he finds an exit, he is confronted by Zerlina and Masetto. Thinking that he is the hated Giovanni, they are about to murder him when, in desperation, Leporello reveals himself. Angrily they determine that they will punish him anyway, but Leporello flees.

Ottavio, now completely convinced of the Don's guilt, swears, in the lovely tenor aria "Il mio tesoro" (No. 13), that he will indeed keep faith with Donna Anna and avenge her father's death.

To a churchyard dominated by a large statue of the Commandant on horseback both Giovanni and Leporello have fled to escape their pursuers. Leporello is still frightened from his recent experience, and the Don attempts to put him in better spirits by telling him of a little adventure he had this evening with a pretty girl who mistook him for Leporello. As the two are talking, the moon breaks through the clouds, flooding the statue of the Commandant with a ghostly light.

A voice solemnly proclaims, "Your joking will end before dawn." At first Giovanni thinks someone must be hiding in the churchyard, but when the voice is heard again, he realizes that it comes from the statue. He forces the terror-stricken Leporello to go over and read the inscription. Stuttering with fright, the servant manages to tell the Don that it says, "Here I wait for vengeance on the impious man who killed me." Not at all dismayed by these words of warning, Giovanni instructs the trembling Leporello to invite the statue to have dinner with him. Under the prodding of the Don's sword, Leporello blurts out the invitation, and the statue nods its head in acceptance.

A room in Donna Anna's castle. Don Ottavio is trying to persuade the still-grieving Donna Anna

to forget her sorrows and marry him, for Don
Giovanni will soon be brought to justice. In the tender aria "Non mi dir" (No. 14), she assures him of
her love but says she cannot marry him now while
her grief is still so poignant. In time, she says, they
will marry.

In the brightly lighted, lavishly furnished ban-
quet hall of Don Giovanni's palace, a private orchestra is playing in the gallery, as the Don placidly
stuffs himself with a sumptuous dinner. At this moment Elvira rushes in and begs the Don to repent
his scandalous past and reform before it is too late.
Giovanni scorns her frenzied warning and continues
with his dinner. Elvira, furious, turns to leave but
suddenly jumps back from the door in terror. Leporello goes to the door to see what has frightened her.
Trembling with fear, he tells the Don that the stone
statue is outside.

There is a heavy knock, and Giovanni orders his
servant to open the door. But Leporello has hidden
himself under a table. The Don himself opens the
door, and the statue dramatically announces that it
has come to dinner, as invited. With a somewhat
shaky bravado the Don orders another place to be
set at the table.

The statue, declining mortal food, invites Giovanni to dine with him. Despite Leporello's pleas that
he refuse the invitation, the Don gallantly accepts,
and the statue puts out its hand to seal the pact.
Giovanni finds himself held in a terrible stony clasp,
and the statue urges him to repent. When the Don
proudly refuses, the statue dramatically pronounces

his doom. Flames leap up and a chorus of hollow voices proclaims his eternal damnation. Finally the whole house is consumed by flames.

Epilogue: Elvira, Anna, Zerlina, Ottavio, and Masetto, accompanied by ministers of justice, appear. Leporello, who has somehow managed to escape the inferno, comes in and tells them what has happened. They all agree that justice has indeed triumphed. And now Donna Anna promises that, after a year of mourning, she will marry Ottavio; Zerlina and Masetto plan to marry more promptly; while Elvira says that she will enter a convent. Last of all, Leporello announces that he will seek a better master.

Faust

FAUST

AN OPERA IN FOUR ACTS

by Charles Gounod

Cast

FAUST .... Tenor
MEPHISTOPHELES . ... Bass
VALENTINE . ... Baritone
WAGNER .... Baritone
MARGUERITE .... Soprano
SIEBEL ....Mezzo-soprano
MARTHA ....Mezzo-soprano

PEASANTS, TOWNSPEOPLE, SOLDIERS, STU-
DENTS, MUSICIANS, CHORUS OF DEMONS,
CHORUS OF ANGELS

Libretto by Jules Barbier and Michel Carré
(based on Goethe's play)

Time .. .. Sixteenth century
Place .. .. Germany

First Performance
Théâtre Lyrique, Paris, March 19, 1859

FAUST

Introduction

T HE SLOW, meditative first part of the Introduction to Faust effectively suggests the monotonous, involved thinking of the aged philosopher. As we first see him he is seated in his gloomy cell, dismally contemplating the meaning of his life. In sharp contrast, follows the refrain from the aria "Even Bravest Heart May Swell" (No. 4)*—heard again in Act 1. The Introduction ends on a quiet, pastoral note.

Act 1

The opening curtain discloses the aged Dr. Faustus, in a philosopher's black gown and long white beard, seated at a table littered with parchments in his study cell in Wittenberg. It is Easter morning, just before dawn, and he complains that all his studying has taught him nothing—not even to die. As day breaks, he resolves on suicide and prepares himself a goblet of poison. A chorus of passing youths and maidens interrupts his suicidal mood (No. 1)—and he begins

*Thematic Guide, p. 325.

to curse everything good on earth, finally calling on Satan for help. A great *crescendo*, a crashing chord —and the Devil actually appears through the fireplace.

At first Faust is frightened by his elegantly dressed visitor; but he is reassured by Mephistopheles' winning manner and by his offer of anything the aged man wants—gold, glory, or power. But Faust wants more than all these—he wants youth. And he bursts into a wild expression of his desire for young love (No. 2).

"Fine," says Mephistopheles. "I can get them for you." And how much will it cost? Almost nothing. Here on earth Mephistopheles will be Faust's servant; but below (and the Devil points down to hell), Faust will be his. With that, the old philosopher is offered a parchment to sign. When he still hesitates, the Devil makes a magical gesture, and in the back of Faust's study appears a vision of a beautiful blonde young maiden. It is Marguerite seated at her spinning wheel. Enraptured by both the vision and the love music that breathes forth (No. 13-b), Faust signs the pact. Immediately Mephistopheles offers him a potion he has just mixed, and when the old man drinks it, he is transformed into a handsomely gowned youth.

The vision of Marguerite fades. Faust again sings of his wild desires (No. 2). And accompanied by the Devil, he rushes out in search of adventure.

(Scene 2) The setting is the square of the German village of Leipzig, where a colorful fair is reaching its climax. While soldiers, students, and villagers festively sing the praises of light wines and beer (No. 3), Marguerite's brother, Valentine, wanders disconso-

lately into their midst. Chided about his sour look, Valentine says that he is worried over his orphaned sister, who will be left uncared for when he leaves Leipzig for battle.

Several young men—among them Siebel, Marguerite's extremely youthful admirer—eagerly volunteer for the attractive assignment of caring for her. And Valentine, slightly cheered, sings the aria "Even Bravest Heart May Swell" (No. 4). The holiday spirit of the afternoon is now brought back with a round of drinks.

Just as a young student, Wagner, begins the rollicking "Song of the Rat," Mephistopheles appears and joins in the festivity by announcing that he knows an even better song. He bursts into "The Calf of Gold" (No. 5), describing how everyone dances about the pedestal of gold while Satan leads them on. Satan, in this case, does lead them on, for the soldiers and students join lustily in the chorus without understanding its irreligious connotations.

The song ended, Wagner promptly offers the stranger a drink. The Devil accepts, but first seizes the student's hand, points to the life line on the palm, and predicts that he will lose his life in battle. The foolish Siebel, fascinated by this fortunetelling, thrusts out his hand, and Mephistopheles obliges by telling him that hereafter any flower he touches will wither at once. No more bouquets for Marguerite, adds the Devil. When Valentine angrily protests this bandying about of his sister's name, the Devil calmly responds by predicting that the soldier will be killed.

But it is time to drink now. Mephistopheles takes

the drink Wagner has offered him, but instantly spits it out in disgust. He calls on the figure of Bacchus sitting on the wine barrel, which is used as the sign of the inn, to supply something better. Magically, sparkling wine spurts from the barrel, everyone fills his glass, and the Devil proposes a toast—to Marguerite. The quick-tempered Valentine draws his sword and challenges the stranger, who also draws and describes a circle on the ground about himself. As soon as Valentine steps inside the circle, his sword breaks in half.

Now the crowd knows with whom it has to deal. Led by Valentine, they sing the "Chorale of the Swords" (No. 6), in the midst of which they reverse their weapons, showing Mephistopheles the sign of the cross in the handles. He cowers in fright. But when all have left the stage, he regains his courage in time to greet Faust, who now joins him. The philosopher immediately inquires about Marguerite, and the Devil obligingly tells him that he can meet her at the dance, which begins at once.

The rhythms of a waltz come from the orchestra (No. 7-a), the gay crowd joins in, and, as Mephistopheles predicted, the beautiful Marguerite appears. Delighted, Faust gallantly steps forward and offers to escort her home (No. 8); but the simple village girl declines. The waltz rhythms return, and the first act ends with the dancing reaching a delirious tempo.

Act 2

The scene is the flower-filled garden of Marguerite's home, where Siebel comes to gather a bouquet for her. He stops before a rosebush in the center of the stage and in the famous "Flower Song" (No. 9) begs the flowers to speak to Marguerite of his love. But when he picks one of the blossoms, it withers, as Mephistopheles had prophesied. Wisely, Siebel dips his hand into a bowl of holy water beneath a statue of the Virgin, where Marguerite prays every evening, and the next flower remains fresh and beautiful.

As Siebel dashes off to other parts of the garden to pick a bouquet, Faust and Mephistopheles enter. A moment later Siebel returns, leaves his gift at the door of the house, and shyly steals away.

Faust is left alone while the Devil goes off in search of a gift which will be more persuasive than Siebel's token. He is now so deeply under the spell of the place that he has a moment's compunction about carrying out the planned seduction. He sings his great "Cavatina" (No. 10).

Mephistopheles returns, bearing a jewel box, which he promptly deposits next to the bouquet. As the Devil hastily takes his protégé off, Marguerite enters the garden. She is musing aloud about the handsome young stranger she met at the fair, and at several points in the ballad "The King of Thule" (No. 11), which she sings at her spinning wheel, she stops to reconstruct the scene—how embarrassed she was, how she blushed, how like a *grand seigneur* he seemed.

Suddenly she spies the bouquet which she recognizes at once as having come from Siebel, and then the ornate casket. At first she scarcely dares touch the beautiful box—but there is a tiny key, and, gathering her courage, she uses it. Delighted, she ornaments herself with the trinkets she finds there, as she sings the spectacular "Jewel Song" (No. 12).

As she naïvely speculates on the effect she might have on the handsome young stranger if he could but see her now, Martha, a middle-aged town gossip, drops in. She is exclaiming over the jewels and assuring Marguerite that they must be the gift of some unknown lover, when Mephistopheles suddenly enters to ask for Lady Martha Schwerdtlein. That is Martha, of course, and he announces with mock gravity that her husband is dead and sends a greeting. As Martha performs a comic faint in the Devil's arms, Faust slips into the garden and begins complimenting Marguerite on how beautiful she looks in her jewels.

The stage slowly darkens as night falls, and at one side of the garden Mephistopheles with saturnine humor woos the eager Martha, while at the other side, Faust's and Marguerite's relationship progresses tenderly. The Devil slyly watches the two lovers and, ridding himself of the foolish Martha, he steps behind a rosebush and invokes night to aid him in his designs on Marguerite's virtue. For a moment the bush glows with a reddish light, and then Mephistopheles disappears.

The two lovers express their mounting feelings in an exquisite love duet (Nos. 13-a, 13-b), which begins with a faint protest from Marguerite that it is late and she must be getting into the house. But Faust presses his suit passionately, and the two embrace for their first kiss. Their voices blending almost indistinguishably, they whisper the word *éternelle*.

Marguerite is panic stricken by the strength of her own emotions. She begs Faust to leave and not to break her heart. His feeble better nature has a temporary triumph as he tenderly promises to go, asking only to see her again the next day (No. 10). "Yes, at dawn—tomorrow—always," answers Marguerite. She throws him one more kiss and goes into the house.

Mephistopheles is disgusted. "Lunkhead," he calls Faust, "stop a moment and listen to what she has to tell the stars." At this moment Marguerite opens the window, looks out at the soft night, and pours out her heart. Faust, completely forgetting his promise, rushes to the window and embraces Marguerite with a long, passionate kiss.

As the curtain slowly descends, Mephistopheles throws himself on a bench howling with laughter. He now believes he has both souls safe in his grasp.

Act 3

(*Scene 1—customarily omitted*) Some time has passed, and Marguerite, deserted by Faust, has become the laughingstock of the other girls of the town. As she sits disconsolately at her spinning wheel, she sings the aria known as "The Spinning Wheel Song." At the end of this the faithful Siebel comes in to comfort her with the sweet and once very popular melody "When All Was Young" (No. 14). But Marguerite is too distraught for human comforting, and goes to the church to seek God's help.

It is the interior of the cathedral, and Marguerite is seen kneeling apart from her neighbors. As she prays, the voice of Mephistopheles tauntingly mocks her, reminding her of her innocent past, while the church choir solemnly begins the *Dies Irae*. Then suddenly Mephistopheles himself appears out of an open tomb. Marguerite is horrified and tries all the harder to pray, her voice rising higher and higher. The Devil pronounces a curse on her—and terrified, she faints. The worshipers gather around in excitement and finally carry her away.

The campaign which had taken Valentine off to war has ended, and he and the other soldiers have just returned to Leipzig. As they arrive in the village square, women rush in to welcome their men, and the "Soldiers' Chorus" (No. 15) is sung. Then the throng departs, leaving Valentine and the young Siebel alone together. Although Siebel is unable to tell Valentine the truth about his sister, he does arouse the soldier's suspicion by his embarrassed and evasive attitude. As Siebel escapes to the church, Valentine enters his own house to see what has happened during his absence.

Night is beginning to descend as Faust and Mephistopheles arrive before Marguerite's house. Apparently the philosopher's conscience has been plaguing him, for he has insisted on returning, despite the Devil's objections. As the two stand before the doorway of the house, Mephistopheles brings out a guitar and

sings an insulting serenade to Marguerite (No. 16).
Valentine bursts from the house in anger, demanding
to know what is going on, but the Devil merely mocks
him. Enraged, Valentine runs his sword through the
guitar. Mephistopheles then calmly inquires whether
he has an ear for music.

Valentine can stand no more of this persiflage.
Which of the two, he challenges, is going to die for
these insults to his honor? Faust feels obliged to take
up the challenge. In the ensuing duel, Faust, with the
Devil's aid, runs his adversary through.

The two hurry away, as neighbors, hearing the
noise of the duel, rush to Valentine's aid—too late.
When Marguerite appears, Valentine turns on his
sister and curses her. "And should God pardon you
at last," he ends, "be cursed here on earth!" Everyone
recoils in horror at the blasphemy, but Valentine,
with death already rattling at his throat, only repeats his curse. The crowd sinks to its knees in
prayer, as the curtain descends.

Act 4

(Scene 1—often omitted) The setting is the Wal-
purgis Night revels in the Harz Mountains. Mephistopheles has taken Faust to watch the spectacle,
which is performed to the Ballet Music. At the Devil's
command Cleopatra, Laïs, and other queens of antiquity come to join them. But a vision of Marguerite
appears to the doomed philosopher, and, conscience
stricken, he demands to be taken to her.

Gone literally mad after Faust's desertion and

her brother's death, Marguerite has killed her illegitimate child, and is now to be hanged. The scene opens in her prison cell, where Mephistopheles and Faust find her asleep on a pallet of straw on the floor.

Awakened by the visitors, Marguerite's first impulse is to throw her arms about Faust, and she cries pitifully that at last he has come to save her. Faust assures her that nothing can part them now, not even Mephistopheles. But the frenzied girl's mind begins to wander. She relives in her imagination her first sweet meetings with Faust, and the orchestra plays, one after the other, the themes of these meetings (Nos. 7-b, 8, 13-b). Futilely, the philosopher pleads with her to come with him from the prison.

Mephistopheles now bursts in, urging them to hurry. Marguerite, recognizing him, shrinks away in fright and prays wildly to the angels of heaven. The emotions of the three are vividly portrayed in the great final trio of the opera (No. 17-a). Then Marguerite, in her frenzy, imagines Faust's hands to be covered with blood. Dying, she cries, "Go! You fill me with horror!"

As the Devil is gloating over what he believes to be his seizure of one more soul, a chorus of angels answers Marguerite's prayer, declaring that she is saved. A vision suggesting the apotheosis of Marguerite appears on the back wall of the prison, and an Easter hymn of forgiveness sounds out over organ and orchestra.

As the curtain falls, Mephistopheles sweeps Faust away, as though to take him straight to hell.

LOHENGRIN

AN OPERA IN THREE ACTS

by Richard Wagner

Cast

LOHENGRIN .... Tenor

ELSA OF BRABANT .... Soprano

ORTRUD .... Soprano or Contralto

FREDERICK OF TELRAMUND .... Baritone

KING HENRY .... Bass

HERALD .... Baritone or Bass

COUNTS AND OTHER NOBLES, LADIES OF
HONOR, PAGES, MEN AND WOMEN

Time . ... Tenth century

Place . ... Antwerp

First Performance

Hoftheater, Weimar, August 28, 1850

LOHENGRIN

Prelude

THE PRELUDE begins with six tonic chords in A major played high in the violins and flutes, and so soft that they can scarcely be heard. Then the violins alone give out the motive of the Holy Grail (No. 1).* Gradually other instruments are added, and the music rises to a tremendous climax, with the trumpets and trombones spreading out a great *crescendo* on the Grail theme. Beautifully it all fades away until there is nothing but the ethereal whispering of the violins.

Act 1

On the banks of the Scheldt River near Antwerp, King Henry the Fowler is enthroned beneath the judgment oak, surrounded by his Saxon retinue. Across the field Brabantine lords are grouped about their leader, Count Frederick of Telramund, whose wife, Ortrud, is seated by his side.

---

*Thematic Guide, p. 330.

The King's herald signals for trumpeters to sound the royal summons (No. 2), and then he solemnly announces that the King of Germany has come on affairs of state. As the trumpeters again sound their horns, the King rises and reveals that he has come to bid the Brabantines join him in battle against the Hungarians, who, now that a nine-year truce has ended, are eager for war. But, to his dismay, he has found that Brabant is filled with turmoil and unrest, and he calls on Telramund for an explanation.

Now Telramund, after paying homage to the King, relates that when the Duke of Brabant died, he appointed him the guardian of his two children, Elsa and Godfrey. One day the two children went walking in the woods; but only Elsa returned. Convinced by her guilty manner that Elsa had killed her brother, Telramund continues, he renounced the right, granted to him by the old Duke of Brabant, to marry her, and took to himself another bride—Ortrud. Dramatically Telramund accuses Elsa of fratricide and claims the rulership of Brabant.

The crowd is shocked by this terrible accusation, and the King himself can scarcely believe what he has heard. Excitedly, Telramund elaborates on his story, declaring that Elsa killed her brother so that she might rule the dukedom with a secret lover.

This is too much for the King, who silences Telramund with a sharp gesture and asks that the accused be brought forward so that he may proclaim a judgment. As the royal summons is sounded once more, the King hangs his shield on the judgment oak and swears not to use it until a verdict has been rendered. The Saxon and Brabantine nobles echo his oath, and the herald calls upon Elsa to appear.

The beautiful Innocence theme, played entirely by the woodwinds, is heard as Elsa, accompanied by her ladies in waiting, steps forward (No. 3-a). Her appearance and manner so impress the nobles that they marvel that one seeming so pure could be accused of such a crime. Solemnly the King asks whether she is indeed Elsa of Brabant, and she nods assent. When he asks if she knows the charge against her, she gives Telramund and Ortrud a shuddering glance, but still refrains from speaking. The King demands that she admit her guilt, and Elsa, as though in a trance, murmurs, "My poor brother."

The King urges Elsa to speak, and she begins the famous aria "Elsa's Dream" (No. 4). In this she tells how she prayed to God for help, crying out in anguish—a cry that echoed back to her—and she was suddenly overcome by sleep. While in this trance-like sleep, the vision of a knight appeared and tenderly consoled her. An exciting theme of military character, known as the Lohengrin motive (No. 5), accompanies her description of the knight, and she closes her recital to music based on No. 3-b, declaring that this unknown knight shall defend her innocence.

Everyone is deeply moved, and the King calls on Telramund to reconsider his charges; but Telramund angrily challenges anyone who doubts his word to take up a sword against him. The Brabantines cry out that they fight only on his side, and Telramund calls on the King to remember how well he had served him in the war against the Danes. Henry acknowledges Telramund's trustworthiness, and announces that the issue must be decided through trial by combat.

Symbolically Henry thrusts his sword into the earth, as the brasses trumpet out the Trial by Combat motive (No. 6). Then, turning to Elsa, he tells her to choose a champion. Elsa responds that the knight of her dream will be her defender. Her father's dukedom and her hand in marriage will be his reward.

Again trumpeters sound the royal summons (No. 2), and the herald calls in stentorian tones for the champion of Elsa of Brabant to appear. There is no answer, and Elsa begs the King to have the call sounded once more. Again there is no response, and Elsa falls to her knees and prays to God to send her hero once more in the time of her need. Her ladies in waiting pray with her in close harmony, but Elsa's voice rises above them all, and at the end of the prayer the Lohengrin motive (No. 5) is heard softly in the orchestra.

Excitedly the men nearest the river bank exclaim that they see a boat drawn by a swan coming up the river, and in the boat is a knight in magnificent armor. Elsa, still on her knees, remains in the foreground, not daring to look back. A grand climax of welcome to the strange knight works up, at the end of which Lohengrin makes his first move to leave the boat. Silence falls on everyone as the violins breathe the motive of the Grail (No. 1).

With one foot still in the boat, Lohengrin bows toward the swan and sings it a soft farewell (No. 7).

The crowd expresses its awe in a tender melody, and Lohengrin advances to the King, bows, and announces that he has come to defend the accused maiden. Then he turns to Elsa and asks if she will put aside all fear if he acts as her champion. When she replies that she has already lost all fear, he asks a second question: Will she become his wife if he is the victor? Fervently she answers that she will.

And now Lohengrin has one demand to make. Solemnly he tells her that she must never question from whence he comes, what his name is, or what sort of man (No. 8) he may be. Almost in a trance, Elsa replies quickly that she will never ask, and Lohengrin, taking her in his arms, declares that he loves her.

As the crowd sings its tender expression of awe, the knight leads Elsa up to the King and places her under his protection, declaring solemnly that Elsa is guiltless. Once more Telramund is urged to retract his terrible charge—but Telramund would rather die than take back his accusations.

Three Saxon nobles and three Brabantines now measure out the fighting grounds, and the King prays to God to give his judgment of this combat (No. 9). The crowd echoes his prayer, and the signal is given for the trumpeters to sound the summons for the start of the fight. To the accompaniment of the Trial by Combat theme (No. 6), the two lunge at each other. And in the brief battle that follows, Lohengrin fells Telramund. Standing over his helpless opponent, the knight proclaims himself victor and announces that he will spare Telramund's life.

In a stirring closing chorus the crowd joyfully hails the victor, as Telramund and Ortrud lament.

Act 2

The curtain rises on the Cathedral of Antwerp, opposite which are the women's quarters of the citadel of Antwerp. To the back the Pallas, the knights' quarters, can be seen. It is night, and on the steps of the great cathedral sit Ortrud and Telramund, clothed as beggars. They are silent as the orchestra plays a low, ominous prelude. In contrast, gay festal music is heard from the Pallas.

Finally Telramund gloomily mutters that they had better leave. But Ortrud, fiendishly plotting revenge, says they cannot leave now. Turning on her angrily, Telramund blames her for their present outcast state. As he despairingly cries that he would rather have died than suffered such disgrace, the festal trumpet calls from within the Pallas lend ironic contrast.

Ortrud's scorn drives Telramund to even greater fury, and he recalls how she herself told him that she had seen Elsa drown her brother. Sardonically Ortrud tells him that if he had shown as much fight against the stranger as he is now showing against a woman, he would have been the victor. But they may yet find revenge, she adds. And as she spins her plans, Telramund begins to weaken.

The secret spell around this unknown knight, Ortrud says, is not invulnerable, for if he should reveal his name and lineage, he would lose all of his magic powers. They must persuade, or tempt, Elsa to betray Lohengrin. Not only that, Ortrud continues, but if the knight should shed just one drop of blood through the smallest wound, all of his supernatural strength would vanish. Telramund, feeling that his defeat had come about through trickery, is completely won over and is quite willing to swear vengeance.

The theme of Elsa's happiness is heard now in the orchestra (No. 10), and on the balcony of the women's quarters Elsa appears. Sweetly she sings to the night air of her joy over her approaching marriage to Lohengrin (No. 11). Seeing a chance to further her plans, Ortrud calls to Elsa. So realistically does she feign repentance and despair that Elsa is touched and bids Ortrud wait while she comes down to let her into the house.

While Elsa descends the steps inside, Ortrud drops her mask of humbleness and, in a wild frenzy, calls on the pagan gods, Wotan and Freia, to aid her.

Elsa appears, and Ortrud throws herself at her feet. Deeply moved, the young girl raises her enemy, asks her forgiveness for the unhappiness she has caused her, and promises that after her marriage she will intercede with Lohengrin on behalf of Telramund. Ortrud, feigning the greatest gratitude, says that, in return for Elsa's kindness, she feels she must warn her that perhaps Lohengrin may be taken from her by the same magic which brought him.

Elsa is too filled with the rapture of her love to become seriously worried, however, and she pities Ortrud for never having experienced that complete trust and faith which come with true love. Ortrud, in an aside, scornfully remarks that this loving trust will be the very weapon with which she will find her revenge. The two voices blend in a duet that, despite Ortrud's ominous mutterings, is one of the warmest passages in the opera (No. 12).

As Elsa leads Ortrud into the women's quarters, Telramund comes out from his hiding place and muses over his wife's evil scheme.

Day begins to dawn, and from the towers near and far trumpets sound, bringing servants into the courtyard to begin their morning chores. Four trumpeters enter from the Pallas to deliver a royal summons, and knights and courtiers fill the yard in answer to the call. In a rousing chorus they sing of the promise and happiness this day will bring.

Now a herald comes forth with the latest news, given in three sections, each dutifully hailed by the noblemen. First: Telramund has been banished, and anyone who aids him shall suffer the same fate. Second: That strange knight, who has earned the hand of Elsa and with it the dukedom of Brabant, does not desire to be called a Duke, but prefers to be addressed as Guardian of Brabant. And third: Today the wedding shall be celebrated, but tomorrow all must prepare for battle, for the bridegroom plans to follow the King in his campaign against the Hungarians.

As the throng joyously hails these pronouncements, four of the nobles, adherents of Telramund, discontentedly but quietly protest. As they huddle together, Telramund, emerging from his hiding place, joins them. Frightened by his sudden appearance, the four hurry him away before he can be seen by the throng.

Four page boys clear the way for Elsa, whom they announce; and the prenuptial procession begins, the women filing out of their quarters and approaching the cathedral to a slow stately measure (No. 13). As the procession nears the steps of the church, the music mounts to a resounding climax. Suddenly Ortrud advances to the top of the steps and demands her rightful place—before Elsa. Dramatically she reminds everyone that before Lohengrin came, Telramund was honored before all. And who is this man they are now honoring? Not even his bride can name him!

Elsa, rising to the occasion as best she can, spiritedly defends her knight and calls on the people to judge if he is not a noble and good man. The crowd acclaims Lohengrin. But Ortrud cannot be silenced, and she accuses Lohengrin of having used magic and sorcery to gain his victory over Telramund. Even Elsa, she points out, must have some misgivings about this unknown man, for she does not dare ask his name.

This last accusation goes unanswered as the royal summons announces the arrival of the King and Lohengrin, accompanied by Saxon nobles. In tears, Elsa rushes to Lohengrin and begs his protection. Angrily, he orders Ortrud away and then leads Elsa toward the cathedral.

At this moment, Telramund rushes forward and denounces Lohengrin as a sorcerer. He demands to know the knight's name and rank. When Lohengrin refuses to answer, he turns to the King and bids him ask. Before the King can reply, Lohengrin announces that Elsa is the only person who can make him reveal his identity. He turns to her for what he hopes will be confirmation of her faith in him. But Elsa, confused and bewildered and already beset with doubts, is evasive in her response. The King now advises Lohengrin not to reply to Telramund, and the knights express their confidence in their new leader. Unnoticed, Telramund sneaks up to Elsa and whispers that he will be near at hand that night. For if he can but scratch Lohengrin, the secret will be out. Falteringly Elsa refuses to have anything to do with him; and when Lohengrin sees who is talking to his bride, he orders Telramund away.

Now the procession, to an ever-mounting *crescendo*, starts into the Cathedral. At the top of the steps Lohengrin takes Elsa into his arms. But her happiness is far from complete, for over her lover's shoulder she sees Ortrud, her arm raised as though in victory—while the trumpets and trombones in the orchestra ominously sound the warning motive (No. 8).

Act 3

(Scene 1) The brilliant Prelude to Act 3, deservedly one of the most popular pieces in the concert repertoire, glowingly sets the mood for the wedding celebration which is to follow (No. 14). The festal music is interrupted briefly by a reiteration of the warning motive, and finally modulates quietly into the even more famous Bridal Chorus, commonly

known as the "Wedding March from *Lohengrin*"
(No. 15).

The curtain rises on Elsa's and Lohengrin's bridal
chamber. Torchbearing pages enter, followed by
ladies in waiting conducting Elsa in from a door on
the left, while King Henry and the men escort Lohengrin in from the right. The two lovers, left in the
center, are relieved of their outer garments, and the
entire assemblage, singing the Bridal Chorus, wishes
them well and finally leaves.

As the last faint echo of the music fades away in
the distance, Lohengrin takes his bride in his arms
and begins a magnificent duet which combines the
most tender love melodies with the clear tracing of
Elsa's upsurging curiosity about Lohengrin's name,
and his growing dismay as his efforts to avoid the
fatal question fail, one after the other.

In answer to Lohengrin's question—"Is she happy
to be his bride?"—Elsa responds with a love melody
of great warmth and restraint (No. 16), which is finally taken up by Lohengrin. But when the unsuspecting husband tenderly pronounces his bride's
name, the mood changes, and Elsa asks whether he
cannot tell her his name in the privacy of their love
so that she may pronounce his as he has hers. Lohengrin reproaches her tenderly in a lovely aria (No. 17),
but Elsa persists.

"Entrust me with the secret of the place you came
from, and you will see how well I can guard the
knowledge," Elsa argues. Her husband's attempts to
reassure her only strengthen her curiosity, and she
expresses the fear that the magic which brought him

to her may suddenly take him away. Indeed, she becomes so filled with fear that she imagines she sees the swan coming to take her lover from her. All of Lohengrin's frantic imploring does no good now. With the music mounting in excitement, she pronounces the fatal questions in precisely the words that had been forbidden her.

At this very moment Telramund and his four followers stealthily enter the room with drawn swords. Elsa sees them just in time to warn her husband, who mortally wounds Telramund with one magical blow. As the terrified followers sink to their knees, Elsa faints away.

Sadly, Lohengrin places Elsa on the couch and then directs the four men to take the body of Telramund to the King's judgment seat. Summoning two women in waiting, he instructs them to dress Elsa for an appearance before the King, where she will finally learn the answer to her questions. Once more the warning motive (No. 8) is heard, and the curtain falls.

(*Scene 2*) The Saxons and Brabantines have gathered before the judgment oak, where, to their amazement, the four nobles now bring the body of Telramund. Presently Elsa enters, pale and weak, accompanied by her ladies in waiting.

When Lohengrin, clad in armor, arrives, the throng greets him joyfully, for they are eager to have him lead them into battle. Quickly Lohengrin explains that he comes not as a warrior, but as a complainant. Uncovering the body of Telramund, he asks if he was not justified in killing this man who attacked him in his bridal chamber. The nobles vigorously proclaim the justice of the act, and Lohengrin goes on with his second charge: Elsa has broken her oath and has demanded to know his name and from whence he comes. Now he must give the answers before them all.

Accompanied by the theme of the Holy Grail (No. 1), Lohengrin begins his "Narrative" (No. 18). He tells about the castle of Monsalvat, where the Grail is guarded by a band of holy knights. Each year a dove descends from Heaven to strengthen the mystic powers of the Grail. Those who guard it receive magical powers, and no matter to what distant lands the knights are sent on their deeds of goodness, the power remains undiminished so long as the knights remain unknown. The Grail has sent him here: he is the son of the reigning King Parsifal, and he is called Lohengrin (No. 5).

The King and nobles express their sorrow as Lohengrin tenderly takes Elsa in his arms and chides her for what she has done. Elsa can scarcely comprehend the tragedy that has overtaken her, and she begs Lohengrin to stay. The throng joins her in her pleas, but Lohengrin replies that it is mandatory that he leave. Then he assures the King that, although he cannot lead them in the battle against the Hungarians, the campaign nevertheless will be victorious.

Suddenly the swan is seen on the river, and Lohengrin begins his last farewell. He turns to Elsa and tells her sadly that had he only been able to stay with her for one year, the Grail would have sent her brother back. Giving her his sword, his horn, and his ring, he bids her keep them for her brother, should he ever return. He kisses the half-fainting Elsa passionately, and sings his last heartbroken *Leb' wohl*. Then he rushes to the river bank.

Only Ortrud remains unshaken. And, in a burst of fiendish triumph, she reveals that she recognizes, by a little chain about the swan's neck, the animal as Elsa's brother, whom she had magically turned into a swan.

At the river bank Lohengrin sinks to his knees, and as the theme of the Holy Grail (No. 1) comes from the orchestra, a white dove descends from the clouds. The dove takes up the chain, and suddenly the swan disappears—in his place stands young Godfrey. "Behold the Duke of Brabant," cries Lohengrin. He steps into the boat and is slowly drawn down the river.

Elsa and Godfrey embrace, and then the distraught girl rushes to the river bank and calls frantically after her husband. But her cries are futile, for Lohengrin, his head bowed, slowly disappears. As the curtain falls, Elsa sinks lifeless into her brother's arms.

LUCIA DI LAMMERMOOR

(The Bride of Lammermoor)

AN OPERA IN THREE ACTS

by Gaetano Donizetti

Cast

LORD HENRY ASHTON	Baritone
LUCY	Soprano
SIR EDGAR OF RAVENSWOOD	Tenor
LORD ARTHUR BUCKLAW	Tenor
RAYMOND BIDE-THE-BENT	Bass
ALICE	Mezzo-soprano
NORMAN	Tenor

LADIES AND KNIGHTS, PAGES, SOLDIERS,
DOMESTICS

Libretto .... by Salvatore Cammarano
(based on the novel by Sir Walter Scott)
Time . ... .Late sixteenth century
Place . ... Scotland

First Performance

Teatro San Carlo, Naples,
September 26, 1835

LUCIA DI LAMMERMOOR

Act 1

(*The Departure*)

HE FIRST SCENE opens upon the somber grounds of Ravenswood Castle. A group of Lord Henry Ashton's retainers are assembled in hunting array. They are excitedly discussing with Norman, the Captain of the Guard at Ravenswood, a plan for scouring the woods in search of the stranger recently seen roaming about. The retainers leave in a body, while Norman stays behind to confront Sir Henry Ashton, who now approaches frowning haughtily.

Ashton is in a glowering mood, bitter at the thought of the ancient glory long departed from his house. He is obsessed with the notion that his dispossessed foeman, Sir Edgar of Ravenswood, watches in scorn while Ashton now rots among the ruins of Ravenswood. Only a brilliant marriage which he has arranged for his sister Lucy can retrieve Ashton's position. But so far, he exclaims bitterly, his sister has dared disobey him.

Lucy's tutor and confidant, Raymond, intervenes on her behalf, counseling patience. For Lucy, still in mourning for her mother, has no mind at the moment for thoughts of love and marriage. This naïve view provokes Norman's scorn, and in response to Lord Henry's question, he relates how Lucy, not long after her mother's death, was assaulted by a wild boar while wandering through a lonely pathway. Her rescuer was none other than the Ashton enemy, Edgar of Ravenswood. And since that time she and Edgar have been meeting regularly each morning in a secluded spot near by. The news stuns Ashton. During the aria in which he swears every kind of vengeance upon the traitor (No. 1),* Raymond seeks to placate him, while Norman avers that he spoke only to protect Ashton's honor.

The returning huntsmen confirm Norman's story, for they report that they had come upon Edgar during their search of the woods, and that he had dashed past on horseback, pale and noiseless as a shadow. Vows of vengeance burst afresh from Ashton's lips, and when Raymond pleads for faith in Lucy's innocence, Ashton replies that his suit is in vain (No. 2). Only Edgar's lifeblood will assuage him. And while the chorus echoes Ashton's sentiments, Raymond sadly reflects that days of grief will soon be upon them.

The setting now shifts to the entrance of a park, and Lucy emerges from the castle, accompanied by Alice, her faithful companion. They are in a state of agitation. Lucy is fretting that her lover has perhaps already forgotten her; Alice is worried at so risky a love affair and so imprudent a place for a meeting between the two.

---

*Thematic Guide, p. 333.

A fountain in the foreground makes Lucy tremble, for there is a dark legend that tells how, on this very spot, a Ravenswood once murdered the maid that loved him. Once in the darkness and silence of the night, relates Lucy, she heard the maid sigh and saw her wave her hand (No. 3). This, to Alice, is an evil omen, and she pleads vainly with Lucy to forego her fatal love. But Lucy can think only of the ecstasy of having her lover with her (No. 4), and Alice must be content with hoping that her fears will prove unfounded.

When Edgar appears, Alice re-enters the castle, and Lucy hears from her lover the unwelcome news that he must leave for France immediately. However, he must first find Ashton, make peace with him, and ask for Lucy's hand in marriage. Lucy knows her brother only too well and when she advises that their love be kept secret, all of Edgar's resentment against his enemy bursts forth. What more can Ashton want? asks Edgar bitterly; for Ashton has already slain his father and taken his ancestral home. By the tombs of his ancestors he had once sworn vengeance (No. 5), and now he plans to fulfill the vow.

Still overwrought, despite Lucy's attempt to calm him (No. 6), Edgar, with sudden determination, places a ring upon her finger, bidding her swear that she will be his. Their voices rise in a duet as they pledge themselves to each other. Just before parting, Lucy promises to pray for him (No. 7), and once again their voices join in a mutual avowal of love.

Act 2

(*The Marriage Contract*)

Ashton and Norman are engaged in conversation in Lord Henry's apartments at Ravenswood Castle. After a lapse of several months, Ashton has finally ventured to invite friends and kinsmen to celebrate the wedding he plans for Lucy and Lord Arthur Bucklaw. He dreads Lucy's stubborn resistance, despite Norman's assurances that absence will have estranged her from Edgar. Moreover, continues Norman, Edgar's letters to Lucy were intercepted, and the report spread that he had married another.

Lucy enters, pale and listless, with eyes fixed upon her brother. When Ashton remarks upon her pallor and suggests that a gayer demeanor would be more fitting for the occasion, she replies that he knows the reason for her grief and begs him to renounce his horrible enmity (No. 8). In his turn, he exhorts her to be dutiful. But when she remains adamant, he produces in desperation a forged letter which purports to prove Edgar's infidelity. Her last hope gone (No. 9), she declares that only death can comfort her, reiterating the sentiment while Ashton urges her to forget her infatuation.

Festive music is heard in the distance. The nuptial hour approaches, declares Ashton; but to Lucy it is the hour of her doom. Desperately trying to fix the distracted girl's attention upon him, Ashton outlines the urgent political considerations which compel this marriage with Bucklaw. His party has been defeated, and only Bucklaw can save him from the hated Mary who will soon rule Scotland. In an energetic aria, he accuses Lucy of coldly consenting to his ruin (No. 10), and to the same music she pleads for pity. Finally, when she sinks exhausted upon a chair, Ashton leaves to look after the necessary preparations. Lucy has not overtly consented, but she is obviously too distracted to resist.

Raymond now approaches and asks Lucy to go through with the marriage for her brother's salvation (No. 11). She reproaches him for the cruel suggestion, but he urges her to forego all hope of happiness on earth. In the ensuing duet, while she implores her tutor to counsel her and weeps afresh over Edgar's infidelity, Raymond tells her that her sacrifice will be rewarded in Heaven.

A change in scene reveals a hall festively prepared for the prospective bridegroom. After the welcoming bridal chorus (No. 12), Bucklaw expresses his joy and joins with the assembled company in a chorus of congratulation. Taking Bucklaw aside, Ashton warns him that Lucy will seem somewhat distraught. Her mother's death, he explains, still weighs heavily upon her; and Bucklaw must be content when Ashton reiterates the explanation, although disturbing rumors of Edgar and Lucy have reached his ears.

When Lucy arrives, her despondent appearance is glossed over by Bucklaw, who promptly goes to the table and signs the marriage contract. But Ashton has difficulty forcing Lucy to collect herself sufficiently to do the same. No sooner has the deed been signed than the door opens on a cloaked intruder. When the entire company challenges him, he reveals himself in a thunderous voice as Edgar. Amid general consternation, Alice and several other ladies help the fainting Lucy to a seat. In an aside, Edgar and Ashton begin the famous sextet with a recollection of the vengeance each has pledged upon the other (No. 13).

Turning to Alice, Lucy laments that the comfort of death is denied her, while Raymond also in an aside, implores Heaven's mercy upon them in this hour. Four voices are now engaged, and when Alice adds her lamentations, and Bucklaw, his plea for heavenly guidance, the full sextet rises over the chorus of the kinsmen and guests, who pray that Lucy will be shielded from all harm.

Sword in hand, Edgar defies the company, who close in upon him with drawn swords. Only Raymond's intervention prevents what would obviously have been murder. When he shows Edgar the marriage contract as evidence that he no longer belongs here, Edgar turns to Lucy for a denial of her signature. She can scarcely speak, and stifling his rage at her apparent treachery, Edgar returns the ring she gave him as an engagement pledge.

Scarcely aware of what she is doing, Lucy removes Edgar's ring from her own finger. He snatches it from her, throwing it down and stamping on it. Then he curses her and the whole Ashton race, upon whom he swears to be revenged. Horrified by his embittered malediction, the company orders him to leave quickly for his own safety (No. 14). Throwing away his sword, Edgar offers his breast for them to strike;

while Lucy, her voice joined to his, falls on her knees and begs for his life (No. 15).

Again the sextet rises above the chorus: the assembled company commanding Edgar to leave; Bucklaw reiterating the advice; Alice pleading with him to heed it; Lucy continuing to beg for his safety; Raymond urging that all forego rashness and anger; while Ashton bitterly accuses his enemy of having perverted an innocent maiden's affections; and Edgar, in an ecstasy of self-sacrifice, continues to offer himself as a victim to their swords.

Act 3

(Scene 1—Nowadays customarily omitted in performance.) Alone in his rudely furnished chamber in Wolfscrag tower, Edgar paces about, listening to the storm outside and reflecting how aptly it mirrors his tempestuous fortune. Ashton appears, come to avenge his honor; but Edgar reminds him that this place holds the spirits of Ashton's many victims, and bitterly bids him beware lest they rise to confound him.

With savage joy in the obvious torture he is inflicting, Ashton reports the details of Lucy's marriage, until Edgar, with haughty impatience, bids him say plainly why he came. To arrange a duel between them, replies Ashton. And after several impassioned defiances are flung back and forth, they agree to meet at dawn near the moldering tombs of Ravenswood. They join voices in a closing duet, each professing his joy that the hour of vengeance is at hand.

The scene now reverts to the hall in Ravenswood Castle. Dance music is heard in the adjoining rooms, and toward the rear of the stage wedding guests stand about, conversing in groups. They are united in an optimistic choral declaration signifying that strife is now over, and fate smiles once more, when Raymond enters, pale and scarcely able to stand. Gesturing to the company to gather around him, he tells how he had heard screams of anguish from the bridal chamber, and entering, discovered Lucy holding the dagger with which she had just murdered her husband (No. 16). Her eyes are vacant; she is hopelessly mad. After the company comments in chorus upon this tragedy, Lucy enters, dishevelled and dressed in a plain white gown.

In a rambling monologue, she calls for Edgar. She is seized by a fit of trembling, enjoins her lover to rest beside her near the fountain, and then in terror sobs that the specter stands between them. Suddenly calm—for she has found her Edgar again—she gently bids her beloved take shelter near the rose-strewn altar, and with mounting excitement describes the wedding ceremony which she imagines she is living through with him. Now that she believes herself married to Edgar (No. 17), she paints an ecstatic picture of their happiness together, while the company interjects doleful comments upon her delusion.

Ashton rushes in, horrified by the news of the crime, and instantly begins upbraiding Lucy for her perfidy, when he notices her strange pallor. Overcome by the realization of her madness, Ashton calls upon Heaven for pity. But his glowering looks and bitter tone have taken root in Lucy's disordered mind, and she is soon lost in a reliving of the bitter scene when her lover rejected her. She pleads with Edgar not to look so darkly upon her, nor speak so wrathfully, for he knows she must obey her brother. In a frenzied assurance that she is ever faithful, her voice rises above the lamentations of Raymond and Ashton. For a moment she imagines with horror that Bucklaw stands beside her. Falling on her knees she begs Edgar not to leave her, while the bystanders accompany her outcries with grief-stricken exclamations.

A hush falls upon the company as, in a sweet song, she enjoins that there be no weeping and asks that a flower be placed on her grave (No. 18). As the others again join in chorus, her voice soars over theirs, now happily affirming that she will wait in Heaven for her beloved. At the climax of the scene she falls swooning into Alice's arms. Ashton rushes off in consternation, after asking Alice and Raymond to provide her with whatever comfort they can. As Lucy is led away, Raymond turns upon Norman and accuses him of having been the root of this mischief with his malicious talebearing. Commending him to the vengeance of Heaven, Raymond follows Lucy off stage, while Norman, cowed and flustered, leaves by the opposite exit.

The final scene takes place outside Wolfscrag Castle near the tombs of Ravenswood. Alone among the graves of his ancestors, Edgar watches Ravenswood Castle illuminated in the distance and imagines Lucy surrounded by a rejoicing throng. He reflects wearily that he is the last of his line, and that his life is a desert without her. Embodying his sentiments in an aria bidding earth a last farewell, he asks only that his grave be forgotten even by the one who betrayed him (No. 19).

The sorrowing company emerging from Ravenswood Castle now cross the stage, and in response to Edgar's questions they inform him of Lucy's madness and of her death. A bell tolls the death knell, and when Edgar hears that Lucy in her final hour called for him, he is overcome with grief. Raymond restrains him from rushing off to Ravenswood; and Edgar, controlling himself, prays that her blessed spirit look down upon him in pity (No. 20). He is resolved to live no longer. And despite attempts to calm him, he stabs himself, while the onlookers gasp in horror. Reiterating his desire to be parted from Lucy no longer, Edgar dies, while the chorus implores Heaven's mercy upon him.

MADAME BUTTERFLY

AN OPERA IN TWO ACTS (LATER IN THREE ACTS)

by Giacomo Puccini

Cast

MADAME BUTTERFLY (CHO-CHO-SAN)	Soprano
SUZUKI	Mezzo-soprano
KATE PINKERTON	Mezzo-soprano
B. F. PINKERTON	Tenor
SHARPLESS	Baritone
GORO	Tenor
PRINCE YAMADORI	Baritone
THE BONZE	Bass
YAKUSIDÉ	Baritone
THE IMPERIAL COMMISSIONER	Bass
THE OFFICIAL REGISTRAR	Baritone
CHO-CHO-SAN'S MOTHER	Mezzo-soprano
THE AUNT	Mezzo-soprano
THE COUSIN	Soprano
TROUBLE	Mute

CHO-CHO-SAN'S RELATIONS AND FRIENDS, SERVANTS

Libretto by Luigi Illica and Giuseppe Giacosa
(based on a story by John Luther Long
and a play by David Belasco)

Time Early twentieth century
Place Nagasaki, Japan

First Performance
La Scala, Milan, February 17, 1904

MADAME BUTTERFLY

Act 1

THE STORY takes place near the harbor of Nagasaki forty years before that city was destroyed by an atomic bomb. To a gay and busy little theme (No. 1)* the curtain rises as Goro, a bowing and scraping Japanese marriage broker, shows Lieutenant Benjamin Franklin Pinkerton, U.S.N., the home he has rented. It is a wonderful little place, in which rooms can be made to appear and disappear just by sliding a partition in or out. Like a tower, as Goro says, it jumps out of the earth—and can disappear as quickly. The contract for the rent is just as conveniently evanescent: for though it runs for nine hundred and ninety-nine years, it can be canceled at a month's notice. And equally convenient is the marriage contract that Pinkerton has negotiated through Goro: good for nine hundred and ninety-nine years, but it can be annulled any month during that time.

Lighthearted and carefree—the traditional attitude of the American sailor—is the way Lieutenant Pinkerton enters on this business. Quickly he interviews the

*Thematic Guide, p. 338.

staff of three servants Goro has lined up for him, and is enchanted with their names—Miss Gentle Breeze of Morning (known as Suzuki), Ray of the Golden Sunbeam, and Sweet-scented Pinetree. He is a little less enchanted with Goro's account of his future bride's family, which Goro enumerates in detail to another busy little theme (No. 2). But his spirit perks up when the American Consul Sharpless, at Nagasaki, enters to discuss the forthcoming match (No. 3).

To the accompaniment of a couple of drinks of whisky, the Lieutenant explains to Goro the delightful elasticity of Japanese houses and contracts. And after the orchestra has enunciated a phrase from *The Star-Spangled Banner*, he sings a little song in praise of that peculiar American brand of imperialism which believes in traveling all over the world to make money —and women (No. 4).

In vain Sharpless tries to make the carefree, egotistical Pinkerton take a more serious attitude. "An easygoing gospel," he warns, "but likely to end in heartbreak." "Is the bride pretty?" Goro, who has been eavesdropping, answers the last question: not only is she a garland of flowers and a bright-shining star, but she is costing Pinkerton only a hundred yen —less than fifty dollars.

Now Sharpless takes Pinkerton aside and asks him whether he is crazy drunk to do this. Gaily, with an almost untranslatable pun, Pinkerton replies that it depends on just how "fried" he considers him to be. Anyway, he cannot say whether it's love or a whim —she is so enchanting that he cannot resist her (No. 5). His misgivings mounting, Sharpless says that she visited the Consulate the other day, and though he did not see her, her voice had such mystery that it touched him to the heart. It would be sinful to wreck so trusting a heart. Pinkerton merely says that a middle-aged fellow like the Consul can't see that it is no great harm to introduce her to the delights of love. And giving Sharpless another drink, he proposes a toast to the day when the Lieutenant shall be married in a *real* wedding.

At this moment Goro breathlessly announces the coming of the bride and her party, and we hear them off stage approaching, with Butterfly's voice soaring above the rest as she sings to her coming happiness. It is eloquent music, and the melodies are heard again later in the opera, especially in the famous love duet that closes the first act (Nos. 6, 7, and 8).

It is quite an entourage that Butterfly has brought, and their relationships to her, as well as her own history, are revealed in a series of questions from Sharpless, answers by Butterfly, and comments from Pinkerton and the members of the entourage.

Butterfly, it seems, comes of a family that has seen better days. Her mother is poor through no fault of her own; her father committed suicide on the invitation of the Mikado. One uncle, an important official known as "the Bonze," has absented himself because he disapproves of the marriage; another uncle is present but, as usual, tipsy. And her younger relatives and friends, who see Pinkerton for the first time, disagree on the quality of his looks, one of the girls even claiming that he had been offered first to her but that she had refused him. Butterfly herself, it turns out, is only fifteen years old (a pretty advanced age, in her opinion), and Sharpless, along with the audience, is utterly charmed with her childlike sincerity and directness.

Pinkerton has become somewhat impatient with the alien fussiness of the whole procedure—particularly the posturings of his prospective mother-in-law—and Goro manages to restore some semblance of order by procuring drinks and sweetmeats for the company. Then, in a quiet little interview with her fiancé, Butterfly takes from her full sleeves her "lady's trifles"—handkerchiefs, pipe, buckle, mirror, fan, a jar of make-up (which she promptly throws away when Pinkerton disapproves), the dagger her father had used to commit hara-kiri (which she regards most sacredly), and some little images representing her ancestors in the religion of ancestor worship in which she has been brought up. But casting these aside, she whispers to Pinkerton (lest the others hear) that yesterday she had gone to a Christian Mission, and that she wishes to adopt the religion of her new husband —she will kneel in the same church with him and give up her own people.

Now, on the prompting of Goro, the Commissioner reads out the marriage contract pompously; the bride, groom, and witnesses all sign—and the Commissioner and Sharpless leave. The marriage ceremony is thus quickly over, and a toast is drunk to the happy pair (No. 9).

But this is suddenly interrupted by someone off stage angrily cursing Butterfly by her Japanese name —"Cho-cho-san! Cho-cho-san! You abomination!"

(No. 10). It is the Bonze, Butterfly's clergyman uncle who, in a towering rage, accuses her of having become a Christian, and thunders curses at her in Japanese: "Kami sarundasioc!" All her relatives and friends renounce her; and when Pinkerton angrily orders them from the place, they leave hurriedly, expressing their horror and hatred even after they have gone.

Butterfly has been standing through all this, her face hidden in her hands, and now she breaks into tears. Pinkerton then takes her hands in his own, telling her that all her relatives and all the Bonzes in Japan are not worth one tear from her beautiful beloved eyes.

Slowly the girl's fright ebbs, and quiet descends on the scene . . . evening begins to fall. Suzuki is heard saying her Japanese prayers, as the servants slide the partitions of the house to prepare the marriage chamber. And with her lord and master sitting by smoking a cigarette, Butterfly changes her wedding garment for one of pure white and sits on a cushion arranging her hair. Finally she murmurs, "They have renounced Butterfly; they have renounced her—and she is happy." Then she sings of her growing happiness, and Pinkerton becomes increasingly enchanted with his strange little child-bride. First tenderly, then more and more urgently, he urges her to come with him into the house. And with voices rising in passionate unison as they sing to the descending night, they slowly enter their new home together. It is one of the most sweeping melodic love duets in all opera (Nos. 11, 12, 6, 7, 8).

Act 2 — Part 1

It is three years later in Butterfly's house, and early in the morning Suzuki is praying to a figure of Buddha that Butterfly may weep less. For in all this time they have not heard from Pinkerton, and their money is running low. Butterfly is contemptuous of Suzuki's Japanese gods and stoutly maintains that her husband's god will take care of them. Why, she asks, did he have the Consul provide this house if he did not intend to return? But Suzuki, far from convinced, says that she never heard of a foreign husband's returning. Butterfly is so angry at this that she seizes Suzuki and virtually forces her to admit that Pinkerton will prove faithful to his promise.

Then Butterfly breaks ecstatically into her famous aria, in which she graphically describes how one day they will see first some smoke, then a ship; then she will not go to the harbor to meet him but will wait on the hill—partly to tease him, and partly not to die of that first meeting. He will call, he will come, he will use all the old endearments. Suzuki shall see! (No. 13).

When Suzuki is dismissed, Goro and Sharpless appear in the garden, but it is the Consul who comes in alone. Butterfly, who has not seen him in a long time, is utterly delighted with the visit, and makes such a fuss over the middle-aged gentleman—offering him a seat (too low for him), a pipe (he doesn't use one), a cigarette, a light—and prattles away so cheerfully that poor Sharpless cannot get down to the business that brought him.

The fact is that Sharpless has a letter from Pinkerton announcing his marriage to an American girl. But before he can tell her, she asks at what time of the year robins nest in America, for it was at that season that Pinkerton had promised her he would return. Goro overhears this last question (which Sharpless evades) and enters, laughing. The fact is that the marriage broker has long taken the measure of the American naval officer and has been urging Butterfly, much to her annoyance, to make another match through his kind offices.

Goro's latest candidate for Butterfly's hand enters a moment later with a snatch of the Japanese national anthem (No. 14) and followed by two servants. It is a prince, no less, Prince Yamadori, who, though he has been married and divorced several times, promises to be faithful to Butterfly. Firmly Butterfly declines the polite offer, and points out that though it might be legal for her to marry again in Japan, the divorce laws of her own country are more stringent —and her own country is, of course, the United States. Declining a cup of tea, the Prince makes one last slightly grotesque appeal and leaves, accompanied by his servants and Goro.

Now at last Sharpless has his opportunity to read her the sad news in the Letter Duet which follows (No. 15). But at each phrase Butterfly shows such eagerness and confidence that finally Sharpless puts aside the letter and asks what she would do if Pinkerton were never to return. "Either become a geisha girl again," says Butterfly, "or—better—die."

Painfully embarrassed, Sharpless gives up trying to

tell her the news and instead urges her to accept the hand of Yamadori. Butterfly almost faints over the implications of such advice coming from this source, but rallies and tells Sharpless it is utterly impossible, for see . . . and she brings forth her little son (No. 16), of whom she is inordinately proud—as he looks far more American than Japanese. "No!" she passionately cries, while the music suggests a Japanese fate (No. 17), she could not possibly now go back to being a geisha girl. She could not sing and entertain. She could only die.

Calming down a little, Butterfly tells Sharpless that the child's name is Trouble—but will be changed to Joy when his father returns. The father knows nothing of the existence of the child, but she urges Sharpless to write him. Sharpless, who knows that Pinkerton's ship has already been sighted off Japan, promises that Pinkerton shall be told. He hastily leaves, utterly defeated.

A moment later Suzuki roughly drags in Goro, who has been skulking about and has been spreading evil rumors about the doubtful paternity of Trouble. He tries to defend himself by saying that in America such children are shunned by everyone. Butterfly is so angered that she shouts, "Liar! Liar!" at him and threatens to kill him with her father's old dagger. The little fellow barely makes his escape, and Butterfly whispers endearments and promises to her little son.

Just then a cannon is heard in the harbor, and Butterfly, seizing a telescope, looks down the hill at the back and sees a white man-of-war with the American flag and the name *Abraham Lincoln*. It is Pinkerton's ship. "You see, you see!" she cries, "my love and faith have triumphed!" And she makes Suzuki help her in the delightful task of decorating the room with cherry blossoms, lilies, violets, and white roses as they sing the charming Flower Duet (No. 18). They then set about decorating both Butterfly and the little boy, as the sun begins to set.

As night comes on more rapidly, the screen to the veranda is drawn, and Butterfly makes three holes in it. One is for little Trouble, seated on a cushion before the screen; one, a little higher, for Suzuki, who sits next to him; and the last, much higher, for Butterfly herself, who plans to stand through the night as she keeps her vigil watching the harbor. The rays of the moon light up the screen; the orchestra and a humming chorus give the tender music of the Letter Duet (No. 15); Suzuki and the baby fall asleep; but as the curtain ascends, Butterfly remains standing at her post, rigid and motionless.

Part 2

During the orchestral interlude that separates the two parts of this act, and even before the curtain rises, we hear the sounds of sailors calling offshore from the *Abraham Lincoln*. It is dawn as the curtain rises; the baby is still asleep on its cushion, and so is Suzuki, but Butterfly remains standing just as she had been. With a start, Suzuki wakens and urges Butterfly to take a rest. The mother picks up the child and sings it a tender little lullaby (No. 16) as she walks out. She is scarcely in her room when Pinkerton and Sharpless surprise Suzuki by coming in and urging her to speak quietly.

The girl tells them how Butterfly has kept her vigil and reveals the way the room has been decorated against Pinkerton's arrival. But suddenly she sees an American lady walking in the garden. "Who is she, who is she?" she keeps asking, sensing at once that it may be Pinkerton's wife. Sharpless finally tells her the truth, for Pinkerton lacks the moral courage, and Suzuki falls to her knees in anguish. Sharpless, raising her, explains that they have come thus early hoping to enlist her aid and advice, but Suzuki is so distraught she can hardly speak to them. The Consul virtually has to force Suzuki to go out and ask the new Mrs. Pinkerton to come in; and when she has gone, Pinkerton tells Sharpless he cannot possibly stay here. He presses some money into his friend's hand, sings an emotional farewell to the place where he had known only flowers and love (No. 19), and runs away.

Kate Pinkerton now comes in, promising Suzuki that she will take care of the child as if she were his own mother; but they are interrupted by Butterfly, who has heard voices. She searches eagerly everywhere for her husband, and then suddenly sees Kate. A few questions asked of Suzuki and Sharpless, a few evasive answers, and the truth slowly and horribly dawns on Butterfly. Kate tries to be sympathetic, and asks whether Pinkerton can have his child. Yes, says Butterfly with a fateful finality (No. 17), if he will come to get him in half an hour.

The day is shining brightly after Kate and Sharpless have gone, and Butterfly decides it is too cheerful for what she plans to do. She orders her sobbing servant to close the screen and pull the curtains, and then go to play with the child. Having lighted the lamp in front of a statue of Buddha, she takes the white veil from it and throws it across the screen.

Finally Butterfly takes the dagger from the wall near the Buddha, kisses the blade piously, and reads the words inscribed on it: "Death with honor is better than life with dishonor." It is the message the Mikado had sent her father when demanding his suicide. But just as she is about to press it to her throat, her little child runs in, pushed from the door by Suzuki's hand. She covers the baby with kisses, sings him a passionate farewell (No. 20), and then carefully seats him on a stool. She gives him an American flag to play with, gently bandages his eyes, and taking the dagger with her, disappears behind the screen.

A moment later the knife is heard falling, the white veil is snatched from the screen, and Butterfly totters out with it about her throat. She reaches toward the child and is feebly embracing him, when Pinkerton's voice is heard off stage calling, "Butterfly! Butterfly!" Then, as the orchestra thunders out the most fateful music of the opera (No. 17), Pinkerton and Sharpless rush in. They are, of course, just too late, for Butterfly has died. And as Pinkerton falls sobbing to his knees, Sharpless takes up the child and kisses him. Quickly the curtain falls.

The Marriage
of Figaro

THE MARRIAGE OF FIGARO

(Le Nozze di Figaro)

AN OPERA IN FOUR ACTS

by Wolfgang Amadeus Mozart

Cast

COUNT ALMAVIVA	Baritone
FIGARO	Bass
DOCTOR BARTOLO	Bass
DON CURZIO	Tenor
DON BASILIO	Tenor
ANTONIO	Bass
COUNTESS ALMAVIVA	Soprano
SUSANNA	Soprano
CHERUBINO	Soprano
MARCELLINA	Soprano
BARBARINA	Mezzo-soprano

Libretto by Lorenzo da Ponte
(based on the play by Pierre de
Beaumarchais)
Time Latter half of the eighteenth century
Place Almaviva's estate near Seville

First Performance
Burgtheater, Vienna, May 1, 1786

THE MARRIAGE
of
FIGARO

Overture

THE JOYOUS Overture delightfully sets the tone of swift-running comedy for the whole opera. Its principal themes (Nos. 1 and 2)* are never used in the opera itself but are completely in character and might—had Mozart been less prodigal of his genius for melody—have been economically employed as musical material for two more of the many wonderfully melodic arias and concerted numbers which adorn the score.

Act 1

The curtain rises (following a light and engaging overture) upon a half-furnished apartment which Figaro and Susanna are to occupy after their marriage. At the moment Figaro is measuring the room, trying to fix upon the most convenient location for the bed which is the Count's wedding present to them, while Susanna stands before a mirror trying on

---

*Thematic Guide, p. 342.

a hat. (Much of the duet is carried on over a lilting orchestral figure No. 3.)

Surprised that Susanna does not appreciate the apartment the Count has put aside for their use, Figaro points out its advantages. Should the Countess require you at night, it is but two steps to her chamber (No. 4). And should the Count call for Figaro's services, then the summons can be answered in a trice. But Susanna shrewdly remarks, knowing the Count better than Figaro does, that should his lordship send Figaro off on an overnight errand, then it is still only three steps from the Count's bedroom to hers. For his information, she continues, the Count has already focused his roving eye upon her, and Don Basilio, the singing teacher, has already been pressuring her to accede to the Count's wishes.

The *droit du Seigneur*, which the Count regretfully renounced, he now plans to renew upon her. Just then the Countess rings for Susanna, and when she leaves, Figaro reflects in a light, sly aria that if his lordship would dance, he (Figaro) will call the tune (No. 5). When it comes to cunning, Figaro is surely a match for his master.

Following Figaro's departure, old Bartolo arrives accompanied by Marcellina, his elderly housekeeper. He has never forgiven Figaro his part in the farce that robbed him of his ward Rosina, who is now the Countess, and whom Bartolo had himself intended to marry.* For her part, Marcellina is in love with

---

*For this part of the story, see *The Barber of Seville.* Beaumarchais' play, on which the present opera is based, was a sequel to *The Barber.*

Figaro, and flourishing a contract (Figaro owes her money), outlines a plan whereby she can have her Figaro and he (Bartolo), his revenge. If Susanna can be persuaded to reject the Count's advances, then the latter, in his anger, may perhaps help Marcellina force Figaro to marry her.

The "revenge" aria which Bartolo now sings (No. 6) is a masterly characterization of this pompous and rather pitiable fool who imagines, despite his rich experience to the contrary, that his astuteness, acuteness, and discernment will suffice to dispose of Figaro readily. Susanna's return, after Bartolo's exit, precipitates a neat exchange of compliments between her and Marcellina, which soon degenerates from mock courtesy to outright malicious name calling.

Marcellina, worsted in the verbal duel, retires, and Cherubino, the Count's page, rushes on stage, imploring Susanna to intercede for him with the Countess, his godmother. Last night the Count, moral enough where his servants are concerned, caught him with Barbarina, the gardener's daughter, and promptly dismissed him. This adolescent Don Juan can scarcely keep the object of his affections in focus. One moment it is Barbarina, another it is Susanna (for, he exclaims, he will never see her again if he is dismissed). Finally it is the Countess, whose ribbon he snatches from Susanna, sighing with envy over the duties Susanna performs for her mistress (robing and disrobing her, binding her tresses, pinning her bodice).

In return for the ribbon he offers Susanna a song composed for her, for the Countess, for Barbarina, for Marcellina: in brief, for any and every woman. He sings a breathless little aria about the anguish and delight of love (No. 7), and hearing the Count approach, conceals himself behind the sofa on which the Count seats himself upon his arrival.

Intimating that by now Susanna must have learned his intentions from Don Basilio, the Count proposes a meeting in the garden that evening. But his suit is interrupted by the sound of Don Basilio's voice; and the Count, also deeming it unwise to be found in Susanna's room, moves to hide behind the sofa. Just in time Cherubino vacates without detection, allowing the Count to replace him and in turn taking the Count's place upon the sofa. Hastily covering Cherubino with one of the Countess's dresses, Susanna turns to confront Basilio, who has come to urge upon her the advisability of submitting to the Count's embraces. Moreover, continues the old scandalmonger, Cherubino has been seen prowling around this room, and the manner in which he looks at the Countess while at table is bound to stir up trouble. He (Basilio) would, of course, never think of creating scandal, but everybody is talking.

Unable to control his curiosity any longer, the Count reveals himself and demands to know what this talk is all about. In reply Susanna pretends to faint; but when they propose putting her on the sofa, she promptly recovers. The Count's grievances against Cherubino are now double: his infatuation with the Countess, and the affair with Barbarina, which he begins to relate. Coming to the part at which he lifted the tablecloth in Barbarina's room and discovered his page hiding under the table, the Count illustrates the scene by lifting the dress from the sofa. To his amazement, Basilio's delight, and Susanna's mortification, he uncovers Cherubino.

Quickly recovering, the Count begins to exploit the situation. First he orders Basilio to fetch Figaro, so the latter may see how his intended bride disports herself. But when Susanna quickly explains what Cherubino was doing there, it suddenly dawns upon the Count that his overtures to Susanna had been overheard. Cherubino now has a hold over him, and even though the page insists that he tried not to listen, the Count realizes that the play has been taken out of his hands.

Just then Figaro arrives with a crowd of peasants, who sing a chorus of praise to the Count. Figaro is holding a bridal veil, and it impresses him as the strategic time to maneuvre the Count into a public renunciation of the *droit du Seigneur*. He invites the Count to place the veil upon Susanna's head, but the nobleman counters with a speech, as pretty as it is empty, in which he artfully manages to postpone the action to some future date.

The peasants leave after another chorus of praise. Only Cherubino is downcast; and when the Count refuses to hear his plea for forgiveness, a gentle reminder of his page's infinite capacity for silence forces the Count to concede that, for the while, it is best to have Cherubino on his side. Ostensibly extending his pardon, the Count appoints him an ensign in his regiment. Since the regiment is going abroad, Cherubino is thus neatly disposed of. This strikes Figaro as a rather humorous assignment; and the act ends in a mock military tone as he tells Cherubino that his days of philandering are now over (No. 8).

Act 2

The scene changes to a handsomely furnished room, where the Countess is seated alone, recollecting her former bliss and invoking the aid of the God of Love to restore her husband's errant affection in the first serious—and very beautiful—aria in the opera (No. 9). When Susanna arrives, the conversation turns to the infidelity and jealousy of men; but upon Figaro's appearance they discuss the plan which he outlines for trapping the Count. On his own initiative he has sent the Count an anonymous letter (much to the Countess's dismay) advising him of a meeting between the Countess and her lover this night. Further, Susanna is to agree to meet the Count in the garden, and Cherubino, dressed in girl's clothing, is to take her place. When matters are sufficiently advanced, the Countess is to surprise her husband in the garden. Figaro takes himself off, gaily singing a fragment of his earlier aria (No. 5) in which he reiterates that if the Count would dance, it will be to Figaro's guitar.

Cherubino must now be rehearsed for his forthcoming performance with the Count, but when he arrives, he is first prevailed upon to sing his charming song about love ("Voi che sapete") (No. 10). The Countess commends him warmly, but Susanna, locking the door, promptly gets down to the business of trying woman's apparel on Cherubino. His commission, they discover, has not yet been sealed by the Count, and while Susanna is fitting him out and giving him instructions, both women comment on the prettiness of their little darling. As Susanna rolls up his sleeves, the ribbon he had taken from her is revealed, and the Countess, recognizing it, is touched by the boy's confusion and his obvious devotion to her.

Suddenly the Count's knock is heard on the door. Cherubino darts into the anteroom, Susanna hides in the alcove, and the Countess goes to the door to admit her husband. The locked door and a noise from the anteroom (Cherubino has overturned a chair) rouse the Count's suspicions. He demands to know who is locked in the anteroom, and the flustered Countess assures him it is Susanna.

During the ensuing trio, the Count calls out to Susanna to answer, the Countess urges her to remain silent, while Susanna, hidden in the alcove, comments upon the seemingly inextricable situation they are now in. Finally the Count, determined to know who is within and aware that it is best not to make a scandal before the servants, goes off to fetch some tools to force open the door himself. As a precaution against trickery, he closes all doors and takes the Countess with him.

No sooner are they gone than Susanna rushes from the alcove calling to Cherubino to get out quickly. He does so, but finding all exits locked, and in a panic over the prospect of facing the Count again, he runs to the window and jumps out. Susanna looks out after him, but noting that the little rogue is already a mile away, she hastily makes for the anteroom and locks herself in.

Unaware of the change in the situation, the Countess confesses to the Count upon their return that Cherubino is hidden in the anteroom. There is no point to his jealous rage, she assures him, for Cherubino is only a child. Somewhat mollified, yet determined to teach this irritating imp a lesson, he draws his sword, opens the door, and stands confounded as Susanna gravely emerges. Her ironical comments leave him speechless. And as he gropes around in the anteroom to make sure that Cherubino is nowhere concealed, Susanna takes advantage of his momentary absence to assure the bewildered Countess that Cherubino has made good his escape.

Aided by Susanna, the Countess quickly assumes the role of an unjustly accused wife. Between the two the Count is soon reduced to hang-dog contrition. But the letter purporting to reveal an assignation between the Countess and her lover still rankles, and when they explain that it was some of Figaro's tomfoolery, he is all for venting his bewildered anger upon his valet. However, he is compelled to forgive Figaro if he would have the Countess forgive him.

Everything is neatly ironed out when Figaro makes his appearance, inviting the Count to join the wedding festivities already in progress. Still somewhat suspicious of the explanation offered him about the letter, the Count shows it to his valet, who of course blandly denies all knowledge of the document. The women quickly set Figaro straight, and dropping the pretense of innocence, he joins his voice to theirs in imploring the Count to hasten the wedding. Once again at a loss, the Count turns the trio into a quartet by muttering that Marcellina is now his last resource.

Just then Antonio, the gardener, enters. He is half drunk and blathering wildly about things that people throw out of windows. When men start throwing themselves out, breaking his carnation vases in the process, then the limit has been reached. This story arouses the Count, but Figaro, catching the signal from the women, promptly announces that he was the one. This Antonio can scarcely credit, since the person who jumped seemed a boy half Figaro's size. Such optical illusions are common, explains Figaro, but the Count promptly pounces on this and declares that it was Cherubino. Since Cherubino is supposed to be in Seville, Figaro ironically agrees that of course it must have been the page just returned from town on horseback.

However, when the gardener seriously insists that no horse came flying through the window, the Count, grimly hanging on to his sanity, turns fiercely to Figaro and demands a forthright explanation. It is simply this, explains Figaro nursing a suddenly sore ankle: not wanting to meet the Count because of the faked letter, he took the only exit available—which was through the window. Well, then, says Antonio, here are the papers you dropped. Before Figaro can get a look at them, the Count seizes them from the gardener, takes a quick look—the papers are Cherubino's commission—and craftily asks Figaro to identify them. Figaro plays for time, fumbling among the papers he extracts from his pockets. Taking a whispered hint (relayed from the Countess to Susanna and from Susanna to him), he finally declares that it is the license the young man gave him because it required a seal. The Count checks and finding that the commission does indeed lack a seal, he tears up the document in a rage.

Bartolo, Basilio, and Marcellina now arrive, and much to the Count's delight, Marcellina announces that Figaro has contracted to marry her. Susanna, Figaro, and the Countess are dumfounded; Bartolo, Basilio, and Marcellina are triumphant; while the Count joyously declares that he will hear the case and see that justice is done. As the curtain falls, all are united in a septet in which each simultaneously expresses his or her view of the matter.

Act 3

In a room elegantly decorated for the wedding festivities, the Count paces back and forth, turning over in his mind the puzzling details for which he still seeks an explanation: Susanna hidden in the anteroom, a man jumping out of a window, his wife's agitation. . . . He suspects his servants, for "what won't the rabble dare do nowadays?" The letter still worries him, although the Countess, he feels, is above suspicion. His own tarnished honor causes him a twinge or two, however.

While he pursues his scattered thoughts, Susanna and the Countess enter in the background, and between them arrange for the Countess to impersonate

Susanna at the latter's rendezvous with the Count. When the Countess retires, Susanna approaches the Count. He suspects that Susanna has told the Countess of his secret plan to renew his *droit du Seigneur* with her, in which event he intends to revenge himself by marrying Figaro to Marcellina.

After some careful conversation, heavily weighted with innuendo, they agree in a beautiful duet (No. 11) to meet in the garden that night. Just as the Count is congratulating himself, Figaro appears, and the Count overhears Susanna whisper to him that their suit has been won without a lawyer. After they leave, the Count gives vent to his anger at being made a plaything by his servants, and in a powerful aria (No. 12) assures the pair that they will know of his wrath.

The trial is now at hand, and Don Curzio (a lawyer), arriving with Marcellina, Bartolo, and Figaro, states Marcellina's claim. Figaro borrowed a thousand pieces of silver from her, and he must now either pay the old lady or marry her. But, argues Figaro, he really is of gentle birth and hence must have his parents' consent. Unfortunately, he doesn't know who they are, since he was stolen when a child. His only clue (and thus far, a meaningless one) is an odd mark on his arm.

"A spatula under your right elbow?" asks Marcellina. And when it turns out that she has described it correctly, then the absurd truth is at last revealed. Marcellina is Figaro's mother, and Bartolo, his father. Both fall on his neck, and Susanna, entering to find Figaro in Marcellina's arms, instantly decides that the wretch has already betrayed her. In the magnificent sextet which follows, the welter of confused exclamations and explanations finally resolves into a general chorus of rejoicing.

The trial over, and the stage clear once again, Barbarina enters with Cherubino, whom she invites to her cottage to meet the prettiest girls in the village. To escape the Count's notice, she decides that she will dress Cherubino in her clothes, and they go off. The Countess arrives upset over the deception she has agreed to practice upon her husband. Her love for him remains firm, and in the beautiful aria "Dove sono" she recalls her vanished happiness. Flown forever, love's sunny splendour (*Dove sono i ben momenti*, No. 13).

After her exit Antonio and the Count cross the stage in conversation, the gardener informing his master that Cherubino has returned. As they disappear the Countess returns with Susanna. In a lovely "Letter Duet," she dictates to her maid a note to the Count confirming the rendezvous in the garden (No. 14). The note is sealed with a pin, Susanna affixing a written instruction that the seal is to be returned.

A group of peasant girls now enter (Barbarina and Cherubino in girl's clothes among them) and address themselves to the Countess, to whom they offer flowers. The "fair stranger" (Cherubino), whom Barbarina passes off as her cousin, attracts the Countess's attention, and Susanna agrees that the resemblance to someone they know is remarkable. But Antonio steals in quietly, pulls off Cherubino's headdress and substitutes an ensign's cap, thereby exposing him to the Count, who again turns upon his wife in jealous anger.

The Count's threat to Cherubino is quickly checked by Barbarina, who coyly reminds the Count that when His Excellency embraced her, he promised her anything she would ask. She asks now to marry Cherubino, and the Count, publicly trapped, can only mutter that fiends and devils are in league against him. For whatever comfort it will offer him, the Count tries once more to ensnare Figaro with questions about the window episode. Figaro does not know that the Count has discovered it was Cherubino; and when confronted with Cherubino's confession, Figaro can only say that if one man can jump out of a window, so can another.

The hall now fills with wedding guests. The bridal march is begun and a fandango is danced. As Susanna kneels before the Count to receive the bridal veil, she slips the note, sealed with a pin, into his hand. When the ceremony is over, Figaro, dancing with Susanna, notices the Count prick his finger on the pin. He observes to his partner that someone has been sending their master a love letter. The Count now asks the company to disperse and reassemble at nightfall when the celebration will really be under way. The company complies after a short chorus in praise of the Count.

Act 4

The last act opens on the palace garden with arbors on either side. It is night, and Barbarina, with a lantern, hunts frantically for the pin the Count gave her to return to Susanna with a message regarding the assignation. When she explains her loss to Figaro (who enters with Marcellina) and innocently betrays the rendezvous among the pines, Figaro storms off, convinced that Susanna is unfaithful. He will avenge not only himself, but the whole race of gullible husbands.

Deeming it best to apprise Susanna of Figaro's mood, Marcellina leaves, pausing first for a brief aria. Her place on stage is taken by Figaro, who returns with Bartolo and Basilio. The latter two are instructed to conceal themselves if they would discover why he is so distraught. They consent, but not until Basilio has delivered an aria dealing with his own youthful follies and the wisdom the years have brought him. Alone, Figaro gives vent to his outraged feelings (No. 15), "Ye men, will nothing school ye" (*Aprite un po' quagl'occhi*). His torment increases as he overhears Susanna ask the Countess—they have entered disguised in each other's clothing—for permission to wander by herself among the pines.

This is the place for the projected rendezvous, and as Susanna pours out a song of love for Figaro ("Deh vieni, no tardar," No. 16), he misconstrues it as addressed in eager anticipation to the Count.

Cherubino now appears, looking for Barbarina. But seeing the Countess, whom he mistakes for Susanna, he begins to press his embraces upon her. The Count arrives and steps between the two in time to receive the kiss Cherubino intended for the disguised and embarrassed Countess. Almost automatically he sends his fist in Cherubino's direction, but just then Figaro pokes his head between them and takes the Count's blow on his own ear. The comedy of errors now proceeds apace.

The Countess (who the Count thinks is Susanna) allows her husband to make love to her, accepting a ring as a token of his affection, and docilely allowing him to conduct her to the dark pavilion. Meanwhile, Figaro comes across Susanna, whom he first mistakes for the Countess; but in the process of explaining to her that she can catch the Count with Susanna in a most compromising situation, he realizes—Susanna has forgotten for a moment to alter her voice—the deception that is afoot.

Relieved that it is really Susanna before him and not the Countess, Figaro determines to carry on with the farce and to repay Susanna in kind for the anguish she caused him. Therefore he begins to make extravagant love to her, addressing her as the Countess and leading her to believe that he has forgotten all about Susanna. Unable to bear this any longer, Susanna resumes her natural voice and begins to rain blows upon him, which delights Figaro, for this he takes as a prime token of her affection.

Once reconciled, the two plan a further diversion for the Count, and when he returns, looking for the supposed Susanna whom he has lost in the dark, he finds the woman he believes to be his wife listening favorably to the ardent proposals Figaro is addressing to her on his knees. Hastily calling for help—Basilio, Bartolo, and Antonio answer his summons—the Count seizes Figaro (who pretends to be terrified) and accuses him of an attempted seduction of the Countess.

Amid the general amazement that follows this charge, the Count goes to the pavilion intending to bring out the Countess. (Susanna took refuge there upon the Count's arrival.) Instead, he drags out Cherubino—then Barbarina—then Marcellina—and finally Susanna, still dressed as the Countess. Maintaining her disguise, Susanna pleads for forgiveness, but the Count will have no mercy shown his errant wife. Ultimately the real Countess arrives and the deception is revealed. It remains for her to forgive her humble and supplicating husband (No. 17), and then all on stage unite in a final chorus of reconciliation and rejoicing.

PAGLIACCI

AN OPERA IN TWO ACTS

by Ruggiero Leoncavallo

Cast

NEDDA (in the play "Columbine") Soprano
CANIO (in the play "Pagliaccio")... Tenor
TONIO (in the play "Taddeo") ..... Baritone
BEPPE (in the play "Harlequin") .. Tenor
SILVIO .... Baritone

PEASANTS AND VILLAGERS

Time . ... August 15, in the late 1860's
Place Near Montalto, a village in Calabria

First Performance
Teatro dal Verme, Milan, May 21, 1892

PAGLIACCI

Prologue

BRIEF ORCHESTRAL introduction sets forth the four principal musical themes of the opera. Beginning with a lively melody suggestive of the strolling players (No. 1),* it moves to a more somber strain which is associated with Canio's utter despair (No. 2). This is followed by the love theme sung out by the violins (No. 3), and it subsides into the low strings giving out *misterioso*, the theme used for Canio's suspicions and jealousy (No. 4).

As the gay *pagliacci* theme is picked up again, Tonio, the misshapen clown, sticks his head through the curtain and begs a word with the audience. This play, he explains, is to be a powerful and realistic tale of human emotions. The story to be unfolded is a memory of something that really happened, and let no one forget that under the poor costumes breathe men of flesh and blood with the same human emotions as everyone else. With the words, "Well, let's begin," the clown disappears and the curtain rises on

---

*Thematic Guide, p. 344.

Pagliacci

Act 1

It is mid-afternoon of the day of the Feast of the Assumption (August 15). At the meeting of two roads outside a village in the province of Calabria, Italy, a gay crowd of villagers have gathered to await the arrival of the *pagliacci*, the strolling players. Tonio, who has arrived ahead of the troupe, regards the gay townspeople scornfully and proceeds to lie down in the shade of an impromptu stage which is in readiness for the evening's performance.

As the crowd's excitement reaches a happy climax, a donkey cart, led by Beppe, the juvenile lead, comes along the road. In the brightly painted cart are Canio, in the costume of Pagliaccio, and Nedda, his wife, who is dressed as Columbine. Canio, stirring the crowd to even greater excitement, is beating a huge bass drum. Then, when he has secured everyone's undivided attention, he proceeds to outline the plot of the evening's play. He ends with a sprightly waltz tune (No. 5), inviting everyone to come. This theme is taken up by the happy throng.

As Tonio obligingly starts to help Nedda down from the cart, Canio angrily bops him on the head. The crowd roars with laughter, and Tonio, muttering blackly, hobbles off. At this point some of the villagers invite the players to have a drink with them in town. All start to leave except Tonio, who is busy rubbing down the donkey.

One of the townspeople laughingly suggests to Canio that he had better be wary, for Tonio may now have an opportunity to pay court to his wife. Canio warns that no one had better try that, for although on the stage a husband may be lenient about such flirtations, it is quite different off stage (No. 6). The theme associated with Canio's intense jealousy is heard in the orchestra (No. 4), and Nedda shudders. But the villagers are in too good a mood to be serious about this, and Canio, to bring back the full happiness of the day, laughs with them and then runs to Nedda and kisses her fondly.

At this point a group of bagpipers passes, reminding the villagers that it is time for church. As the townspeople slowly leave, they sing the charming "Bell Chorus" (No. 7).

Nedda, left alone, is still agitated by her husband's warning, and she wonders anxiously if he really suspects her. The themes of love and jealousy effectively sound from the orchestra and suggest that perhaps Canio has good reason for his suspicions.

But Nedda is too lighthearted a person to allow such gloomy thoughts to occupy her very long. Looking up to the bright summer sky, she sings a carefree song to the birds. It is the "Balatella," or "Bird Song" (No. 8). While she is singing, Tonio appears and sits down to listen. Nedda sharply demands that he go join the others in their drinking. When Tonio pleads his love for her, Nedda laughs derisively and tells him to save his love-making for the stage. But Tonio is not easily dissuaded and he becomes more ardent. When he attempts to kiss her, Nedda darts away, grabs a whip, and furiously strikes him with it. Enraged, Tonio swears he will have his revenge. As he limps away, Nedda, unimpressed by his threats, hurls more insults after him.

Now a young and handsome villager, Silvio, arrives, announced by the love theme in the orchestra (No. 3). At first Nedda is alarmed that he should come here in broad daylight, but Silvio laughingly informs her that there is no need to be worried, for all of the other men are in the village drinking. Petulantly, Nedda tells her lover of Tonio's unwelcome advances and of her dissatisfaction with this life she must lead. Silvio urges her to run away with him. Nedda's protestations are not quite convincing, and when Silvio becomes more insistent, she succumbs in a passionate exchange of vows to the love theme (No. 3).

Meanwhile, Tonio has been watching the two lovers from a distance. Seeing a chance to execute his revenge, he has summoned Canio to observe his wife's faithlessness. The husband arrives just in time to hear Nedda arranging a rendezvous with her lover. He rushes out but catches only a glimpse of the fleeing Silvio. As Canio dashes away in pursuit, Tonio gloats over Nedda with satisfaction, promising that he will presently do even better.

Canio returns, puffing from the futile chase, and angrily demands to know the name of his wife's lover. Nedda refuses to betray Silvio, and Canio, enraged, takes out his knife. He is on the point of killing Nedda when Beppe arrives, just in time to restrain his master. With a parting word to Tonio that he try to calm Canio, Beppe leads Nedda into the theatre.

Tonio's manner of calming the irate husband is

indeed effective. He tells him to bide his time since the lover may come to the evening's performance, and if he does, he will surely betray himself.

With these words of consolation, Tonio goes to prepare for the play, and Canio, head bowed, considers his fate. He sings the famous laugh-clown-laugh aria (Nos. 9 and 3). Though his heart is breaking, he says, the show must go on. And overcome by a fit of sobbing, he finally forces himself to enter the theatre as the curtain goes down.

Act 2

It is the evening of the play, and the crowd is excitedly filing in for the performance. Tonio busily directs the villagers to their seats, as Beppe and Nedda help collect the admission fees. Silvio enters and, after a hurried word with Nedda, slips into his seat.

A loud bell announces that the play is about to begin, while the audience becomes more and more excited, demanding silence of one another with great gusto.

And now it is time for the play-within-a-play device, which vividly serves to contrast the artificialities of the stage with the realities of life. As the curtain rises, a minuet is heard in the orchestra, and Nedda, as Columbine, is seen waiting for Taddeo (Tonio) to arrive with refreshments for the rendezvous she has arranged with her lover. The sound of a guitar offstage announces the arrival of Harlequin, played by Beppe, who sings a serenade to his love (No. 10).

Now Taddeo returns, bearing a chicken. He puts down his supplies and begins to make love to Columbine. As his pleading becomes more earnest, Harlequin vaults in through a window and gives Taddeo a healthy kick, to the great delight of the audience. Comically, Taddeo blesses the lovers and then leaves. He is to keep watch outside and warn the lovers if Columbine's husband should return.

The lovers are planning to elope that evening, and Harlequin gives Columbine a sleeping potion which she is to administer to her unsuspecting husband. As the two gaily prepare for their little feast, Taddeo rushes in and announces that Pagliaccio is coming. As Harlequin slips away, Pagliaccio enters, just in time to hear his wife bidding her lover a fond adieu.

Columbine's words—"Till tonight, I shall be forever yours"—are the exact ones which Nedda had used that afternoon in bidding good-by to Silvio. Canio is taken aback, but he forces himself to go on with the play. Pointing to the two places set at the table, he accuses Columbine of having a lover. She replies mildly that it was only Taddeo, and to prove it, opens a door and reveals the clown. With exaggerated irony Taddeo says, "Believe her, for those faithful lips would hate to utter a lie."

The impact of these words causes Canio to forget his part, and he angrily demands to know the lover's name. Frightened by her husband's forcefulness, Nedda makes a valiant attempt to bring him back to the play. But Canio has now thrown aside all pretense. He falls into a chair and sings an expressive melody in which he says that he had built all his hopes on Nedda, but she has betrayed him and he must defend his honor (No. 11). The audience applauds mightily. For this, they think, is a marvelous bit of acting.

Frantically, Nedda tries to force Canio to go on with the play, but he persists in demanding her lover's name. Beppe appears at the back of the stage and is about to interfere, but Tonio restrains him. Nedda cries that she will never betray her lover. And Canio, blind with anger, draws his knife and violently thrusts it into her. Dying, Nedda calls for Silvio. The lover rushes onto the stage, and Canio stabs him to death. With a terrible dramatic irony, Canio turns to the audience and brokenheartedly mutters, "The comedy is over."

Rigoletto

RIGOLETTO

AN OPERA IN THREE ACTS

by Giuseppe Verdi

Cast

THE DUKE OF MANTUA	Tenor
RIGOLETTO	Baritone
SPARAFUCILE	Bass
COUNT MONTERONE	Baritone
MARULLO	Baritone
BORSA	Tenor
COUNT CEPRANO	Bass
AN USHER	Bass
GILDA	Soprano
GIOVANNA	Mezzo-soprano
MADDALENA	Contralto
COUNTESS CEPRANO	Mezzo-soprano
A PAGE	Mezzo-soprano

CHORUS OF KNIGHTS, LADIES AND PAGES OF
THE COURT

Libretto by Francesco Piave
(based on the play *Le Roi s'amuse*
by Victor Hugo)

Time Sixteenth century

Place Mantua

First Performance

Teatro la Fenice, Venice, March 11, 1851

RIGOLETTO

Act 1

FOLLOWING a short and dramatic prelude (Nos. 1 and 2),* the curtain rises on a splendidly furnished room through which pages, servants, elegantly attired ladies and their escorts pass on their way to several brilliantly lighted rooms which open onto the rear of the stage. Dancing is in progress in the inner rooms, for which an orchestra behind scenes furnishes appropriate music (Nos. 3, 4, and 5). This is the palace of the Duke of Mantua whose favorite pastime is the seduction of the wives and daughters of members of his court.

The Duke enters attended by Borsa, one of his courtiers, to whom he is imparting the details of his latest adventure. For three months he has been pursuing a beautiful young girl who lives in an obscure street and in a humble house to which every night a mysterious person is admitted. A group of ladies and gentlemen cross the stage, and the Duke's attention is drawn from the prospective consummation of this affair to pleasures immediately on hand.

Count Ceprano's lovely wife is marked as the

*Thematic Guide, p. 347.

Duke's next conquest, and Borsa's warning that he may be overheard is shrugged off with cynical indifference toward the Count's knowledge of his intentions. The well-known "Questa o quella" aria follows (No. 6), in which the Duke expounds his attitude toward women: no one is dearer to him than any other. As for husbands and lovers, they are fit only for derision.

While the company assembled is engaged in a minuet, the Duke tries his persuasions upon the Countess Ceprano; and when the pair leave arm in arm, Rigoletto (the Duke's hunchbacked court jester) proceeds to bait the understandably nervous husband. With a gesture of impatience Ceprano leaves Rigoletto to entertain the company with his malicious humor, the orchestra all the while continuing with its elegant ballroom music (No. 4).

After Rigoletto leaves, and a Peregodino has been danced, Marullo, another of the gentlemen of the court, arrives. While the orchestra reverts to Nos. 3 and 5, he recounts with considerable relish the news that Rigoletto, the hunchbacked and ill-favored fool, has been discovered possessed of a mistress. Rigoletto returns with the Duke (No. 4 in the orchestra), suggesting to his master several ways in which he might rid himself of the Count Ceprano—arrest, exile, decapitation. Ceprano is present, of course, and the Duke pats him on the head at this last suggestion.

A sentence or two more from Rigoletto is as much as the Count can stand. His sword is out, but the Duke intervenes. As the courtiers group together to discuss possible vengeance upon Rigoletto for his innumerable insults, the Duke warns his jester that he may yet go too far, Rigoletto replying that the Duke's favor is sufficient protection. The dancers come out from the inner rooms, and their merrymaking dominates the stage for awhile.

Off stage a voice, peremptory and desperate, is heard demanding admittance. As old Count Monterone pushes his way onto the stage, the courtiers in chorus cry out the name of the intruder. He has come to denounce the Duke for the seduction of his daughter; but Rigoletto, pretending to give him audience, sets upon him with jeers and taunts "like a hound upon a lion dying." (The phrase is Monterone's.)

Turning with contempt from fool to master, the old Count calls down a father's curse upon both the Duke and his despicable jester. This seems to strike the one vulnerable spot in Rigoletto's otherwise impenetrable armor of cynicism and malice, for he stands apart, obviously unnerved, while the outraged assembly roars its disapproval of Monterone, who is hastily seized by two halberdiers and led away.

(*Scene 2*) It is night. And Rigoletto, wrapped in a cloak, walks towards his house, which stands to the left of a deserted street. A door leads into a walled-in courtyard with a garden seat and a tree. Above the wall, a series of arches support a veranda which is reached by a staircase and also by a door opening upon it from the first floor. Off to the right of the street, a high wall and an angle of the Ceprano Palace are visible.

Still distraught by the curse laid upon him (No. 1),

Rigoletto replies abruptly to another cloaked figure who, to a sinister theme (No. 7), has followed him onto the stage. It is Sparafucile, a professional assassin who offers his services to Rigoletto for a price. After taking the man's address and dismissing him, Rigoletto notes that they are equals: Sparafucile stabs with a sword in darkness, and he (Rigoletto), with the tongue of malice in daylight. Returning to the curse which keeps tormenting him—its motive (No. 1) sounds intermittently in the orchestra—he pours out his hatred for the young, rich, and handsome Duke for whom he must play the fool, and for the courtiers, whose viciousness debased him.

His whole personality changes the moment he enters the courtyard, and Gilda, his daughter, comes out to greet him. In the ensuing scene between them, it is clear that Rigoletto has reared his daughter in complete ignorance of the world and of his place in it. She is patently his refuge, the personification of innocence in an evil world. Yet the mystery that attends her way of living—she is forbidden to go abroad, she knows neither kindred nor even her father's name—prompts her to question Rigoletto, particularly since tonight she senses his troubled and abstracted mood.

However, only when Gilda asks about her mother does Rigoletto break down and tell her of the angel who married him despite his deformity, and who died soon after Gilda's birth (No. 8). This reopening of an ancient wound affects them deeply, and Gilda's consolations (No. 9) soon flower into an affecting duet between the two.

Yet she cannot help renewing her questions. He avoids revealing his name, as he tells her, for fear of his many enemies. But when she questions the close seclusion in which she is kept, his obvious panic prompts her to reassure him that his injunctions on that score have been most strictly obeyed. A twinge of conscience, uttered apart, assails her for her silence concerning the handsome stranger who has been following her lately. Rigoletto is sufficiently disturbed to check with Giovanna, to whose care Gilda is entrusted during his absence. Receiving her assurances that no one has seen him enter and that the door to the terrace is always locked, he eloquently enjoins her to be vigilant for Gilda's safety (No. 10).

A noise outside arrests Rigoletto's attention and, as he goes outside to investigate, the Duke, disguised as a student, slips into the courtyard through the door Rigoletto has momentarily left open. Tossing Giovanna a purse and gesturing to her to be silent, the Duke hides behind a tree. From this vantage point he observes Rigoletto's return and learns from the ensuing conversation that his court fool is the father of the lovely young prey he has been stalking these last months.

Rigoletto now takes leave of his daughter (No. 10). And Giovanna, remembering the Duke's purse, settles Gilda's misgivings concerning the recent deception practiced upon her father. The Duke emerges, dismisses Giovanna, and proceeds to captivate the young girl with his elegant love-making (No. 11). He has progressed to the point of spinning a story intimating that he is a poor student named Gualtier

Maldè, when voices outside (Ceprano's and Borsa's) bring Giovanna hastily back.

Fearful of Rigoletto's return, Giovanna directs the Duke's exit through the house, but not before Gilda and her lover have taken affectionate leave of each other. The famous "Caro nome"—an aria at once tuneful, technically formidable, and dramatically descriptive of Gilda's emotions—now follows (No. 12). Gilda begins it while still in the courtyard gazing after her departed lover, and continues it as she enters the house and re-emerges on the veranda with a lamp to follow his progress down the street.

Ceprano and the group of courtiers, who have now joined him outside, catch sight of Gilda on the veranda and comment upon her remarkable beauty. She re-enters the house still singing, the concluding strains of the aria growing fainter as from an ever increasing distance within the house.

Attention now shifts to the courtiers who have come to abduct Gilda, supposing her to be Rigoletto's mistress. It strikes them as an especially neat joke to enlist Rigoletto's aid when the latter, returning, runs into them in the dark street. His fears for Gilda's safety are dispelled when Marullo allows him to feel and identify the crest on Ceprano's key, and he readily falls in with what they tell him is a plan to carry off Ceprano's wife.

Rigoletto allows himself to be masked by Marullo who, at the same time, surreptitiously binds a handkerchief over his eyes and gives him the ladder to hold underneath the veranda. During a chorus in which the conspirators, *sotto voce*, enjoin speed and silence upon one another, several ascend the ladder, break open the door from the terrace to the first floor, and return with Gilda whom they have gagged. They depart, leaving Rigoletto alone. He does not hear Gilda's muffled outcry nor the courtiers' shout of triumph in the distance. But reflecting that the "jest grows tedious," he passes his hand over his eyes and suddenly realizes that what he mistook for an exceptionally dark night was really the bandage placed over his mask.

Completely horrified, Rigoletto tears both mask and handkerchief from his face. And by the light of a lantern left by one of the courtiers, he recognizes the scarf which Gilda dropped during the abduction. He storms into the house—and returns dragging Giovanna out with him. For a while his voice fails him, and he makes mute, agonized gestures of an outcry. After repeated efforts he forms the Curse motive (No. 1) aloud, and, with the realization that Monterone's vengeance has overtaken him, falls fainting to the ground.

Act 2

The Duke, pacing an antechamber in his palace, is fretting over Gilda's disappearance. He had returned later that night and found the doors locked and the house deserted. In an uncharacteristically tender and serious aria, the melodious "Parmi veder," he imagines her weeping for him in loneliness (No. 13). This change of mood is not lost upon his courtiers, for when they arrive to tell the story of the hoax perpetrated upon Rigoletto (No. 14), the Duke, realizing immediately that it is Gilda they have brought to him, bursts forth with genuinely enraptured lyricism (No. 15), "Now hope renewed" *(Possente amor)*, which leaves them amazed.

A moment after the Duke departs through the center door, the orchestra preludes Rigoletto's arrival with a haunting little melody (No. 16) which ambles along casually, pathetically, and almost literally with a limp to it. It mirrors perfectly Rigoletto's affected nonchalance as he wanders about prying wherever he can for some sign of Gilda's presence; meanwhile, abstractedly exchanging sarcasms with the snickering courtiers.

A messenger arrives from the Duchess, inquiring for the Duke. And when the courtiers hurriedly pack the messenger off with the information that the Duke cannot be disturbed, Rigoletto suddenly guesses the truth. He makes for the door; but the courtiers, even though now aware from Rigoletto's outburst that Gilda is his daughter, bar his exit. In a truly magnificent fury, he curses their callousness and corruption *("Cortigiani, vil razza dannata,"* No. 17). Then suddenly broken with misery, he weeps before them and begs for pity.

Gilda, at last, rushes out of the inner room onto the stage, and throwing herself into Rigoletto's arms, she tells her horrified parent that she has been dishonored. Turning imperiously to the courtiers, he orders them out and (to the grimly majestic motive of the curse, No. 1) charges them to inform the Duke that he, Rigoletto, forbids him to enter.

The courtiers retire confounded, and Gilda now narrates the story, hitherto concealed, of the handsome young stranger (No. 18). As they finish comforting each other in an ornate duet, Monterone, under guard, is led across the stage. He stops before the Duke's portrait hanging on the wall, reflecting bitterly that his curse has been in vain; but when he leaves, Rigoletto, taking his place before the portrait, swears vengeance sufficient for the two of them (No. 19).

Act 3

The curtain rises on a desolate spot on the banks of the Mincio, which is seen in the background. On the left stands a ruined house, its front open to the audience. A broken staircase leads up from the ground floor to a loft containing a battered couch. Gilda and Rigoletto are on the road outside the house; within sits Sparafucile polishing his belt. In the hope of destroying the love Gilda still bears for the Duke, Rigoletto bids her look through a fissure in the wall and observe the proceedings within.

Unaware that he is being watched, the Duke, who enters disguised as a cavalry officer, sends Sparafucile for some wine and breaks gaily into his famous song about the fickleness of women, "La Donna è mobile" (No. 20). After he has furnished the wine and summoned his sister Maddalena down to entertain the Duke, Sparafucile leaves the house. He confers briefly outside with Rigoletto on the murder of the Duke, which they have planned together, and then he goes off in the direction of the river.

The situation—with Maddalena coyly eluding the Duke's embraces and Gilda and Rigoletto outside, the one watching and exclaiming and the other bidding her forget the scoundrel—soon builds into a remarkable quartet (Nos. 21 and 22). Sending Gilda off with instructions to disguise herself as a youth and take horse for Verona, Rigoletto now completes arrangements with Sparafucile for the Duke's murder, giving him part payment in advance and promising to come for the body at midnight.

A tempest is brewing (suggested by an off-stage chorus of men's voices singing a series of sliding chromatic harmonies with mouths closed); and the Duke, despite Maddalena's earlier caution to be gone, readily accepts Sparafucile's offer to take shelter here for the night. Since he is tired and wants an hour's rest, Sparafucile leads the Duke to the upper floor and, commending him to Heaven's protection, leaves him and goes below. As the Duke dozes off singing snatches of the "La Donna è mobile," Sparafucile sends Maddalena to fetch his dagger, which she does unwillingly, stopping on the upper story to look in on the sleeping young stranger, who has excited her sympathy and affection.

In the meanwhile Gilda returns in male attire. Listening in on the conversation between Sparafucile and his sister, she hears her attempt to dissuade the assassin from murdering the Duke. He, however, stands upon his professional dignity, especially when Maddalena suggests that it would be just as easy to murder the hunchback. He makes it clear to her that he is neither a robber, cheat, nor bandit. Murder happens to be his line of work, and like an honest craftsman he cannot think of deceiving his employer. However, when she persists and threatens to awaken the Duke, he compromises with his conscience and agrees to murder instead the first passing stranger and substitute the body for that of the Duke.

The climax comes with the fusion of the three voices—Maddalena rejoicing that her love has saved the stranger, Sparafucile worried about his conscience, and Gilda determined to offer herself as the sacrifice. The wailing of the storm (again the muffled chorus off stage) is heard as Gilda knocks, and Sparafucile conceals himself behind the door which Maddalena opens. As she enters and the door closes behind her, storm music thunders out from the orchestra, and darkness and silence cover the tragedy swiftly enacted on stage.

It is now midnight, and Rigoletto returns relishing the hour of his vengeance. He is in the process of dragging toward the river the sack Sparafucile has brought out to him, when he hears the Duke's voice merrily singing the "La Donna è mobile" (No. 20). For a moment he fears that he has gone mad, but the Duke's voice has a convincing vitality, and opening the sack, he discovers the body of his daughter.

Gilda has just enough breath left to ask his forgiveness and to promise that she and her mother will wait for him in Heaven (No. 23). She dies in his arms. And Rigoletto, crying out that the curse has been fulfilled, tears his hair and falls senseless on the body of his child.

THE RING
of
THE NIBELUNGS
(Der Ring des Nibelungen)

I.
THE RHINEGOLD
(Das Rheingold)

II.
THE VALKYRIE
(Die Walküre)

III.
SIEGFRIED

IV.
THE TWILIGHT
OF THE GODS
(Die Götterdämmerung)

THE RHINEGOLD

(Das Rheingold)

AN OPERA IN FOUR SCENES

by Richard Wagner

Cast

WOTAN		Baritone
DONNER	GODS	Bass
FROH		Tenor
LOGE		Tenor
FRICKA		Soprano
FREIA	GODDESSES	Soprano
ERDA		Contralto
FASOLT	GIANTS	Bass
FAFNER		Bass
ALBERICH	DWARFS	Baritone
MIME		Tenor

RHINE MAIDENS

WOGLINDE	Soprano
WELLGUNDE	Soprano
FLOSSHILDE	Mezzo-soprano

Time ....Antiquity

Place . ...Legendary Germany

First Performance

Hof-und-National Theater, Munich,
September 22, 1869

I. THE RHINEGOLD
(Das Rheingold)

T HE RHINEGOLD, the first of the *Ring* tetralogy, sets forth the sequence of events whose consequences are unfolded in the three remaining operas. In brief, this prologue-opera details how Wotan, seeking a dwelling place for the gods and a secure and sumptuous stronghold from which he might wield his power, contracted with the giants for the building of the fortress-palace Valhalla. Freia, the goddess of youth, was left with the giants as security until such time as payment for their labor should fall due. Eventually Wotan satisfies the debt with gold stolen from the Rhine Maidens.

(Scene 1) The original thief was the dwarf Alberich, one of the race of Nibelungs, who came upon the flirtatious Rhine Maidens one day while they were guarding their treasure. To him they foolishly imparted the secret of its power; namely, that a ring woven from the gold would secure for its wearer measureless might and command over the world's wealth. But he who would fashion such a ring must

first renounce love. Goaded by the Rhine Maidens' refusal to submit to his embraces—although they tantalizingly keep his expectations at fever pitch—Alberich does indeed renounce love, seize the treasure, and subsequently fashion from it the Ring.

(*Scene 2*) Two of the giants, Fasolt and Fafner, appear before Wotan to demand payment. Freia so pleases Fasolt that he would gladly keep her in lieu of gold, but Fricka (Freia's sister and Wotan's wife) intercedes on her behalf. Moreover, Freia can scarcely be surrendered, for as guardian of the golden apples of eternal youth, her ministrations prevent Wotan and the gods from growing decrepit and eventually extinct. Loge, the god of fire, suggests that the Rhine treasure be offered in payment; and when he reveals that it is now in Alberich's possession, it becomes clear to god and giant alike that they may both fall victim to the dwarf's malice.

(*Scene 3*) Upon Loge's urging, Wotan accompanies him into the nether reaches of the earth where they find Alberich, now in possession of the treasure, the Ring, and the Tarnhelm, a helmet of invisibility which was fashioned by his brother, the dwarf Mime. Playing on his vanity, they persuade Alberich to change himself—with the Tarnhelm's aid—first into a serpent and then into a toad. Wotan instantly steps on the toad, and Alberich, thus secured, is compelled to surrender his possessions. But in his fury, the dwarf lays a curse upon the Ring: murder shall ever follow it and it shall enslave and consume its possessor.

(*Scene 4*) The complete treasure, Ring and Tarnhelm included, is demanded by the giant Fafner, and upon the advice of Erda (goddess of earth and wisdom), Wotan turns it over to him. No sooner has Freia been exchanged for the gold than the brother giants quarrel over the division of shares. During the fight, Fasolt is killed—the curse is already at work—and Fafner departs, dragging with him the gold and his brother's body. As the gods cross the rainbow bridge into Valhalla, the sound of the Rhine Maidens' voices drifts up from the valley below.

THE VALKYRIE
(Die Walküre)

AN OPERA IN THREE ACTS

by Richard Wagner

Cast

SIEGMUND	Tenor
HUNDING	Bass
WOTAN	Baritone
SIEGLINDE	Soprano
BRÜNNHILDE	Soprano
FRICKA	Mezzo-soprano
VALKYRIE	Sopranos and Altos

Time ... Antiquity

Place ... German forests

First Performance

Hof-und-National Theater, Munich,
June 26, 1870

II. THE VALKYRIE
(Die Walküre)

Although Fafner, with the aid of the Tarnhelm, has changed himself into a dragon and now slumbers in guardianship over his treasure, Wotan fears that Alberich may yet regain the Ring and use it to destroy the gods. In order to secure it for himself, but this time without recourse to treachery or violence, Wotan has determined to beget a hero who shall unwittingly accomplish this mission for him.

Since the close of the previous opera, Wotan has had nine daughters by Erda, the earth goddess. These daughters are known as the Valkyrie, and their mission is to transport bodies of slain heroes to Valhalla where, reanimated, they stand guard over the fortress of the gods. He also has reared, in alliance with a mortal woman, a race of Wälsungs *(Volsungs)*, one of whom, Siegmund, he intends as the hero who will reclaim the Ring for him.

Wotan is known to Siegmund and his sister Sieglinde only as Wolfe, their father who lived with them in the woods. During a raid by an enemy tribe, Sieglinde was carried off later to become Hunding's bride, and when Wolfe also disappears, Siegmund is left alone in a friendless world. The opera opens as Siegmund, in the course of his wanderings, comes by chance upon Hunding's hut.

Act 1

As a storm rages outside (No. 1),* and the thunder roars (No. 2), the curtain rises upon a hut constructed around the trunk of a huge ash tree which stands in the center of the stage. Off to the right is a hearth, and behind it a storeroom, while to the left, steps lead up to an inner room. A table with a broad bench and some wooden stools complete the furnishings. As Siegmund enters exhausted, a motive associated with him is sounded in the orchestra (No. 3). Exclaiming that he must rest, regardless of whose hearth this may be, he throws himself down on a bearskin rug.

Sieglinde enters and, bending over the motionless stranger—her pity motive (No. 4) in the orchestra—wonders over his valiant appearance and his extreme exhaustion. Suddenly raising his head, he asks for a draught. After she has fetched it, he drinks, signs his thanks, and then stares fixedly at her, the cellos meanwhile eloquently depicting the awakening of their love for each other (No. 5).

The stranger asks to whom he is indebted; and learning that she is Hunding's wife and this his home, he explains that he is weaponless, wounded, and in flight from his foemen and the storm. Moved to pity (No. 4), she fetches a horn of mead to refresh him, but he insists that first it touch her lips. They gaze

---

*Thematic Guide, p. 351.

in silence upon each other (the love motive, No. 5, in the orchestra), and then, abruptly declaring that she has given comfort to an ill-fated one, he prepares to leave. But she restrains him, for this, too, is a house of ill-fortune. Softly her pity motive (No. 4) sounds over the theme of the Wälsungs' woe (No. 6), and Siegmund, turning back from the door, tells her that his name is Wehwalt ("Woeful") and that he shall await Hunding here.

For awhile neither speaks, but the sound of Hunding outside, leading his horse to the stable, brings Sieglinde quickly to the door. She opens it just as Hunding—a grim, armed figure—enters, his motive (No. 7) blaring sternly out of the orchestra. When the stranger's presence has been explained, Hunding sheds his armor and orders the meal set. The physical resemblance between his wife and the stranger has not escaped him. (They are, indeed, unknown to each other, brother and sister; and the orchestra, at this point inserting the motive, No. 8, which in *The Rhinegold* was associated with Wotan's treaty with the giants, suggests both Wotan's parentship and the root source of the present complication.)

During the ensuing conversation, Siegmund, apparently loath to reveal his identity, is persuaded to do so when Hunding—aware of the constant exchange of glances between his wife and the stranger—remarks that his wife would also like to know. They are all three now at table, and Siegmund, still referring to himself as Wehwalt ("Woeful"), tells them of his twin sister whom he scarcely knew, and of the days when he went hunting with their father Wolfe in the forest. Once returning, they found their home destroyed, the mother dead, the sister gone.

In a later encounter with the Neidings, Siegmund was separated from Wolfe, and while he relates how he sought for his father in vain, the strains of the Valhalla motive (No. 9) sounding softly in the orchestra, identify Wolfe with Wotan. Suspicion, feuds, and ill-fortune have dogged him ever since. No one, remarks Hunding, would willingly welcome a man so in disfavor with the fates. But when Sieglinde bids him continue, Siegmund tells how he lost his weapons in a recent attempt to save a young girl from her kinsmen who were compelling her into a loveless marriage.

As Siegmund goes to the hearth, and Sieglinde, deeply moved, stares at the ground in silence, the moving theme of the Wälsungs' woe (No. 10) rises out of the orchestra. There is a riotous race, says Hunding suddenly, at war with his own. His kinsmen called upon him for vengeance, but he arrived too late, and now returning finds his foeman a guest in his home. For the night Hunding offers his hearth for shelter, but upon the morrow he bids Siegmund be prepared to fight for his life.

Turning toward the storeroom Sieglinde pauses (No. 10), and then with quiet resolution (No. 4) fills a drinking horn into which she shakes some spices. However, before entering the bed chamber she turns and with her eyes indicates to Siegmund a particular spot in the ash tree. (The sword motive, No. 11, which was heard in the closing scene of the *Rhinegold*, conveys her meaning.) An angry gesture of dismissal from Hunding compels her to leave, and then Hunding himself exits, after first removing his weapons from the tree (No. 7) and again warning Siegmund to arm himself for the morrow.

Left to brood by himself while the rhythm of Hunding's motive (No. 7) throbs relentlessly in the orchestra, Siegmund recalls how his father had once promised him a sword for his hour of need. Just then a flicker of firelight illuminates a sword hilt buried in the ash tree. But Siegmund, obsessed by thoughts of Sieglinde, fails to comprehend what the brief flame has shown him.

When the fire dies out, Sieglinde reappears; her draught has put Hunding into a deep sleep and she has come to tell her beloved guest the secret of the sword. Upon her wedding night, while she sat neglected among the revelers, an old man in gray entered (the Valhalla motive, No. 9, identifies him as Wotan), and buried a sword (No. 11) up to its hilt in the ash tree. His gaze rested threateningly upon all present, but he looked at Sieglinde with compassion and love. After his departure all attempts to draw the sword proved vain. And while the Valhalla motive (No. 9) sounds again, Sieglinde declares that she then realized who the old man was, and at last knew who one day would claim the sword. Siegmund is her long awaited deliverer who, embracing her, ardently exclaims that he too has suffered disgrace, and that vengeance for both of them is now at hand.

The door leading to the forest suddenly flies open. But Siegmund quiets Sieglinde's sudden terror, draws her down beside him to the couch, and sings to her of the waning of winter and the coming of spring (No. 12). "Thou art the spring," she replies ecstatically to the melody of the love motive (No. 5). The full moon now shines in upon them from the forest as they cling to each other, singing of their new found felicity (No. 13).

To the accompaniment of the Valhalla motive (No. 9), Sieglinde tries to express the strange feeling that she has always known the beloved stranger whom first she saw today. Siegmund's voice is as an echo from her childhood, yet she heard it only recently when an echo gave back her own voice in the forest. His eyes are as the eyes of the old man who looked lovingly upon her on her wedding night as if she were his child. With mounting excitement she declares that he shall no longer be known as Wehwalt; for the sword was meant for him, and now in love she christens him "Siegmund." Leaping up in passionate acceptance of the name, he seizes the sword (No. 14) and names it "Nothung" (Needful). He draws her to him and Sieglinde passionately throws herself on his breast, exclaiming that she shall be both bride and sister to him—and thus shall the Wälsungs flourish forever. Exultantly they rush through the open door into the moonlit forest.

Act 2

After a brief though stormy orchestral prologue (towards the end of which the famous Ride of the Valkyrie motive, No. 15, is heard), the curtain rises on a wild rocky place revealing Wotan and Brünnhilde, both fully armed. He is instructing her—she is the leader of the Valkyrie, and his favorite daughter—to haste to the scene of the impending battle between Siegmund and Hunding.

Siegmund and Sieglinde are in flight from her grim husband, and Brünnhilde's orders are to guard the Wälsung. As for Hunding, even his corpse is not welcome in Valhalla. Uttering the fierce cry of the Valkyrie (No. 16, "Hojotoho"), Brünnhilde leaps from rock to rock, and arriving upon the highest crag, turns back to call to Wotan a warning of Fricka's approach. As her Valkyrie cry (No. 16) trails off in the distance, Fricka makes her appearance, accompanied by the motive symbolic of her anger (No. 17).

During the domestic dispute that follows, Wotan defends his partiality toward the Wälsung pair on the grounds of their holy love for each other, while Fricka reminds him that this "holy love" is not only adultery, but incest. Wotan's own numerous infidelities are thrown up to him (Siegmund, Sieglinde, Brünnhilde, and the Valkyrie are listed as cases in point), and Fricka concludes with an impassioned plea that Wotan finish his holy work by destroying her too.

As calmly as he can, Wotan explains his need of Siegmund as the hero who, of his own free will, will effect the salvation of the gods. But Fricka dismisses this as a mere sophistry, for there is no free will involved on Siegmund's part when Wotan constantly intercedes for him. Siegmund may have drawn the sword with his own hand; but, argues Fricka, it was

Wotan who created his need for it, prepared the sword for him, and directed him to the spot where it was hidden. Rapidly pursuing her advantage, for moral right is on her side, Fricka demands to know whether Wotan will shield the pair who have defied her. (She is the goddess under whose protection lies the sanctity of marriage.)

The motive of Wotan's defeat and dejection (No. 18) sounds intermittently in the orchestra, as he is compelled to promise not only that he will remain neutral, but that Siegmund shall die. As Fricka leaves, she encounters Brünnhilde returning. Brünnhilde's Valkyrie cry (No. 15) is cut short as she sees Fricka, and after a brief interval during which the two women regard each other in silence, Fricka tells the Valkyrie that her father awaits her with new instructions.

While Fricka departs and Brünnhilde anxiously comes forward, Wotan remains lost in gloomy brooding, his dejection motive (No. 18) now the dominant feature in the musical background. A sudden outburst of anger and despair from Wotan terrifies the Valkyrie, and, casting aside her armor, she sinks to her knees before him in solicitude. He strokes her hair with unconscious tenderness, and in reply to her questions, begins the long story of what had transpired during the preceding opera: his treaty with the giants, Alberich's theft of the Rhinegold, the Ring, and his plan to retrieve it, Erda's counsel, and his union with the Earth goddess who bore him Brünnhilde and her eight sisters.

As the god of treaties, he is enslaved by a pact

of his own making. And now that Fricka has destroyed his plan to use Siegmund, the destruction of the gods looms threateningly ahead. Rising with bitterness and wrath, he orders her, despite her horrified protests, to see that Fricka is vindicated and Siegmund slain. Turning his wrath upon Brünnhilde for daring to question his decision, he reminds her that she is a mere instrument of his will: the furies that rage within him he shall unlease upon her should she disobey him. And insisting that Siegmund must die, he storms out, leaving her confused and alarmed.

As Brünnhilde stoops slowly to rearm, commenting upon the unwonted heaviness of her weapons, the motives of Wotan's dejection (No. 18) and of the Valkyrie ride (No. 15) arise as a reminder of the grim task before her. Moving toward the rocky pass, she looks over into the gorge and watches Siegmund and Sieglinde below. By the time they appear on stage, Brünnhilde has already entered the cavern and is lost to view. Sieglinde, distraught and staring wildly about her, endeavors to go on, but Siegmund forcibly persuades her to rest.

For a moment, while the love motive (No. 5) appears in the orchestra, Sieglinde yields and presses herself lovingly to Siegmund. But her sense of guilt now overmasters her, and starting away from him wildly, she begs him to desert her—for she is sinful, loathsome, accursed. His attempts to quiet her are vain, for horn calls accompanied by the rhythm of the Hunding motive (No. 7) rouse her terror of Hunding, his kinsmen, and their vengeful hounds close in pursuit of them.

Sieglinde stares madly before her, calls for Siegmund, her "radiant brother," and again gives way to a terrorized vision of Hunding's dogs tearing fiercely at her beloved. At the climax of her hysteria, she collapses in his arms; he lets her slide down gently so that her head comes to rest in his lap, and he kisses her softly while the love motive (No. 5) sounds once more.

Brünnhilde reappears, leading her horse from the cavern. As she advances, regarding Siegmund solemnly, the orchestra gives out two motives in succession (Nos. 19 and 20)—associated with fate and death. They continue to sound as Brünnhilde calls to Siegmund to tell him that she appears to heroes only before their death. He must come to Valhalla with her, where Wotan awaits him and lovely maidens shall be at his service. Shall his sister-bride go with him, he asks? And when the answer is that he will not find Sieglinde there, he tenderly kisses his still unconscious sister, and with quiet dignity tells Brünnhilde that she may greet for him Wotan, Wälse, the heroes, and the beautiful maidens, but he shall not follow her to Valhalla.

As Siegmund bends to kiss Sieglinde, the love motive (No. 5) is heard; but upon the conclusion of his declaration, the fate motive (No. 19) makes its soft, but inexorable appearance. Bit by bit, Brünnhilde impresses upon him his inevitable doom: it is the will of Wotan, and as for his sword, its power has been withdrawn. Bent over Sieglinde in an agony of pity, he cries shame upon one who would bestow a sword and in treachery render it useless.

To Valhalla Siegmund will not go; rather shall Hell hold him for its own. And when the Valkyrie asks whether for a helpless wife eternal bliss is worth rejecting, he bitterly upbraids her. He bids her feast, if she will, upon his sorrow, but be silent about Valhalla and its loveless delights. Deeply touched, Brünnhilde begs him to leave Sieglinde with her for the sake of the child she is to bear. But as Siegmund, determined that his beloved shall always be with him, points his sword at her, Brünnhilde suddenly reverses Wotan's command, to stop the murder, and tells Siegmund that both he and Sieglinde shall live.

Brünnhilde rushes off, leaving Siegmund exultant. As the stage darkens, Siegmund bends tenderly over Sieglinde once more, bidding her slumber on, setting her down gently, and kissing her farewell. As Hunding's horn sounds, Siegmund rises and hastily disappears into the storm-clouded background to meet his foe.

Stirring restlessly in her sleep, as she dreams of her childhood, Sieglinde gives utterance to phrases about her father and mother and the burning house. She calls upon her brother for help, as she starts out of her dream with the cry "Siegmund." Frozen with terror, she hears the voices of Hunding and Siegmund calling to each other in the distant darkness. Their voices grow nearer, and as she rushes towards them, a bolt of lightning illuminates Brünnhilde protecting Siegmund with her shield and urging him to strike.

At the moment a red glare breaks, revealing Wotan holding his spear in front of Siegmund. As the latter strikes, his sword shatters against Wotan's spear and

Hunding drives his spear into the Wälsung's breast. Turning in terror as Siegmund falls, Brünnhilde lifts Sieglinde onto her horse with her and instantly disappears.

The clouds divide, and Wotan is seen gazing mournfully upon the slain hero, while Hunding draws his spear from his body. In terse phrases, Wotan tells Hunding to kneel before Fricka as her slave. Then with a contemptuous wave of his hand, he strikes Hunding dead. As he remembers Brünnhilde's disobedience, his anger suddenly flares up; and after a brief, embittered outburst, Wotan rides off in pursuit of the Valkyrie as the curtain falls.

Act 3

The famous Ride of the Valkyrie (No. 15) opens the third act. When the curtain rises, a rocky, storm-clouded summit is revealed, with four of the Valkyrie perched on crags calling their wild greetings (No. 16) to one another. From time to time, one more appears bearing a slain warrior to Valhalla, until eight are assembled chorusing with savage joy. Only Brünnhilde remains unaccounted for, and soon she too appears, but with Sieglinde riding with her.

Brünnhilde frantically appeals to her sisters for help, as she rapidly outlines for them her disobedience to Wotan's command and the punishment that she fears when Wotan finds her. They are too much terrified of Wotan to be willing to render any aid, even if only to help her get Sieglinde to safety. As Brünnhilde warmly embraces her, Sieglinde starts up from her apathy and urges the Valkyrie to have no thought of her welfare. Death now is her only desire; but when Brünnhilde reminds her that she must live for the child she is to bear, Sieglinde suddenly becomes alert and pleads that her child be rescued.

Brünnhilde quickly checks with the Valkyrie who recently came from the east. Learning that Fafner in the guise of a dragon sleeps on his gold in a cavern there in the forest, she decides that eastward would be the safest direction for Sieglinde to go, since Wotan will never venture there. She sends Sieglinde off, bids her remember the glorious hero she shall bear (the Siegfried as Hero motive, No. 21), and gives her the splinters of Siegmund's sword, which she had salvaged from the battlefield. Sensing the symbolical significance of this gift, Sieglinde ecstatically thanks Brünnhilde to the theme that thereafter is associated with the triumphal redemption of love (No. 22).

As Sieglinde hastens away, a fearful storm approaches; a fiery light begins to glow, and Wotan's voice (heard through a speaking trumpet) calls out to Brünnhilde. Turning again to her sisters for help, she moves with them as, chorusing in terror, they draw together and hide her among them.

Magnificent in his anger, Wotan strides in, storming at the Valkyrie for daring to shield Brünnhilde. Vainly they plead with him to calm himself, but (as the orchestra again and again thunders out the theme of his despair, No. 18) Wotan continues to rage over Brünnhilde's disobedience. Ultimately Brünnhilde steps forth, humble yet determined, and halting a few paces from him, bids the god pronounce sentence upon her.

Brünnhilde has sentenced herself, says Wotan; for she was created to serve purely as an instrument of his will, and now that she has disobeyed him, she can serve as a Valkyrie no longer. Furthermore, he continues, after she exclaims in horror, she who was once his favorite daughter is to be banished from the company of the gods and from his sight forever. The Valkyrie sisters wail, while Brünnhilde, dumfounded, asks if he means to take away all that he had bestowed upon her.

On this rock, decrees Wotan, shall she lie in defenseless slumber; the first mortal who finds her shall despoil her of her godhood. While Brünnhilde lies kneeling before him, the Valkyrie descend to surround her, begging Wotan to recall the terrible curse. But Wotan is determined that as punishment for defying the king of the gods, Brünnhilde shall be compelled to obey the mere mortal who shall claim her as wife. They recoil from her—and she falls with a cry to the ground. As the motive of Wotan's despair (No. 18) thunders out once more, he commands them to fly from the accursed one, lest misfortune fall upon them too. With wild shrieks they hasten to obey, a flash of lightning revealing them upon their steeds in frenzied flight. Twilight falls; the dark clouds clear away; Brünnhilde and Wotan remain in silence, their positions unchanged, while a new theme of the Wälsungs' love (No. 23) sounds softly in the orchestra.

Brünnhilde quietly asks if her sin were indeed sufficient to warrant such shame. She rises to a kneeling position before him and begs that he look into her eyes to see if he can discover there such hidden guilt as would compel him to cast off his child. When he refers to her disobedience, she pleads that in truth she carried out his real desire; that when he bid her slay Siegmund, it was Fricka's command, and not truly his own. She knew Wotan's love for the Wälsung, and his need of him; and when she looked into Siegmund's eyes and saw his defiance and despair, she was moved by the pity and the love (No. 23, in the orchestra) which Wotan himself had instilled in her. Wotan's word only did she defy, but in so doing, remained true to his need and his love that moved within her. Anger now drained from him, Wotan admits that she did what he desired, but could not himself do. As he pours out once more the story of his sorrows, Wotan laments that no longer can he and Brünnhilde be together.

Brünnhilde accepts her punishment as inevitable. Then she plays upon his pride in the Wälsungs, reminding him that Siegmund's unborn son will surely be a hero—and if she must be won by a mortal, at least no craven human should be permitted to claim her. But Wotan can no longer protect her. She must lie weaponless and in slumber (the strange harmonies of the Magic Ban, No. 24, accompany his words) until awakened to be the wife of a mortal. Then let the rock be surrounded with horrors, she demands, so that only the most fearless of heroes will dare ascend it. (The Siegfried as Hero theme, No. 21, accompanies her request, while leading up to it we hear the slumber motive, No. 25.)

Brünnhilde embraces Wotan's knees and fervently begs that if he cannot grant her wish, he put her to death. When she pleads at least for a circle of fire to ward off craven-hearted humans, he turns at last, overcome with emotion. Then he raises her from her knees and begins his deeply moving farewell. The circle of fire shall be drawn around the rock, he promises, and the hero who wins her (the Siegfried motive, No. 21) shall be freer even than Wotan who is a god.

As Wotan holds her in a long, silent embrace, the theme of the Wälsungs' love (No. 23) rises, followed by the slumber motive (No. 25) which continues to be elaborated in the orchestra when he resumes his farewell. Holding her head in his hands, he kisses her eyes. She sinks into unconsciousness (Nos. 24 and 25), and he places her upon the ground, covering her with the great shield of the Valkyrie. For a moment, he gazes upon her in silence. Then, with determination, he strides to the center of the stage, points his spear at a great rock, and calls sharply upon Loge, the fire god. He strikes the rock thrice, and after the last time a spurt of flame issues from it, which with his spear he spreads till the mountain is ringed with fire. (The famous Magic Fire Music, No. 26, has in the meantime engulfed the orchestra.)

Wotan cries out, prophetically to the melody of the Siegfried theme (No. 21), that no mortal who fears his spear shall cross the flaming mountaintop, the god, gazing in sorrow upon his daughter, turns and disappears through the fire.

SIEGFRIED

by Richard Wagner

Cast

SIEGFRIED	......	Tenor
MIME	......	Tenor
WOTAN	......	Baritone
ALBERICH	......	Baritone
FAFNER	......	Bass
ERDA	......	Contralto
BRÜNNHILDE	......	Soprano

Time ...... Antiquity

Place ...... German forests

First Performance

Festspielhaus, Bayreuth, August 16, 1876

III. SIEGFRIED

In the interim between the *Valkyrie* and *Siegfried*, Sieglinde has died in childbirth, and her son Siegfried has been raised by the dwarf Mime, the brother of Alberich.

Act 1

When the opera opens, Siegfried is a strapping young man, much given to badgering little Mime about. It has already occurred to the dwarf that this young hero can reclaim for him the Tarnhelm and the Ring, and with these Mime can then make himself master of the world. His problem, however, is to fashion a sword to fit the needs of his young ward.

Every sword Mime has made thus far, Siegfried has splintered at a blow. The "Nothung" sword is the only one that will serve, but thus far the welding of its splinters (which Sieglinde bequeathed to the dwarf) has proved beyond Mime's ability. During a conversation with Wotan, who arrives disguised as the Wanderer, Mime learns that Nothung can be refashioned only by one who knows no fear. After carefully questioning Siegfried and learning that such an emotion is indeed foreign to him, Mime sets the young hero to the task, which, of course, he accomplishes quite readily.

Act 2

Alberich, who sits brooding before Fafner's cave, waiting for an opportunity to regain the Ring, also receives a visit from the Wanderer. Recognizing him as Wotan, Alberich bitterly upbraids him for his earlier treachery (recounted in *The Rhinegold*) and warns Wotan that when the Ring is his again, he shall gladly use it for the destruction of the gods. He knows of Wotan's plan to foster a hero to reclaim the Ring, but Wotan calmly assures him that the boy whom Mime will bring to the cave will accomplish this mission in complete ignorance of, and freedom from, the god's will.

Alberich tries desperately to win out over Wotan before Siegfried arrives, and he calls to the giant to tell him that a hero is coming to take his treasure from him. But Fafner, now transformed into a dragon, is unimpressed. Urged by Alberich to surrender the Ring, for that is all the hero wants, since then the remainder of the treasure will be forever his, Fafner merely replies: "I lie and possess; let me slumber." In high spirits, the Wanderer leaves with Alberich's curse sounding after him.

Mime brings Siegfried to the dragon's cave, and then retires while the young man stretches out to listen to the forest murmurs. As Siegfried lies there, he wonders about his father. He vainly tries to understand the song of the birds, which he feels will reveal to him much that he does not now comprehend. After a while Fafner appears, and in the ensuing battle is slain by Siegfried; but before he dies, the dragon asks Siegfried, who has goaded him, to commit this murder.

Assured that Siegfried acted freely, in response to an impulse to fight, the dying monster warns the young hero that the two giants to whom the treasure was originally given are now dead, and that the one who blindly impelled Siegfried to this murder also plots Siegfried's doom. A bit of the dragon's blood spatters on his hand, and as Siegfried involuntarily puts his hand to his mouth to suck away the blood, he finds that suddenly he can understand the mysterious language of the birds. One of the forest birds, perched on the tree above, tells Siegfried of the treasure within the dragon's cave and of the power of the Tarnhelm and the Ring.

While Siegfried is in the cave, Mime and Alberich emerge from their hiding places and quarrel as to who should have the Ring. But neither will attempt to take it from Siegfried; and when Mime later tries to wheedle it away from him, Siegfried, having been warned by the bird to distrust the dwarf, gravely responds that he regrets having slain the dragon, and that he hates, more than the dragon, the one who impelled him to this murder.

The dragon's blood now enables Siegfried to interpret Mime's unspoken thoughts, and while the dwarf cajoles him, Siegfried hears underlying his smooth and fawning words the true hatred the dwarf bears him.

He realizes that the dwarf means to kill him to secure possession of the Tarnhelm and the Ring, and in disgust with Mime's hypocrisy in offering him a sleeping potion, Siegfried strikes Mime dead. The bird now tells him that a wonderful bride awaits him, and Siegfried leaps up joyously to follow the bird through the forest.

Act 3

During a conversation between Wotan and Erda, the earth goddess to whom he comes for comfort and guidance, we learn that Wotan has finally reconciled himself to the death of the gods, and has willed his inheritance to Siegfried, the young Wälsung whom he has chosen, but who knows him not. Led by the forest bird, Siegfried appears and is closely questioned by the Wanderer.

Finally, bored and irritated by the old man who seems determined to keep him from the mountaintop where his promised bride lies sleeping, Siegfried shatters the Wanderer's spear that bars his way. Exclaiming that he no longer has the power to stay him, the Wanderer disappears, leaving Siegfried to find his way to Brünnhilde and awaken her with a kiss. She rises sorrowfully and bids him leave her; but as he soothes her, love for him begins to stir within the erstwhile Valkyrie. As the opera closes, the two lovers joyfully throw themselves into each other's arms.

THE TWILIGHT
OF THE GODS

(Die Götterdämmerung)

by Richard Wagner

Cast

SIEGFRIED	Tenor
BRÜNNHILDE	Soprano
GUNTHER	Bass
HAGEN	Bass
GUTRUNE	Soprano
WALTRAUTE	Mezzo-soprano

RHINE MAIDENS, VASSALS, WARRIORS, WOMEN

Time	Antiquity
Place	German forests

First Performance
Festspielhaus, Bayreuth, August 17, 1876

IV. THE TWILIGHT OF THE GODS

(Die Götterdämmerung)

Act 1

The final opera opens upon Brünnhilde's rock, where the three Norms, demigoddesses of Fate, are reading from the strands of the Cord of Fate the history of Wotan, Valhalla, and the Gods. As the strands begin to unravel, their agitation increases. And when the rope finally breaks, they vanish in terror, their wisdom at an end, the future now dark and unknowable.

As the dark stage brightens, Siegfried and Brünnhilde enter, rapturously absorbed in their love for each other. The erstwhile Valkyrie—now a mortal woman, willingly bound to her hero-husband by her weakness and love—is about to send him off to perform his destined deeds of glory. They exchange gifts: Siegfried places the Ring upon her finger, and Brünnhilde gives him Grane, the steed she rode as a Valkyrie.

During the celebrated orchestral interlude depicting Siegfried's journey down the Rhine, a change of scene is effected, and the curtain now rises upon the Hall of the Gibichungs. Gunther, the king of this clan, is in conversation with Gutrune, his sister, and with their half-brother Hagen. Their mother is Grimhilde, but Hagen's father is the dwarf Alberich, and Hagen has inherited from the Nibelung a grim cunning and a darkness of spirit.

At the moment, Hagen is occupied with plans to secure Brünnhilde in marriage to Gunther, and the hero Siegfried as a husband for Gutrune. Since only Siegfried can claim the Valkyrie from the flaming mountain, Hagen plans to use the young hero as a tool. A magic potion will cause Siegfried to fall in love with Gutrune, and then he will gladly surrender Brünnhilde to Gunther.

When Siegfried arrives at the Hall in the course of his Rhine journey, the plan is duly put into effect. Under influence of the potion, all memory of Brünnhilde is erased and superseded in his mind by an all-consuming passion for Gutrune. Taking advantage of Siegfried's addled wits, Hagen arranges for Gunther and Siegfried to go off in quest of the Valkyrie, whom Siegfried agrees to win as a bride for his new-found friend.

Before leaving, Gunther and Siegfried drink to their eternal friendship, while Siegfried is neatly distracted from inquiring too closely into Hagen's refusal to join in the pledge. Left alone, Hagen grimly vows that these two who obviously hold him in contempt shall yet be servants to his will.

Meanwhile, Brünnhilde receives a visit from her former Valkyrie sister Waltraute, who, in the course of a famous narrative, tells of the gloom that has fallen over Valhalla. One day Wotan, returning with his spear shattered by the sword of a hero, ordered the ash tree of the world hewn down and its pieces used to build a rampart around Valhalla. Surrounded by the silent gods, Wotan broods upon their doom which is inevitable unless the Rhine maidens regain the Ring Brünnhilde now wears. Angrily refusing to part with the Ring, Brünnhilde asserts that it is a symbol of Siegfried's love, and as such is more precious to her than the happiness of the gods.

Alone again, Brünnhilde settles to await Siegfried, taking comfort in the protecting circle of fire that still rings the mountain. As his horn call sounds, she starts up in eager welcome, recoiling horrified as a stranger emerges from the flames. It is indeed Siegfried who, with aid of the Tarnhelm, now appears in the shape of Gunther. He tears the Ring from Brünnhilde's finger and claims her as Gunther's bride.

Act 2

Back in the Hall of the Gibichungs, Hagen promises his father Alberich to retrieve the Ring for him. When Siegfried returns (now in his own form), he reports the mission accomplished. And while preparations are begun for a gala pagan wedding, Brünnhilde is led in by Gunther. She stares in amazement as Siegfried approaches and sedately greets her as Gunther's bride. In turn, he stands dumfounded when she, seeing the Ring on his finger, bursts into a series of incoherent accusations.

First she charges—and Hagen is quick to call special attention to her words—that the Ring rightfully belongs to Gunther, for it was he who took it from her on the mountain. Then, when the truth dawns upon her, she turns bitterly on Siegfried, denouncing him for his treachery and insisting that he has already taken her as his wife. This latter accusation is misunderstood by the others to mean that before delivering Brünnhilde to Gunther, Siegfried had first dishonored his friend's bride. But the tension is momentarily dispelled when Siegfried, protesting his innocence, gaily goes off with Gutrune.

Under skillful probing, Hagen learns from Brünnhilde that the protective spell which in love she wove about the hero does not cover his back. Siegfried would never turn his back on an enemy—hence she neglected to make him invulnerable there. Winning consent to Siegfried's death from Gunther and Brünnhilde, Hagen gloats upon the Ring and the treasure which shall be his. For Gutrune's sake, Hagen agrees to stage the murder as a boar-hunting accident. The act closes with the re-emergence of the bridal procession—Gutrune radiant, and Siegfried borne aloft upon a shield.

Act 3

The final act opens upon the Rhine Maidens swimming gaily about and chattering of the hero who shall return their treasure to them. When Siegfried appears they attempt to cajole the Ring away from him. But then they bid him keep it, recounting its grim history and foretelling that like the others who possessed it, he too shall die. Unable to impress him with the truth of their story, they swim off, leaving him to his fate.

As their song dies away, Hagen and Gunther appear with their vassals, and to them Siegfried laughingly relates the Rhine Maidens' prediction of his death. For their entertainment, he sings the story of his youth with Mime, describing how he forged the sword and slew the dragon. As Siegfried drains a horn into which Hagen has slipped some herb juice, his memory is suddenly restored, and now his narrative turns to his conquest of the flaming mountain and how he took Brünnhilde as his bride.

Horrified to hear Brünnhilde's accusation thus confirmed, Gunther starts up. But just then two ravens appear. And as Siegfried arises at Hagen's suggestion to gaze after the birds, he turns his back for a moment on Hagen who instantly plunges his spear into the vulnerable place. Griefstricken over his treachery, Gunther kneels by Siegfried's side, while Siegfried, opening his eyes for the last time, sings his greeting to Brünnhilde before he dies. The scene closes with the famous funeral march. Siegfried is borne aloft in solemn procession while night falls and a mist envelops the stage.

The procession returns to the Hall of the Gibichungs where Hagen, in grim triumph, gloats to Gutrune over his slaying of her husband. In the course of a wrangle about the Ring, Hagen completes his work by murdering his half-brother Gunther. All gasp in horror as the hand of the dead Siegfried raises itself threateningly. Then they busy themselves in carrying out Brünnhilde's commands.

The truth is now clear to her, and, as the funeral pyre she ordered built arises, she sings a long and moving farewell to her hero-husband. Taking the Ring from his finger, she signs for his body to be placed on the pyre, and setting it aflame, mounts her horse and plunges into the flaming pyre. As the Rhine swells towards the flames, the Rhine Maidens are seen riding the waves, swimming toward Brünnhilde to reclaim the Ring. Hagen rushes to grapple with the Rhine Maidens for the Ring. Two of them seize him and drag him down with them, while a third holds aloft the recovered Ring.

As the Hall falls in flaming ruins, the interior of Valhalla is seen in a red glow, the gods sitting in silent assemblage. Flames from the funeral pyre spread to the home of the gods, as Valhalla and all in it are doomed. And as the final curtain falls, the motive which has been associated with the concept of Redemption by Love (No. 22) sounds softly in the orchestra.

TANNHÄUSER

AN OPERA IN THREE ACTS

by Richard Wagner

Cast

HERMANN, LANDGRAVE OF THURINGIA Bass

TANNHÄUSER .... Tenor

WOLFRAM VON ESCHENBACH. ......Baritone

WALTHER VON DER VOGELWEIDE .... Tenor

BITEROLF ....Bass

HEINRICH DER SCHREIBER .... Tenor

REINMAR VON ZWETER . ...Bass

ELISABETH ... . Soprano

VENUS .... Soprano

A YOUNG SHEPHERD .... Soprano

FOUR NOBLE PAGES ...... Soprano and Alto

CHORUS OF THURINGIAN NOBLES AND KNIGHTS,
LADIES, ELDER AND YOUNGER PILGRIMS, SIRENS,
NAIADS, NYMPHS, AND BACCHANTES

Time . ... Early thirteenth century
Place .. .. Thuringia

First Performance
Hoftheater, Dresden, October 19, 1845

TANNHÄUSER

Overture

THE OVERTURE clearly suggests the theme of the opera, which is the conflict between sacred and profane love. It opens with the solemn, even-paced "Pilgrims' March" (Nos. 1, 2, and 3).* The beginning is soft and sustained; but it rises to a climax, intoned majestically by the brass, while a pulsating string figure surges in wavelike undulations over it. After the march dies away, the pace accelerates, and a feverish motive (No. 4) flares fitfully through the orchestra. This and similar themes, depicting the wild and luxurious sensuality of Venus and her court, now command the orchestra. A triumphant theme (No. 5), which Tannhäuser later sings in praise of Venus, is heard, followed by the insinuating melody (No. 6) with which Venus tempts Tannhäuser to return to her.

Act 1

The curtain rises upon the interior of the Venusberg (the Hörselberg in Thuringia), revealing the

*Thematic Guide, p. 356.

grotto within which the goddess of love practices her luxuriant and tormenting pleasures. Daylight filters dimly through the rocks over which a greenish waterfall foams wildly. Naiads are bathing in a distant lake, and Sirens repose along its banks. Venus reclines at the opening of the grotto, while Tannhäuser lies with his head in her lap and his harp by his side. The three Graces are posed nearby, and all about lie sleeping Cupids, their limbs entwined.

The Nymphs begin an alluring dance and are soon joined by a group of young men. As a swarm of Bacchantes pour onto the stage, the dancing grows more abandoned. Satyrs and Fauns join in. The Graces, outraged by the voluptuous revelry, rouse the sleeping Cupids who, drawn up in formation, loose arrows upon the wild throng. The wounded sink down exhausted and, as the dissheveled and disorderly revelers retreat, a rosy mist descends to blanket the stage. Only Venus and Tannhäuser remain visible, their positions unchanged, while through the mist is heard the sound of the Siren chorus chanting its enticements from afar: "Come to these bowers . . . come taste our kisses . . . soft caresses shall calm your yearning" (No. 7).

Suddenly Tannhäuser starts as if from a dream. Venus draws him close and asks what has suddenly disturbed him. He imagines he has heard the sound of bells and wonders how long he has lain here, exiled from the world, lost in the voluptuous life of the Venusberg. Suspecting he is growing tired of her entertainments, Venus urges him to dismiss such foolish thoughts and sing again of love. He takes up

his harp with resolution and pours forth an intoxi-
cating song in praise of the goddess and of her pagan
pleasures (No. 5). But his song slows, grows reflec-
tive, and concludes with the wish that he might
leave her. Venus detects a lack of customary ecstasy
in his singing. He tries again (No. 4); but as the
song accelerates to its climax, once more it turns into
a cry to be delivered from her oppressive embraces.

Venus leaps up. Now thoroughly angry, she turns
upon him with accusations of ingratitude and betrayal. He begs the "lovely goddess" not to frown
upon him and, while she rages on, continues both
to protest his love and to reiterate his desire to be
free. Venus, her passion at its height, turns abruptly
away from him. There is a pause; and when she turns
back again, it is with suppressed frenzy—replaced by
a quiet, languorous seductiveness. With sensuous
melodiousness (No. 6), she invites him back to the
"sweet joys" of the grotto, promising him a "feast of
joy" to celebrate the renewal of their love. As she
draws Tannhäuser gently towards her, the distant
Siren chorus sounds again (No. 7), repeating its invitation to partake in unimaginable delights.

This procedure has its effect. In a fit of frenzied
exaltation, Tannhäuser seizes his harp and once more
plunges into his song in praise of Venus (No. 5). But
his harp falls from his hand, and for the third time
his song turns into a plea for deliverance. Beside herself with passion, Venus berates him as a traitor and
a madman. Scornfully she gives him his freedom and
assures him that only misery awaits him in a cold

world among mirthless men. She prophesies that he shall seek comfort in vain (No. 8) and taunts him with the prediction that with pride broken, he will come crawling to her, begging for the very favors he now so stupidly surrenders.

But Tannhäuser retains his self-assurance. Venus' anger turns to despair. If he does not return, she swears, the whole human race shall be doomed to languish without the comforts and blessings of love. "The world shall be a wilderness," she vows, "and its hero a slave." Tannhäuser, however, declares that his farewell is final and adds that he will seek salvation in repentance. Unwilling to lose him completely, and ready to accept any compromise, Venus begs that when he finds no hope among men, he will then turn back to her. "My hope!" declares Tannhäuser. "My hope rests in Mary!" It is the irrevocable rejection of the pagan for the Christian world, and with a despairing cry, Venus vanishes.

Tannhäuser's position remains unaltered during a sudden change of scene. He finds himself in a quiet valley. A shrine of the Virgin is in the foreground, and from the distant hills the sound of sheep bells is heard. A shepherd pipes a merry tune and then sings his salutation to Holda, the gracious goddess of the spring. His piping mingles with the far-off chant of the Elder Pilgrims who are descending from the distant mountain (No. 9).

As the Pilgrims begin the second verse of their chant (No. 2), the shepherd hears them and ceases playing. He listens reverently, and then shouts, "God speed to Rome." Tannhäuser, on his knees, offers praise to the wonder of the Lord's mercy. The procession passes the shrine. As it and the shepherd (accompanying its chant with his piping) move off stage, Tannhäuser, now alone, takes up the burden of the second verse (No. 2), and he bows his head to the ground and weeps. The Pilgrims' chant fades in the distance; the bells have ceased pealing, and ever closer comes the sound of hunting horns.

A procession of another sort is now seen winding down the mountain. It is the Landgrave of Thuringia and his entourage of minstrels to which Tannhäuser had formerly belonged. Upon being recognized, Tannhäuser bows mutely to the Landgrave. But before welcoming him, Biterolf, one of the minstrels, demands to know whether Tannhäuser has returned as friend or foe. The others seem to think it a fair question, but Wolfram, another of the minstrels, silences them. Tannhäuser's manner, he says, provides answer enough. Following Wolfram's example, the others also extend their greetings.

Then from the Landgrave comes the inevitable question: where has Tannhäuser tarried so long? "In strange and distant lands I wandered," he replies, "where neither peace nor rest was ever found." He provides no further detail, except to assure them that he scorns no man and desires only to depart in peace. This reassurance awakens their hospitality. But Tannhäuser, reiterating that the past is closed to him and that henceforth he must travel alone, remains resolved to leave, until Wolfram invokes the name of Elisabeth, the daughter of the Landgrave. Tannhäuser, entranced, repeats the name. Then Wolfram informs him (after asking and receiving permission from the Landgrave) that before his departure from them, his singing had won for him her love. After he had gone, Elisabeth had withdrawn herself from their tournaments and had closed her heart to their songs.

Deeply moved, Tannhäuser embraces Wolfram and the minstrels. In the ensuing ensemble, he sings his joyful recognition of the radiant world (No. 10) so long lost to him. In the meanwhile, the Landgrave's entire retinue (huntsmen and torchbearers) have assembled. A fanfare (twelve horns) is sounded; the procession rides off. As the curtain falls, Tannhäuser's joyful song (No. 10) is enunciated by the orchestra.

Act 2

The Prelude opens with a bounding motive symbolizing Elisabeth's happiness at her hero's longed-for return, followed by Tannhäuser's joyous melody (No. 10) which had closed the previous act. A passage for winds recalls Venus' grim warning (No. 8); but the festive atmosphere is soon restored, and Elisabeth enters the Hall of the Minstrels, as the curtain rises, singing her greeting to this famed place of song (No. 11). She recalls how Tannhäuser's singing had won her, how this Hall had seemed a desert after his departure, and she rejoices that it will soon again sound with the glory of his voice.

Wolfram conducts Tannhäuser into the Hall and remains apart while Tannhäuser throws himself at Elisabeth's feet. Shy, yet eager to welcome him, she bids him rise, gives thanks for his return, and finally she asks the inevitable question (as the Landgrave asked earlier): where has he tarried so long? His reply is longer this time, but no more explicit than before. He vaguely mentions a strange and distant country from which he was delivered by a miracle, mysterious and inexplicable. It suffices.

Elisabeth praises the miracle that restored Tannhäuser to her and is instantly overcome with confusion. All manner of strange longings possess her, and she confesses them with a mixture of innocence and awakened passion. Tannhäuser promptly declares that it was the god of love who wrought the miracle of his restoration; then in an exalted duet they praise this deity and rejoice in their reunion. Tannhäuser now rushes to Wolfram, whom he embraces impetuously. As the two leave the stage, the Landgrave enters, and it is upon his breast that Elisabeth lays her modest head.

The Landgrave pretends a mild surprise to find her present in this Hall and asks whether the projected Tournament of Song has finally lured her here. Her reply is in the form of a vague and ecstatic exclamation. He suggests that there is probably something she would like to tell him. But after the traditional manner of maidens in chivalric romances, she tells him to find the answer in her eyes. The Landgrave is content to wait until Elisabeth will voluntarily speak to him of her love for Tannhäuser. Diplomatically he turns their attention to the noble guests now entering the Hall.

During the reception of the guests, the orchestra

plays processional music (Nos. 12 and 12-a). First
the chorus of Knights and Nobles pay their respects
to the Landgrave (No. 12), and then their Ladies
(in chorus) make their obeisances (No. 12-a). They
join forces for a resounding choral salutation, and
seat themselves in a semicircle to receive the minstrels, who are ushered in with a trumpet fanfare
behind stage. After bowing to the company, the minstrels are conducted to their seats by pages.

The Landgrave rises, salutes his minstrels in a pretty
speech, makes reference to the "gallant minstrel"
(Tannhäuser) recently returned, and suggests that
in his song the minstrel himself dispel the mystery
of his long absence. He offers the theme of Love as
a text for the tournament, and announces that Elisabeth herself will reward the one who improvises most
nobly upon it. The assembled company responds with
another chorus in honor of the Landgrave.

While the orchestra continues with ceremonial music, the pages collect the names of the minstrels (each
on a separate slip of paper) and place them in a golden
cup. Elisabeth draws one of the slips and returns it
to the pages, who read it and announce in chorus:
"Wolfram von Eschenbach."

Wolfram's song, decorous in tone and entirely innocent in text, abounds in such phrases (obviously
addressed to Elisabeth) as "I'll worship thee kneeling
with soul devoted." Just as the assembly concludes
its chorus of approval, one of the wild Venusberg
themes (No. 4) flickers through the orchestra. Tannhäuser has been sitting apart, leaning on his harp,
apparently in a trance. Now he suddenly rises. With-

out awaiting his turn, and oblivious of the company, he informs Wolfram that he too has known the fountain of love. But he cannot approach it without a burning desire to cool his parched lips in its waters. Elisabeth is about to make the customary sign of approval, but she refrains since everyone else remains silent. It is an unheard-of breach of romantic etiquette to sing of love in terms of sensual consummation.

Walther von der Vogelweide, one of the most celebrated of minstrels, reproves Tannhäuser for suggesting that the hallowed waters of love be used to quench the wild flames of passion. But once more, as the assembly concludes its endorsement of Walther's sentiments, the feverish Venusberg theme (No. 4) courses through the orchestra. Tannhäuser has risen again, and this time impatiently. He taunts Walther with never having known the pleasures of love of which he professes to sing. Biterolf promptly denounces Tannhäuser as a blasphemer and offers to settle the issue between them in combat. This offer is roundly applauded by the chorus of Lords and Ladies.

Again the Venusberg motive (No. 4) breaks through, and Tannhäuser, ridiculing the thought that anyone as crude and unprepossessing as Biterolf might know anything of love, adds one insult to another by spurning his challenge. A command from the Landgrave halts the imminent outbreak of hostilities. Quiet is restored as Wolfram, earnestly invoking Heaven's aid, reiterates his earlier sentiments. But Tannhäuser, unable any longer to contain himself, bursts forth with the magnificently impassioned praise of Venus (No. 5) which he had sung earlier while in the lap of the goddess on the Venusberg.

The Ladies promptly quit the Hall. Landgrave, minstrels, and nobles stand together; Elisabeth, pale and trembling, supports herself against a pillar; and Tannhäuser, still entranced, remains alone. Roaring curses and accusations upon him, the indignant company rings Tannhäuser with drawn swords. But Elisabeth, shielding her beloved with her body, shames them from their vengeance. She reminds them of their Christian obligation to show mercy, and demands by what right they dare sit in judgment upon him. They too are erring mortals, and it is not within their power to close the gates of Heaven to a sinner. Her voice rises in prayer (No. 13) that the hope of pardon may not be denied him. Tannhäuser is crushed by remorse, and the nobles and minstrels are overcome by Elisabeth's angelic heroism.

The Landgrave solemnly castigates Tannhäuser for his depravity. Only one hope remains. He must join the Pilgrim band now assembling for Rome. The others take up the Landgrave's admonition, adding that he owes his life to the intercession of an angel, and that their swords will yet find him if he fails to seek absolution in Rome. During this chorus Elisabeth continues her prayer, while Tannhäuser sings of his abnegation and despair. In the distance the chant of the Younger Pilgrims becomes audible. Suddenly rousing himself, Tannhäuser rushes to join them, and the curtain falls with the entire company urging him on to Rome.

Act 3

The Prelude, descriptive of Tannhäuser's pilgrimage, is based largely upon themes (including 2, 3, and 12) already heard in the course of the opera.

As it dies away, the curtain rises upon the valley in which Tannhäuser had originally found himself upon leaving the Venusberg. Wolfram, descending from a forest path, sees Elisabeth kneeling in prayer before the shrine. In the best tradition of romantic renunciation, he hopes that his beloved Elisabeth's prayers for Tannhäuser's salvation may be answered.

The Pilgrims are due shortly to return and, as Wolfram is about to descend farther into the valley, the sound of their joyous singing (Nos. 1 and 2) is heard. Elisabeth too has heard the homeward-bound procession. She rises, anxiously scanning the ranks of the Pilgrims as they file by her and off again into the distance. Tannhäuser is not among the absolved. As their chant dies away, Elisabeth, believing that he will never return, falls to her knees and implores the Virgin to receive her into her bright kingdom (No. 14). She vows to die a maid and begs that the bounty of Heaven may yet be extended to Tannhäuser.

After remaining in absorbed silence for several moments, she rises and, seeing Wolfram, gestures that he is not to address her. Nevertheless, he asks whether he may not guide her home. But mutely signifying her thanks, she indicates that her concern is now with Heaven and that her path must be unattended.

When her retreating figure has faded into the gloom, Wolfram takes up his harp. In the gentle, melancholy dusk that has fallen over the valley, he sings what is perhaps the most famous aria in the opera—the song to the evening star (No. 15).

It has grown dark, and Tannhäuser now enters. Ragged, emaciated, faltering forward with the aid of his staff, he has followed the sad sound of the harp. Wolfram asks the wanderer who he is. "Who am I?" says Tannhäuser bitterly. "I know you right well. You are Wolfram, the expert minstrel." Wolfram now recognizes him and, fearful of his strained and unnatural manner, inquires whether he has dared return without absolution. "Have no fear," replies Tannhäuser, "I am not looking for you or any of your kind."

As the Venusberg motive (No. 4) rises again in the orchestra, Tannhäuser declares that he is seeking the path he once trod with ease. "What path is that?" asks Wolfram. "The path to the Venusberg," is the ecstatic reply. As Wolfram exclaims in horror, Tannhäuser, with a tone of unnatural craving in his voice whispers: "Do you know the way?" Wolfram demands whether he has been to Rome. But the mention of Rome enrages Tannhäuser and he orders him to be silent. As Wolfram persists, Tannhäuser, softly and bitterly says: "Yes, I have been to Rome." That Wolfram should continue to press him for the full story astonishes Tannhäuser, for he had supposed him an enemy.

Reassured, Tannhäuser sinks exhausted; but as Wolfram is about to sit down beside him, he abruptly orders him away. "The place where I rest is accursed," he declares, and then launches into the story of his pilgrimage.

He describes the contrition that obsessed him during his journey, the vision of the angelic Elisabeth that drove him to burden and lacerate his body with inhuman hardships in the hope of expiating his sins. After a pause, he resumes, now telling of Rome as he entered it amid the pealing of bells and with the hope of pardon raising every heart; how crowds prostrated themselves before him who dispenses the Lord's mercy, asking and receiving papal absolution. He too abased himself in dust and tears, confessed his unclean enslavement to the pleasures of Venus, and implored forgiveness. But absolution was denied him, for those who have lived in the hell-fire of the Venusberg are beyond salvation.

He fell down in a trance, and awoke at night alone. Songs of prayer and praise sounded all about him. He rose with loathing, knowing himself an eternal outcast among decent men, and fled. Then did his longing for the delights of the Venusberg return.

The Siren call (No. 4) sounds again, and Tannhäuser raves on, groveling in a frenzy of abnegation to Venus. Wolfram tries vainly to interrupt this madness. But darkness now completely envelops the stage, Tannhäuser's voice growing ecstatic with anticipation as a rosy light begins to seep through and a misty confusion of dancing shapes approaches him. He calls for Venus (No. 6) with increasing desperation, and finally in the rosy light she is seen reclining upon her couch. She welcomes him back with a mixture of satisfaction and scorn. Wolfram attempts to shield Tannhäuser from his erotic assailants, while Venus continues to taunt her returned slave.

Tannhäuser has just torn himself away from Wolfram and is about to fling himself toward the goddess, when Wolfram utters Elisabeth's name. They remain rooted, listening to the chant for the dead that has become audible in the distance, and watching the glow of the torches that have now begun to penetrate the mist. The body of Elisabeth is being borne to its final resting place. Wolfram instantly realizes that Tannhäuser is saved, and Venus, that she has lost him. She vanishes with the mist, and in the dawning light a funeral procession is seen descending into the valley.

Wolfram asks Tannhäuser whether he hears the distant chorus, and the dying Tannhäuser replies simply: "I hear it." The Elder Pilgrims enter, leading the solemn cortege. Elisabeth's hearse is borne by the minstrels, and after it, the Landgrave with his knights and nobles. Wolfram, who has motioned the minstrels to set down the hearse, leads Tannhäuser to it. Tannhäuser slowly sinks beside it and dies, imploring his Saint Elisabeth to pray for him. Torches are inverted and extinguished. As sunlight floods the valley, all join in reverent chorus for the two souls who have entered Heaven together.

TOSCA

AN OPERA IN THREE ACTS

by Giacomo Puccini

Cast

FLORIA TOSCA	Soprano
MARIO CAVARADOSSI	Tenor
BARON SCARPIA	Baritone
CESARE ANGELOTTI	Bass
A SACRISTAN	Baritone
SPOLETTA	Tenor
SCIARRONE	Bass

JUDGE, CARDINAL, OFFICER, SERGEANT, SOLDIERS, POLICE AGENTS, LADIES, NOBLES, CITIZENS, ACOLYTES

Libretto
by Luigi Illica and Giuseppe Giacosa
(based on a play by Victorien Sardou)

Time	June, 1800
Place	Rome

First Performance
Teatro Costanzi, Rome, January 14, 1900

TOSCA

Act 1

THERE IS NO OVERTURE. A grim chord progression (No. 1)* later associated with Scarpia, the dread chief of Rome's police, is followed by a frenetic theme (No. 2) which accompanies Angelotti onto the stage.

Panic stricken, breathless, and disheveled, Angelotti has just escaped in prisoner's garb from the castle of Sant' Angelo, and taken refuge here in the church of Sant' Andrea della Valle. To the right is the Attavanti family chapel, while to the left, upon a dais, stands an easel, the painting on it covered by a cloth. Near by is a basket of food and various painting implements. Glancing fearfully around him, Angelotti heaves a sigh of relief upon recognizing the figure of the Virgin, and muttering that his sister had instructed him to look at the feet of the Madonna, he hastily searches there for the key. Not finding it, he makes a gesture of discouragement, desperately resumes his search, and scarcely stifles a shout of joy when he does find it.

*Thematic Guide, p. 358.

Taking the key, and looking frantically around to see whether he has been observed (No. 2 in the orchestra), Angelotti creeps towards the Attavanti chapel, inserts the key in the chapel gate, opens it, enters, and locks the gate behind him.

A moment later, a sprightly theme (No. 3) ushers the Sacristan on stage with a batch of paintbrushes in his hand. He bustles about his various little chores (No. 4), talking in a loud voice, and nervously twitching his neck and shoulders. Apparently Cavaradossi, the painter, who is working in the church, has given the Sacristan his brushes to clean, for the fussy fellow now complains loudly of their dirt and stickiness. Noting with surprise that the dais is empty (Cavaradossi, in his opinion, should already have been at work) he inspects the basket and finds the food untouched. Just then the Angelus is rung and the Sacristan kneels to intone the prayer.

In the meanwhile Cavaradossi enters, ascends the dais, and uncovers the painting on which he is working—a Mary Magdalen with blue eyes and masses of golden hair. His devotions over, the Sacristan rises and in astonishment declares that the Magdalen is a portrait of the mysterious young woman who has recently come to pray so devoutly in this church. This the painter acknowledges, and to the scandalized Sacristan he tells how, unseen, he watched the fair lady and painted her without her knowledge.

While Cavaradossi begins to paint, the Sacristan fidgets about, picking up discarded brushes. Suddenly the painter stops, takes from his breast pocket a miniature of Floria Tosca, a celebrated singer who is his own beloved, and compares it with the features of the Magdalen. Some of Tosca's features have been blended with those of the devout lady, and while Cavaradossi is bemused by this "strange harmony of contrasts" (No. 5), the Sacristan grumbles under his breath at the painter's scorn for the saints and his jests with the ungodly. These "Voltairian dogs" should be hanged or burned, in his opinion, and asking permission to leave (which Cavaradossi readily grants), the Sacristan then points to the food basket and inquires whether the painter intends fasting. When Cavaradossi tells him that he is not hungry, the Sacristan (while he politely expresses his regret) cannot repress a greedy and joyful glance at the food which will now be his to devour. Taking two pinches of snuff, he is off, leaving Cavaradossi at work with his back to the chapel.

Angelotti, believing the church empty, opens the chapel gate; but the painter, hearing the noise of the key in the lock, turns sharply around, and Angelotti is panic stricken (No. 2 in the orchestra). Then, with a shout of joy, he recognizes Cavaradossi, his friend and an unhoped-for ally. For a moment Cavaradossi does not recognize him, so altered is Angelotti from his imprisonment; but when he does, he looks cautiously around, hastily closes the church door(again the feverish motive of No. 2 in the orchestra), and promptly offers his help.

Just then the voice of Tosca—a beautiful prima donna, and Cavaradossi's mistress—is heard outside calling to her lover to admit her. Assuring Angelotti that it is merely a jealous woman whom he'll dispose of quickly, Cavaradossi instructs him to conceal himself, and, as Angelotti leans weakly against the scaffolding, hands him the food basket and urges him toward the chapel. Meanwhile Tosca's voice outside has grown more impatient. When the church door is finally opened, she rushes in impetuously (No. 6 in the orchestra accompanies her entry), repulses Cavaradossi's attempt to embrace her, and demands to know why the door was locked. "By the Sacristan's order," replies the painter. Tosca is sure that he was whispering to a woman, and despite Cavaradossi's disclaimer, insists that the rustle of a woman's skirts was quite audible. When he offers to embrace her again, she wards him off. "Before the Madonna?" she exclaims with a modesty faintly tinged with sarcasm; and then reverently bedecking the statue of the Virgin with the flowers she brought, Tosca kneels in prayer.

Cavaradossi resumes work on the Magdalen, replying absently to Tosca who, having crossed herself and risen, now informs him that she is singing tonight, and will expect him at the stage door so that they can leave together for his villa. (A suggestion of No. 2, the theme associated with Angelotti's danger, indicates the reason for Cavaradossi's lack of attention.) Perplexed by his abstracted replies, Tosca asks whether the cottage holds no attraction for him. Expatiating upon the natural beauty and peacefulness of the surroundings and their seclusion together there (No. 7), she paints so glowing a picture of an ideal setting for their love, that Cavaradossi is finally provoked into an expression of equally impassioned eagerness to be with her. However, his gaze shifts to the chapel gate and asking her to be off, insists that he must get to work. (Once more Angelotti's theme, No. 2, is heard in the orchestra.)

This abrupt dismissal is the wrong tactic to use with Tosca. Halfway out she catches sight of the painting, and turning back demands to know who the blonde beauty is. "A Magdalen," replies Cavaradossi, "do you like her?" When she jealously pronounces her much too beautiful, the painter, bowing, takes it as a compliment to his art. But Tosca cannot let the matter rest. Insisting that she has seen those blue eyes somewhere—Cavaradossi observes indifferently that they are by no means uncommon—Tosca finally identifies her as the Marchioness Attavanti. (Just then the dissonant pronouncement of No. 2 in the orchestra suggests that a relationship exists between Angelotti and the Marchioness. They are, indeed, as subsequently becomes clear, brother and sister.)

Tosca now works herself into a jealous rage, and not until Cavaradossi swears that he saw the Attavanti only yesterday and sketched her, unseen, is she willing to grant that perhaps there is no clandestine affair between them. Nevertheless, to Tosca's jealous fancy, the blue eyes on the canvas seem to be staring at her in scorn. He presses her to him affectionately, and assures her that she need fear no rival. Although placated, Tosca cannot resist observing maliciously that the Magdalen's eyes had better be black ones. Her jealousy, she admits, is without foundation (No. 8), and in the next duet, avowals of love are exchanged. A promise is exacted, however: that he will admit no pious woman, dark or fair, while he is working; and this time it is Cavaradossi who jestingly exclaims "Before the Madonna!" when Tosca offers her cheek to be kissed. He embraces her nevertheless, and she leaves with the parting caution that the Magdalen's eyes had still better be black.

After a moment plunged in thought, Cavaradossi checks the side door, and, assured that all is quiet, opens the Chapel gate for Angelotti. They greet each other affectionately, the painter explaining to his friend (who has, of course, overheard the foregoing scene) that Tosca, while a truehearted creature, conceals nothing from her confessor, and hence it is best that she knows nothing of Angelotti's presence in the church.

Angelotti explains that his sister, the Marchioness Attavanti, concealed under the altar a suit of women's clothes which should serve him well enough as a disguise. To Cavaradossi, this accounts for the mysterious woman whose recent devotions he mistook as a cover for some amatory escapade. Scarpia's theme (No. 1) rises in the orchestra, as the fugitive tells how his sister undertook to rescue him from that "bigoted satyr and hypocrite . . . steeped in vice . . . sanctimonious, lascivious, and cruel." Scarpia, declares Angelotti indignantly, is "a cross between a confessor and a hangman."

Cavaradossi, ready to forfeit his own life to protect his friend, gives him the package of clothes and the key to his own villa with directions for proceeding thence from the church. Promising to join him there after dark, Cavaradossi tells Angelotti that if danger threatens, the well in the garden connects, via a narrow passage, with a spacious cellar where he may hide in complete safety. A cannon shot from the castle tells them that Angelotti's escape has been discovered. Suddenly resolving to accompany his friend in case help is needed in a fight with Scarpia's police, the painter hastens out with Angelotti just as the Sacristan enters (No. 3), eager to impart what he considers some splendid news.

Astonished and also annoyed to find Cavaradossi gone (No. 4 in the orchestra), the Sacristan imparts the joyful tiding to a crowd of acolytes, penitents, pupils, and choristers who riotously rush in from all directions, eager to hear what has happened. That miscreant Napoleon, declares the Sacristan, has been beaten, smashed to pieces; and this news he relishes as much as he knew it would vex Cavaradossi, whose advanced political opinions are, as far as the Sacristan is concerned, a counterpart of his irreligious remarks. The victory, continues the Sacristan, will be hailed by a torchlight procession, a gala performance at the Farnese Palace, and an appropriate cantata, newly composed, to be sung by Floria Tosca.

The Sacristan orders them off to don their vestments. But they pay him no heed, capering about and roaring lustily: "Double wages. . . . Long live the King!" until Scarpia—his glowering theme (No. 1), sounding ominously in the orchestra—appears unexpectedly, followed by his henchman, Spoletta, and several other police agents. The mere sight of the Chief of Police hushes the revelers. They slink off;

but the Sacristan, who would also like to remove himself unnoticed, is ordered to remain.

Spoletta is dispatched to search every corner of the church, guards are posted at the doorways, and the Sacristan is enjoined to answer questions truthfully. A prisoner of state, explains Scarpia, has escaped and taken refuge here. Upon Scarpia's request, the Sacristan shows him to the Attavanti chapel, and finding it unlocked, tells him that the key is a new one. They enter the chapel and return promptly, Scarpia holding a closed fan which he flutters in nervous irritation. It was a blunder, he mutters, to have fired the cannon and given Angelotti warning. But the fan suggests an accomplice; and, noting in quick succession the Attavanti coat of arms on the fan and the Attavanti portrait reproduced in the Magdalen on the easel, Scarpia demands the name of the painter. "Mario Cavaradossi," replies the Sacristan; and from Scarpia's reaction it is evident that, both as Tosca's lover and as a holder of heretical opinions, the painter has long been an object of the police chief's interest.

The final clue is provided by the now empty food basket which a police agent brings from the chapel. Exclaiming tearfully over it, the Sacristan reveals that he brought it earlier in the day well provisioned for Cavaradossi, but the painter wasn't hungry and, in any case, couldn't have eaten it in the chapel because he didn't have a key. Scarpia quickly deduces that Angelotti consumed the food, but he is more interested in the fact that Cavaradossi is involved, because that gives him a desired hold over Tosca. "A handkerchief lit Othello's jealous fire," he remarks, as

Tosca enters, hunting excitedly for Cavaradossi, "and I have a fan." Concealing himself behind a pillar to which a holy water font is affixed, he motions the Sacristan to stay where he is. The latter remains just long enough to tell Tosca that Cavaradossi simply vanished, and then he too disappears. As the bells sound, calling the faithful to prayer, Tosca, almost weeping, seeks to reassure herself that her Mario really couldn't be untrue to her.

This hint of Tosca's state of mind is all Scarpia requires. Dipping his fingers into the font, he comes forward and with unctuous courtesy offers her holy water. She touches his fingers, makes the sign of the cross, and listens inattentively while Scarpia launches into an elaborate eulogy of her virtue. Her voice, he declares, gives new life to religion, for with it she brings to earth the delights of Heaven. She is, moreover, a genuinely pious woman, for she comes here to really pray, unlike certain wantons who simulate a Magdalen but use the church as a rendezvous with their lovers. The reference is explicit enough; and now with her attention completely riveted, he produces the fan along with a cleverly concocted story of how it was found upon the dais when the lovers, surprised by a casual worshipper, beat a hasty retreat.

Only too easily convinced, especially when she notes the Attavanti insignia on the fan, Tosca gives vent to her grief, heedless of the worshippers who are now streaming into church. The success of his plan encourages Scarpia to offer himself as the agent for her revenge, if he but knew the name of her betrayer. But Tosca is too self-absorbed to listen and, swearing desperately that the Attavanti shall not possess her lover tonight, declares with bitter tears that God will forgive her for the oath which Scarpia reproves her for having uttered in church. He escorts her gently to the door, signaling for Spoletta to follow her and report to him at the Farnese Palace.

The church is now full; and, as the Cardinal and his procession advance to the high altar, Scarpia remarks sardonically: "Go, Tosca, there is room in thy heart for Scarpia." He bows reverently as the Cardinal passes, but for the moment remains too fiercely absorbed to participate in the responses between chapter and congregation which now proceed apace.

In an erotic tantrum, Scarpia envisages Tosca clasped to him mute with rapture, and (while the crowd kneels) he pronounces savagely the dual course he has plotted for Cavaradossi and Tosca: one leads to the scaffold, the other into his arms. During the choral "Te Deum" he stands as in a reverie. Suddenly rousing himself, he cries out: "Tosca, for thee I would renounce God," and as suddenly kneels in an access of religious fervor, joining with the others in the singing of the "Te aeternum Patrem omnis terra veneratur." As the curtain falls, Scarpia's dread motive (No. 1) rises direfully thrice in the orchestra.

Act 2

Scarpia is at table in his apartment on an upper floor of the Farnese Palace, manifestly impatient for his projected meeting with Tosca. She is a good decoy, he murmurs, and by sunrise the two conspirators should be upon the gallows. On one of the lower floors of the palace a fete is in progress, given by Queen Caroline in honor of General Melas. Tosca is scheduled to sing and, checking with Sciarrone (a gendarme), Scarpia learns that a page has already been dispatched for her. He orders the window open, concluding from the dance music below (No. 9) that the company is still awaiting Tosca's arrival.

Framing a note which he knows will fetch Tosca if only for Cavaradossi's sake, Scarpia dispatches Sciarrone to deliver it, launching into an extended monologue in which the type of seduction that amuses him is made clear. The forcible conquest interests him, not the passive surrender. Unskilled in sighs and sentimental rhapsodies, he must plot basely for what he desires; and once the object of his passion has been possessed, then he discards her for other game. The Lord created beauty and wine of various kinds, and, concludes Scarpia, "I choose to taste all that I can of the heavenly produce."

He drinks; and Spoletta now enters, nervously recounting that he followed Tosca to the villa, but the search there for Angelotti proved futile. Hastening to assuage Scarpia's savage anger, he continues with more welcome news: Cavaradossi was at the villa, and since his contempt for their search seemed suspicious, he had the painter arrested and put in irons. "You did wisely," comments Scarpia, as the orchestra softly insinuates a theme (No. 10) soon to be associated with Cavaradossi's ordeal.

Through the open window, the sound of the choir

below (No. 11) tells Scarpia that the cantata has begun, and that Tosca must already have arrived. Quickly dispatching Spoletta to fetch the prisoner, he sends Sciarrone off to bring Roberti (the executioner), a Judge of the Exchequer, and a clerk. When all are present, he addresses himself with elaborate courtesy to Cavaradossi, who refuses an invitation to be seated and angrily demands to know why he has been detained.

Just as Scarpia begins his reply, Tosca's voice is heard rising above the choir. Cavaradossi exclaims upon hearing her voice, but Scarpia proceeds now to charge him with having concealed a prisoner of state in the church of Sant' Andrea, supplied him with food and clothing, and then conveyed him to his villa. Each charge is resolutely denied, and Scarpia is reminded that his minions did not find anyone at the villa. Suavely Scarpia remarks that this proves only how well Angelotti was hidden; but the futile search is a sore point with Spoletta, who interrupts to complain of Cavaradossi's laughter at their endeavors. When Cavaradossi remarks ironically that he is still laughing, Scarpia rises in anger, slams the window shut, and in the now silent room, begins the interrogation in earnest.

Since Cavaradossi persists in his denials, Scarpia switches from an imperious tone to an almost paternalistic gentleness, advising the painter, in his own interest, to speak up. But this too has no effect. Tosca's entry at this point is what Scarpia has been waiting for. She rushes to embrace Cavaradossi, who hastily whispers to her to say nothing of what she had seen in the villa. Solemnly intoning each syllable, Scarpia announces to the painter that the judge will now take his deposition, and signaling Sciarrone to open the door to the torture chamber—a tremendous outburst of the torture motive (No. 10) in the orchestra—turns to Roberti with instructions to apply the usual pressure until further notice. Tosca and Scarpia are left alone, after the others follow the Judge into the torture chamber which adjoins Scarpia's apartment. "And now," says Scarpia, "let us have a friendly chat" (No. 12).

Evidently Tosca is not aware of the ordeal to which her lover is being subjected, for she effects an easiness of manner and a studied indifference toward Scarpia's insinuations concerning Mario and the Attavanti. However, her reiteration that the painter was alone at the villa sounds overemphatic to Scarpia's practiced ears, and ordering the persuasions made more urgent, turns back to Tosca with the suggestion that she can save her lover an hour of anguish. Only then does she realize what is happening within the adjacent chamber. As a groan from within confirms the gruesome details with which Scarpia now regales her, Tosca, in desperation, promises anything in order to stop the torture.

Granted a momentary surcease, Cavaradossi calls out to Tosca to remain silent; but the effect of this plea is nullified when Scarpia reminds her that the ordeal can, if necessary, be resumed. Her rage provokes Scarpia's laughter, and her anguish, the remark that never was Tosca more tragical upon the stage. In a sudden transport of ferocity, he orders the door opened so that she may hear her lover's outcries more distinctly.

The horror is now at its height: Scarpia shouting for the torture to be intensified, Cavaradossi screaming his defiance, and Tosca uttering broken phrases in an agony of indecision. At a sign from Scarpia, Tosca is permitted to approach the door. Appalled by the sight, she begs Cavaradossi to allow her to speak. But he continues to enjoin silence, and fearful that her lover may prevail upon her, Scarpia orders him silenced. While Tosca sobs convulsively, Spoletta, kneeling, begins a prayer for the dead—"Judex ergo cum sedebit." A prolonged outcry from within is more than Tosca can bear. Starting from the sofa, she reveals Angelotti's hiding place.

The torture motive (No. 10) sounds as Cavaradossi is now carried in and deposited upon the sofa, bleeding and in a faint. For a moment Tosca stands motionless, covering her eyes to shut out the gruesome sight; but ashamed of her weakness, she rushes to the sofa, lavishing tears and kisses upon her beloved. Sciarrone, the Judge, his clerk, and Roberti leave; but Scarpia signals for Spoletta and the other agents to remain. The game is far from being over, and Scarpia watches intently while Cavaradossi, reviving, asks Tosca whether he revealed anything under torture. No sooner does she reassure him, than Scarpia (making sure Cavaradossi hears him) orders his agents off to the garden well to find Angelotti.

Just as Cavaradossi turns upon Tosca with an imprecation for having betrayed him, Sciarrone re-enters, spluttering that the royal troops have been defeated by Napoleon at Marengo. This news transforms Cavaradossi and, mustering his remaining strength, he exultantly pours out a defiant song of freedom and death to tyrants (No. 13). Scarpia listens cynically and then joins his voice to Mario's, uttering scorn for the painter's bravado, while Tosca completes the trio with alternate appeals to Mario to be silent and to Scarpia to be merciful. Regardless of Napoleon's victory, Cavaradossi is still in Scarpia's power. He orders the painter taken off to the hangman, and while Cavaradossi is being forcibly removed by the police agents, Tosca is brutally thrust back into the room as she attempts to follow.

Scarpia now calmly addresses himself to his interrupted supper, invites Tosca to join him, and (to the gallant melody of No. 12) bids her devise with him some plan for her lover's liberation. With quiet contempt she asks his price; whereupon he explains that beautiful women do not purchase his favors with money. His tone is at first insinuating, but with rising passion he declares that if her beauty first attracted him, it is her hatred that completely enslaved him. The moment when she clung to Cavaradossi "like an amorous tigress," he tells her, is the very moment he swore to himself he would possess her. Eluding his attempted embrace, she makes for the door; but Scarpia divines her purpose (which is to reach the Queen in the apartment below with a plea for protection), and laughingly reminds her that even the Queen cannot pardon a dead man.

Completely trapped, she reiterates her hatred of him, but this he shrugs off with the remark that hatred

and love are kindred passions. Her cries for help as
he is about to seize her are interrupted by the sound
of distant drums. It is the escort to the scaffold, and
Cavaradossi, he reminds her, has but one more hour
to live. Leaning against the table, he sips his coffee,
listening coldly while, broken with grief, Tosca re-
views her life. For love and art alone has she unsel-
fishly lived, given her devotion to the Madonna, and
filled her days with pious observances and good
works (No. 14), "Love and music" *(Vissi d'arte)*. In
the orchestra, the melody of No. 6 accompanies Tosca's aria. On her knees before Scarpia she begs, first
desperately and then humbly, for mercy; but he remains unmoved.

Just then Spoletta enters with the news that Angelotti swallowed poison as they were about to seize
him (No. 2 in the orchestra). "Let his corpse be hung
on the gibbet," orders Scarpia, and turning to Tosca,
tells her that she must now make her decision. She
nods, weeping; but quickly demands that Cavaradossi
be set free. This Scarpia cannot do, since it must be
generally believed that the painter is dead. However,
he assures her, Spoletta will arrange the details, and
staring fixedly at his subordinate (who understands
the implication behind every tone and gesture), instructs him to arrange a mock execution. Tosca is to
be allowed to see her lover and explain the plan to him
beforehand.

Once more alone with Tosca, Scarpia declares his
part of the bargain fulfilled. But Tosca insists first
upon a safe conduct for herself and Cavaradossi.
While he is at his desk writing one out, she goes to

the table, fills a glass of wine for herself, and carefully takes possession of a sharply pointed knife which she notices upon the table. Scarpia seals and folds the document, and as he advances, crying, "At last thou art mine," she plunges the knife into his breast. "It is thus that Tosca kisses," she declares, taunting him as he begs for help, glorying in his agony, and cursing him as he dies.

Only when he is dead does Tosca utter her forgiveness. Quickly washing her fingers, arranging her hair, and extracting from Scarpia's lifeless hand the important safe conduct, she surveys her handiwork. In a monotone she exclaims: "And yesterday trembling Rome lay prostrate at his feet." Placing lighted candles on either side of Scarpia's head and a crucifix reverently upon his breast, she rises and (to the sound of distant drums), cautiously quits the stage.

Act 3

The curtain rises on a platform of the Castle Sant' Angelo. In the distance, through the clear, star-studded night, can be seen the Vatican and St. Peter's. One of the walls displays a crucifix, while upon a table stands a lantern, a register book, and writing implements. To the right, there is a trapdoor which leads up from a flight of steps to the platform. In the distance, sheep bells and a shepherd's song are heard. As the gray dawn encroaches, a gaoler ascends through the trapdoor onto the stage, lights a few lanterns, leans over the parapet of the platform to see whether, in the courtyard below, the firing squad and prisoner have yet arrived. Exchanging a few re-marks with a sentinel, he then sits down and dozes while he waits.

Cavaradossi enters under armed escort (No. 15 in the orchestra), and when the formalities between the sergeant and the gaoler are over, Cavaradossi signs the register. He is informed that he has but one more hour to live, and that a priest is available if he desires one. He indicates, however, that he would prefer to write a few words to Tosca, and as he is engaged in this, one of the early motives associated with her (No. 8) sounds nostalgically in the orchestra.

After a while Cavaradossi stops writing, lost in memories of the past, recalling in a tender and deeply emotional aria her beauty, her embraces, the miracle of their love, and the bitterness of dying when life is so dear to him. (The music to which this aria—"E Lucevan le stelle"—is sung, is substantially that of No. 15.) Overcome with emotion he bursts into tears, as Tosca arrives escorted by Spoletta. Instructing the sentry to watch the two carefully, Spoletta leaves, taking the gaoler and the sergeant with him.

Without speaking, Tosca lifts her lover's head and shows him the safe-conduct. He is startled to see her, but his enthusiasm is as suddenly dampened when he sees Scarpia's signature on the page. The payment Scarpia exacts for his mercy is well known in Rome. But she gives him an agitated summary of what hap-pened in Scarpia's rooms; and taking her hands in his, he sings in wonder that such gentle hands should have encompassed the tyrant's doom. Tosca now details the preparations she has made for their journey, and then explains the fraud that must first be enacted. He will be fired at with blank cartridges, and he must pretend to die. After the soldiers have retired, he can get up and then they will be off.

The ecstatic duet which follows (in which they lose themselves in previsions of their imminent bliss) comes to an end when Tosca, recollecting the immediate situation, begins to fret over the delay. She repeats her instructions, anxious that he act his part convincingly. Soon enough, however, the firing squad arrives with Spoletta, and after a brief duet between the lovers, Cavaradossi is informed (the church clock having just struck four) that his time is up. Speaking softly to Cavaradossi, and scarcely able to contain her laughter, Tosca cautions him not to rise until she calls him, to be careful to fall lightly, and not to laugh.

While Cavaradossi takes up his position with his back to the castle wall, Tosca stands off to the left watching the preparations. There is a note of anxiety in her reassurances to herself that this is but a farce. As the officer is about to lower his sword, she covers her ears against the explosion, but nods to Cavaradossi as a signal to remind him of what he must do. The soldiers fire, and Tosca exclaims at the naturalness with which her Mario has enacted his death. The sergeant who inspects the body is hindered by Spoletta from administering the customary *coup de grâce*.

While the squad, officer, sergeant, and Spoletta depart through the trapdoor, Tosca watches, fearful lest Mario move or speak too soon. When the appropriate moment arrives, she approaches, bids him rise, and then touching him, discovers that he is dead. As she falls upon his body, a crowd of soldiers led by Spoletta and Sciarrone enter hunting for Tosca.

Scarpia's murder has been discovered; and as Spoletta attempts to seize her, Tosca tears herself loose and leaps to the parapet. As No. 15 storms out from the orchestra, she flings herself into space. Sciarrone, Spoletta, and the soldiers rush to the parapet, leaning over it and staring down in horror as the curtain falls.

LA TRAVIATA
(The Lost Lady)

AN OPERA IN THREE ACTS

by Giuseppe Verdi

Cast

VIOLETTA VALERY	Soprano
ALFREDO GERMONT	Tenor
GIORGIO GERMONT	Baritone
FLORA BERVOIX	Mezzo-soprano
GASTONE	Tenor
BARON DOUPHOL	Baritone
MARQUIS D'OBIGNY	Bass
DOCTOR GRENVIL	Bass
ANNINA	Soprano

GUESTS OF VIOLETTA AND FLORA, SERVANTS,
DANCERS, OFF-STAGE CHORUS OF REVELERS

Libretto .... by Francesco Maria Piave
(based on the novel by Dumas)
Time .... Late 1840's
Place .. .. .In and near Paris

First Performance
Teatro la Fenice, Venice, March 6, 1853

LA TRAVIATA

Prelude

THE BRIEF Prelude begins with the soft, sad theme associated with Violetta's fatal illness (No. 1).* This is followed by a broad, generous melody used with great effect during the second act to express the depth of the heroine's sorrow at having to leave her lover (No. 2). A light theme, suggestive of the love she knew with other men before meeting her Alfredo (No. 3), is heard as a counter-melody, but it fades away before the stronger love theme.

Act 1

In the lavishly furnished salon of Violetta Valery's house in Paris, Violetta, a pleasure-seeking courtesan, is giving another of her brilliant parties. Grouped about her are some of her more intimate friends: Flora Bervoix, Dr. Grenvil, her physician, Baron Douphol, a suitor, the Marquis d'Obigny, and Gastone, Viscount of Letorieres. Violetta has not been well, and her friends solicitously inquire if she is not endangering her health by giving this party. Gaily

*Thematic Guide, p. 361.

Violetta replies that frivolity is the best medicine for her, since she lives for pleasure alone.

The handsome Alfredo Germont, a friend of the Viscount, is introduced at this point. Gastone whispers to Violetta that the young man is deeply in love with her and, though he had never met her before, he lingered near her house each morning during her recent illness.

The jealous Baron Douphol quickly informs Violetta that he dislikes this young stranger, and when the Baron is asked to render a song he sulkily refuses, suggesting instead that Alfredo do the honors. Violetta promptly seconds the suggestion, and Alfredo bursts into a joyful drinking song—"Libiamo" (No. 4). As he sings the praises of wine, wit, and beauty, Violetta and then all the guests gaily join him.

A band begins to play in the adjoining ballroom, and all happily prepare to go in to waltz. Violetta, suddenly feeling faint, remains behind. Her guests express anxiety, but she bids them go dance and she will follow in a moment. Alfredo, worried, stays with her and urges her to guard her health more carefully. If only he could take care of her, he sighs. Earnestly Alfredo tells her of his love—a love that blossomed on that happy day, "Un Di felice" (No. 5) when he first saw her. It has now grown to such proportions that it governs his whole life, he continues, with a warm melody, expressive of his love (No. 6).

Slightly frightened by his intense ardor, Violetta gaily but tenderly tells him that he had better forget her, for she is not worthy of his love. Alfredo's protestations are interrupted by Gastone, who has come in search of his hostess. The waltz rhythms, which had disappeared from the orchestra during the tender love duet, return with him, and Violetta flirtatiously gives Alfredo a flower from her corsage, suggesting that he go now but return when the flower has died.

It is almost morning, and all the guests come in to bid their hostess adieu. Now left alone, Violetta ponders over the strange emotion which Alfredo's avowal of love has aroused in her. In the expressive aria "Ah, fors' è lui" (No. 7) she wonders if she has at last found a love that could fill her empty life. Then, forcing herself to face reality, she concludes that such happiness cannot be for her. It is only a hopeless dream. And she bursts into the dazzling aria "Sempre libera" (No. 8), a rather wild expression of her feverish health and life.

Under her balcony Alfredo interrupts her song with his tender love melody (No. 6). Violetta listens for a moment, and then crying "What folly!" repeats, with mounting emotion, her brilliant paean to pleasure.

Act 2

(Scene 1) The garden of Violetta's house in Auteuil, a suburb of Paris. Three months have passed— an idyllic three months for Violetta and Alfredo, who have been living together in this country house away from the glitter of Paris. Alfredo, alone in the garden, sings of his complete happiness, "De' miei bollenti spiriti" (No. 9). His ideal of love has been more than realized.

The happy song is interrupted by the appearance of Annina, the maidservant, who announces that she is going to Paris on an errand. Although her mission is a secret, it docs not take Alfredo long to discover that Violetta is sending the maid to dispose of all her valuables. Violetta apparently has been supporting this idyllic ménage, and now most of her money is gone. Humiliated when he realizes that he has been living like a parasite off Violetta's money, Alfredo determines to go to Paris himself and obtain funds. He cautions Annina not to reveal his mission to Violetta.

No sooner has Alfredo left than Violetta—a more subdued and simple Violetta—enters the garden. As she begins to go over the bills and papers she has brought, a servant enters, bearing an invitation from Flora Bervoix to one of her parties. Violetta reads the note and, with a smile, tosses it aside. She has no interest in such frivolities now.

At this moment a visitor arrives. It is Alfredo's father, who has come to persuade Violetta to give up his son and spare him from degradation and ruin. Although the elder Germont is impressed by Violetta's modesty and dignity, he insists that she leave his son, not only for his own sake but for the sake of Alfredo's younger sister who cannot marry while her brother is carrying on this shameful affair (No. 10).

At first Violetta thinks that Germont is asking her to give up his son only until the sister has married, but he quickly tells her that it must be forever.

Shocked by this demand, she replies that she would rather die than do what he asks, for Alfredo offers her the only love and protection she has in this world.

Germont, undaunted, has still another argument—and this is the most effective. He points out that this happiness she now enjoys is but transient, for men are fickle, and she has no legal hold on Alfredo. This deeply affects Violetta, for although she loves Alfredo, she unconsciously realizes his weakness of character; and when Germont repeats his plea on behalf of his daughter, she is won over—and utterly grief stricken (No. 11).

Germont, praising her goodness and generosity, offers the only comfort he can—the rather weak assurance that Heaven will reward her for her sacrifice. The two embrace, and Germont leaves.

Violetta has already decided upon a course of action, and she immediately writes a note to Flora—an acceptance of her invitation. She rings for Annina to take the note and then sits down to compose a farewell to Alfredo.

In the midst of it she is surprised by her lover's return. Her confusion as she tries to hide the letter is hardly noticed by Alfredo, for he is agitated by troubles of his own. He tells Violetta that he has had a severely reprimanding letter from his father, whom he expects momentarily.

Brushing aside her own far greater sorrows, she attempts to comfort him by promising that she herself will fall at Germont's feet and ask his forgiveness. But the effort at deception is too much for her, and breathlessly she asks over and over again if he truly loves her. Then, gaining control over her emotions, she tells Alfredo that she will await him and his father in the garden. But before she goes, she sings the passionate love melody of the Prelude, "Amami, Alfredo; amami puant 'io t 'amo" *(Love me, Alfredo; love me as much as I do you)* (No. 2).

As Alfredo muses over Violetta's intense avowal of love, a servant enters and announces that Violetta and Annina have left for Paris. Assuming that she has gone to arrange for the sale of her possessions, Alfredo takes this news lightly. In a moment, however, Violetta's note is delivered, and as he reads it with astonishment, Germont arrives. Trying to comfort his son, he sings nostalgically of their home in southern France, "Di Provenza" (No. 12) and urges Alfredo to return there to find happiness again.

But Alfredo scarcely hears his father's plea, for he now believes that Violetta has left him for the Baron Douphol, and he is burning with jealousy. Then, noticing Flora's invitation on the table, he reads it hurriedly, and pushing his father aside he rushes out.

The rather gaudy party room of Flora's house. The gossip about Violetta's and Alfredo's parting has already reached the Marquis d'Obigny. As the curtain rises, the Marquis is telling Flora, who has been expecting the two lovers, that if Violetta comes it will be with the Baron Douphol.

As Flora expresses her surprise at this development, a group of masqueraders, some dressed as gypsies and some as Spanish matadors, come in to enliven the evening's festivities. Their colorful songs and dances lend an air of frivolity to the party.

Now Alfredo enters and, admitting that he and Violetta have parted, sits down at a gambling table. He plays with Gastone and others, winning each time, and repeating the trite observation "lucky at cards, unlucky at love." A few moments later Violetta, on the arm of Baron Douphol, makes her entrance. The Baron, spying Alfredo, warns Violetta not to speak to him, and she expresses her apprehension in a poignant melodic phrase (No. 13).

Douphol strides to the gambling table and challenges Alfredo to play with him. In the tense game that follows, the Baron loses repeatedly. The tension mounts, and the two men are on the point of challenging each other to a duel when the situation is relieved by an announcement that supper is ready.

As the guests go off, Violetta sends Flora after Alfredo to come to speak to her a moment. When he returns, Violetta begs him to leave so that further trouble may be averted. He scorns the request but promises to go if she will come with him. She replies that she cannot go with him for she has made a promise. Assuming that Douphol had extracted the promise, Alfredo is furious and demands to know whether she loves the Baron. Violetta sees no way out of this tragedy of misunderstanding and says that she does love Douphol.

Unable to control his anger, Alfredo dramatically summons the guests. Throwing his winnings at Violetta's feet, he announces that he is paying her back for whatever money she has spent on him. Overcome, Violetta faints in Flora's arms, and the guests, shocked by his outrageous insult, demand that Alfredo leave.

At this moment Germont enters and, having learned of his son's behavior, renounces him. The others try to comfort Violetta, who has recovered enough to utter a touching melody in which she tells Alfredo that she acted only on account of her love for him (No. 14). As an impressive concerted number brings the act to a close, Alfredo is covered with shame and grief over having now lost Violetta forever, and Douphol challenges him to a duel.

Act 3

Violetta's bedroom in a dilapidated house in Paris. Now fatally ill, Violetta lies asleep on her bed. The faithful Annina, also sleeping, sits by the fireplace. The soft orchestral Prelude features a pathetic melody suggestive of Violetta's illness and impending death (No. 15).

It is early morning when the doctor arrives just as Violetta wakens. He speaks to her cheerfully, but as he leaves he whispers sadly to Annina that death is now only a matter of hours.

Hearing sounds of revelry in the street below, Violetta asks the reason for the gaiety, and Annina reminds her that it is carnival time. Pathetically she directs the maid to take half of the twenty louis she has left and distribute them among the poor.

Now left alone, Violetta takes out a worn letter.

It is from Germont and tells her that Alfredo was not injured in the duel with Douphol and is now abroad. The Baron, though wounded, is now recovering. He has told Alfredo of her sacrifice, he says, and they will soon come to her together to beg her forgiveness.

The letter came a long time ago, Violetta complains—and they still haven't come. Then, gazing in a mirror at her wasted reflection, she realizes that there is not much time left for her. Weakly she sings a pathetic farewell to life and to love—"Addio del passato" (No. 16).

The revelers in the street below are heard again, and Annina returns, excitement glowing in her face. Immediately Violetta senses the news she brings—Alfredo is here. The young man bursts into the room, and the two lovers cling together, singing ecstatically of their happiness and their plans for the future "Parigi, o cara" (No. 17).

It is only when Violetta falls back exhausted that Alfredo notices how ill she is, and he anxiously asks Annina to bring the doctor. But Violetta, realizing that the doctor can no longer help her, tells Alfredo that it is too late. Overwhelmed by emotion he declares that if she must die, he will die with her.

As the elder Germont and the doctor arrive, Violetta gives Alfredo a small picture of herself, bidding him give it to the woman he will one day marry— as a token from one who prays for them both in Heaven. This is too much for Alfredo, who cries out that she cannot die, he will not let her die. And Germont, Annina, and the doctor express their sorrow.

Experiencing a feeling of false strength, Violetta tells them that life is returning, for she no longer feels any pain or faintness. The futile hope is pathetically suggested by a single violin playing Alfredo's love melody, (No. 6). But suddenly she falls back—lifeless.

As the doctor signifies that the end has come, the curtain falls.

TRISTAN AND ISOLDE

AN OPERA IN THREE ACTS

by Richard Wagner

Cast

TRISTAN	Tenor
KING MARK	Bass
ISOLDE	Soprano
KURVENAL	Baritone
MELOT	Tenor
BRANGÄNE	Soprano
SHEPHERD	Tenor
HELMSMAN	Baritone

SAILORS, KNIGHTS, ATTENDANTS

Time	Middle Ages
Place	Cornwall and Brittany

First Performance

Hof-und-National Theater, Munich,
June 10, 1865

TRISTAN AND ISOLDE

Prelude

T HE FAMOUS Prelude is based on a series of themes (Nos. 1-5)* which have been identified in different ways (even by the composer himself), but which are associated, in various parts of the opera, with the hero and heroine, their love and the magic philtre that inspires it, and their great yearning to love and to die. Beginning with brief statements of two intertwined themes (Nos. 1-a and 1-b) and long but eloquent silences between them, the Prelude mounts slowly with ever increasing intensity to a swirling, passionate climax. Quickly it fades away into a few bare octaves in the bass, like dying heartbeats.

Act 1

As the curtain rises on the forward deck of a sailing vessel, the voice of a young sailor is heard from above singing of the wild west wind and the sorrows of an amorous Irish maid (No. 6). Isolde, the Irish Princess, starts up angrily, for she assumes the

*Thematic Guide, p. 365.

reference is to her. Over a symphonic elaboration of No. 6, she laments to her companion Brangäne the degeneracy of her race and the decline of the magic powers (No. 1-b) once possessed by her people.

Isolde vows that the ship, which bears her to Cornwall to become King Mark's bride, shall never reach its destination. She cries out for air, and as Brangäne draws the curtains, the entire length of the ship is revealed. Sailors are busy about their business; knights with their attendants stand about; while Tristan, somewhat apart, gazes thoughtfully out to sea, his old servant Kurvenal lounging at his feet.

Again the voice of the young sailor is heard (No. 6), while Isolde, staring stonily at Tristan, proceeds with bitter irony and unnatural laughter to berate this famous hero as a slave who brings her a corpse to be wedded to his master. Ordering Brangäne to fetch Tristan to wait attendance upon her, Isolde throws herself down upon the couch and remains in moody silence during the whole of the ensuing episode.

After Brangäne delivers her message, Tristan with quiet courtesy replies that he cannot leave the helm; but when Brangäne insists, Kurvenal leaps up and tells her to carry back to her mistress a reminder of Ireland's subservience to Cornwall. She turns away offended, Kurvenal's voice following her as he sings an account of the Irish Morold's ill-fated mission to levy tax upon Cornwall, and the return of Morold's head to Ireland as Cornwall's "tribute" (No. 7). Tristan succeeds in quieting his servant, while Brangäne returns to Isolde and draws the curtains, thus closing off the rest of the ship.

While Isolde seethes, Brangäne delivers an account of her interview with Tristan which Isolde had, of course, overheard. In reply, Isolde relates how, almost dying, Tristan had come to Ireland in disguise to be cured by Isolde's magic. She, recognizing him as the man who had killed Morold, had the sword of vengeance at the helpless man's throat. At that moment, he had looked into her eyes (No. 2-b), and the sword fell from her hand. Thus it came about that in her weakness, she cured the slayer of her kinsman and sent him home with oaths of his eternal gratitude ringing in her ears. (No. 8, which weaves through her monologue, is the motive of Tristan's illness.)

With feverish scorn Isolde now plunges into an account of Tristan's betrayal; how he had returned to Cornwall singing praises of her beauty to King Mark, and had then undertaken to bring her from Ireland, helpless and unwilling, as Mark's bride. Calling curses upon him at the height of her passion, she then allows Brangäne to draw her to a couch, scarcely listening while Brangäne seeks to persuade her that a marriage with King Mark is a most honorable one.

As she stares vacantly ahead, Isolde reveals the true source of her sorrow. How can she live unloved so close to her beloved? she murmurs, and her words clearly refer to Tristan. In a caressing tone, Brangäne reminds her of the magic love potion her mother had prepared to insure Isolde against a loveless marriage.

But Isolde, extracting a vial which the horrified Brangäne recognizes as the death potion, expresses her resolve to die rather than set foot in Cornwall.

Kurvenal enters without ceremony, announces their arrival, and bids Isolde hurry. But with dignity Isolde demands that Tristan first appear and ask pardon for offending her. Hastily embracing Brangäne after Kurvenal leaves, Isolde bids Brangäne prepare the draught of peace (the death potion) and composes herself to await Tristan's arrival.

Tristan enters (No. 9) and respectfully pauses while Isolde stares intently at him. Asking first for her command, Tristan then explains, in answer to her taunts, that he avoided her through fear, that in his country it was thought fitting for the bride-bringer to keep his distance from the bride. When she reminds him that it is also fitting for foes to make atonement before becoming friends, he retorts that a truce between them had long ago been sworn in open field before all.

This truce, however, is not the one Isolde wants to talk about. She had once spared Tristan's life out of pity, secretly resolving at the time (so she now says) to take vengeance upon him at a later date for Morold's death. Morold was her betrothed, she continues, whereupon Tristan, somberly laying his sword at her service, bids her strike. This solution does not please her, for King Mark would no doubt be angry to hear that she had slain the finest of his knights. Rather is the feud to be settled by their drinking atonement together, and as she signs to Brangäne to mix the draught, the voices of the sailors outside are heard preparing for the landing.

Tristan's forebodings are driven from him by Isolde's sarcasms on Mark's reaction if Tristan refuses to drink a truce with the King's bride. He wildly starts up, shouts an order to the sailors, and snatches the cup from her. It is for him, he declares, the drink of "forgetfulness"; and when he finishes, Isolde drains the remainder of the goblet, crying out that her toast is to a betrayer.

Without changing position (Nos. 1 and 2 in the orchestra) they stare at each other, defiance giving way to longing. Ultimately embracing (for it was the love potion, not the death draught that Brangäne had prepared) they remain rapturously oblivious both of the chorus of welcome sounding outside and Brangäne's exclamation of woe within. At last they rouse themselves from their embrace and join voices in an ecstatic love duet. Then they sink back in contemplation of each other as the curtains are thrust apart revealing the gay ship and the castle on shore now close at hand.

Hastily throwing the royal robe over Isolde, Brangäne vainly seeks to rouse the enraptured pair. Kurvenal's noisy arrival finally causes Tristan to bestir himself, but Isolde, realizing what has happened, exclaims in terror and falls fainting on Tristan's breast. As the curtain falls upon the anguished lovers, the men on ship chorus their rejoicing, and the orchestra thunders out the boisterous sailors' song (No. 6) with which the act opened.

Act 2

At the close of the orchestral introduction (Nos. 10 to 13), hunting horns are heard as the curtain rises on the garden before Isolde's chamber, revealing Brangäne in the bright summer moonlight watching the retreating hunt. She warns Isolde that the horns are still audible, and urges her excited mistress not to let her wild wishes deceive her into imagining that the horns are merely (as Isolde maintains) the sound of distant water. Furthermore, continues Brangäne, Isolde must understand that she is being watched. King Mark willingly attributed her pale and listless manner upon landing to the fatigue of the sea journey; but there was one—Melot—who was not deceived. This Isolde can scarcely credit—the motive of her blind ardor (No. 12) in the orchestra—for Melot is presumably Tristan's truest friend. And brushing aside the accusation that Melot reports Tristan's movements to King Mark, Isolde orders Brangäne to put out the light (No. 12).

This signal to Tristan is also symbolic of Isolde's hatred of Light and Day. Her eagerness to extinguish the torch is in her own mind associated with her longing for the comfort of eternal night. Brangäne, however, would keep the torch burning if only to illuminate to Isolde her peril. When she again berates herself for her part in substituting the potions (No. 1-b), Isolde comforts her with the reply that the change in Tristan and herself was the work of the all-powerful *Frau Minne*, the goddess of love. (In the orchestra, the love motive, No. 14, accompanies Isolde's praises of *Frau Minne*.)

Isolde orders Brangäne to the watch tower, then seizes the torch and throws it to the ground where it is gradually extinguished. The orchestra deals in succession with the ecstasy motive (No. 13), the theme of Isolde's ardor (No. 12), and now, after Brangäne has gone and Isolde looks eagerly into the distance, with an elaborate development of the theme symbolizing Isolde's impatience (No. 11).

Tristan rushes in and they fall into each other's arms as their celebrated love duet begins. Their voices soar in celebration of the blissfulness of eternal love. They continue with a discourse on the agonies of daylight and the naked anguish which the sun's rays reveal, as the orchestra develops with considerable power the motive (No. 10) associated with this interpretation of the Day. Night is their comfort and their source of strength, exclaim the lovers (this aspect of Night is musically represented by No. 15). Drawing Isolde gently down on the flowered bank, Tristan sinks to his knees before her. In hushed voices they invoke the night of love to descend upon them.

From the tower, Brangäne's voice rings out, warning that daylight approaches; whereupon they give utterance to their longing for death (No. 16) which would unite them in unbounded peace (No. 17). Once more Brangäne's warning sounds, but the oblivious lovers respond with heightened expressions of their desire to embrace death (No. 18). As Brangäne shrieks, Kurvenal rushes in with drawn sword, urging Tristan to save himself. But Mark, Melot, and the hunting party arrive before Tristan has time to do more than spread his cloak as if to conceal Isolde who, in the meantime, has instinctively averted her face.

"Have I accused him rightly?" asks Melot, triumphantly. But Mark, in a trembling voice (No. 19 in the orchestra), grieves that Tristan should have betrayed him. While Tristan keeps his eyes firmly fixed upon the ground, Mark continues to upbraid him, finishing his extended monologue by asking who can explain the mysterious cause of all his woes. Tristan raises his eyes sympathizingly as he gently says that this question can never be answered (No. 1 in the orchestra). Then he turns toward Isolde to ask if she will now follow him to a land without daylight. Gladly, she exclaims, for this land is his heritage. And as Tristan bends slowly to kiss her on the forehead, Melot leaps at him with drawn sword.

Tristan turns swiftly and reveals that Melot's treachery was motivated by his own love for Isolde. Yet when Melot thrusts at him, Tristan deliberately drops his guard. As he falls wounded into Kurvenal's arms, Isolde throws herself upon him, while Mark restrains Melot from completing the murder.

Act 3

The final curtain rises upon the garden of Tristan's castle in Brittany. Through a break in the surrounding cliffs the wide sea can be seen. In the foreground

Kurvenal bends over the sleeping Tristan, listening anxiously to his breathing, while from outside comes the mournful sound of a shepherd's pipe (No. 20). Raising himself over the breastwork, the shepherd comes into view and inquires of his friend Kurvenal whether Tristan has yet opened his eyes. The old servant shakes his head, muttering that if Tristan did so, it would have been to part from him forever.

As the shepherd withdraws, piping his hauntingly sad melody (No. 20), Tristan stirs. He opens his eyes and murmurs that the old familiar tune has awakened him. He does not recognize his surroundings, nor is he much comforted when Kurvenal tells him (No. 21) he is at home in his own castle. There is in Tristan neither hope nor desire for recovery. He sinks back exhausted, while Kurvenal remains lost in dejection. However, the old servant quickly rouses himself and tells Tristan how he brought him wounded from Cornwall. Remembering that Isolde had cured him upon a former occasion, he had sent for her to try her magic power again. The shepherd stands watch, ready to signal her ship's approach.

Tristan embraces his servant as he struggles to find words. Then, pouring out praises of Kurvenal's loyalty and love, Tristan's eagerness mounts, until in a frenzy he shouts that he can already see Isolde's ship on the horizon. In deepest dejection Kurvenal tells him there is no ship. And now as No. 20 begins again, Tristan relates with increasing sadness how this shepherd's tune sounded when his father died; how his mother heard it as she lay dying in childbirth. The ill-fated draught now obsesses him, and at the height of his agonized memories (No. 22 in the orchestra), he falls back senseless.

Kurvenal, who has vainly tried to soothe Tristan, now cries out in terror, and listening to his master's heartbeat, he grimly remarks on the rewards of love. Tristan, recovering consciousness, faintly asks if Isolde's ship has yet been sighted. After being assured that her arrival will not be long delayed, he muses expressively over a vision of his beloved crossing the sea. At last the shepherd's lively tune (No. 23) causes Kurvenal to leap up joyously and rush to the watch tower. In answer to Tristan's questions, he describes the ship's entry into the harbor; and finally, leaving Tristan to toss on his couch in excitement, Kurvenal goes off to help Isolde ashore.

But Tristan, unable to contain himself, staggers madly from his couch, tearing the bandage from his wound, and collapsing in Isolde's arms the instant she arrives on stage. He sinks to the ground (No. 1), raises his eyes to hers as he utters her name (No. 2), and dies. Scarcely able to credit Tristan's death, Isolde murmurs to her darling that she will heal him. Then, as the truth forces itself obstinately upon her, she slumps senseless across his body.

All this while, Kurvenal has been gazing in silent grief at his dead master. However, when the shepherd appears with the news of a second ship's arrival, the old warrior bestirs himself and angrily gives orders for the defense of the castle. Mark and Melot must have come for vengeance upon Tristan, and even when Brangäne's voice is heard from below calling on him to open up, Kurvenal refuses to believe that a mission intending peace has come from Cornwall. With savage laughter Kurvenal strikes Melot dead, as the traitor seeks to make his way on stage; but Mark and his followers force their way through, Mark all the while pleading vainly with Kurvenal to listen to reason.

During the fight Brangäne climbs the side wall, and now, while she is busy attending Isolde, Kurvenal, mortally wounded, totters toward Tristan and falls dead at his feet. Most expressively Mark pours out his grief over his fallen friend, for he had set out to unite the lovers in marriage as soon as he had heard from Brangäne the true story of what had happened.

Brangäne has by now succeeded in rousing her mistress, but Isolde is oblivious of everything except Tristan's body. Her celebrated "Love Death" *(Liebestod)* begins with the melody (No. 17) previously associated with the lovers' longing for eternal union in death, and as it continues we hear the cognate motive (No. 18) featured prominently in the orchestra. Isolde gently sinks down upon Tristan's body, and as Mark blesses the now united lovers, the theme of Isolde's magic and of her longing (No. 1-b) sounds for the last time.

Il Trovatore

IL TROVATORE

(The Troubadour)

AN OPERA IN FOUR ACTS

by Giuseppe Verdi

Cast

LEONORA	Soprano
AZUCENA	Contralto
INEZ	Soprano
MANRICO	Tenor
COUNT DI LUNA	Baritone
FERRANDO	Bass
RUIZ	Tenor

A MESSENGER, A JAILER, SOLDIERS, NUNS, GYPSIES

Libretto by Salvatore Cammarano
(based on a Spanish play by
García Gutiérrez)

Time Fifteenth century

Place Biscay and Aragon, Spain

First Performance

Teatro Apollo, Rome, January 19, 1853

IL TROVATORE

Act 1

(*The Duel*)

T HE PLOT of this bizarre story of love and revenge unfolds during a civil war in fif-
teenth-century Spain. Count di Luna (outside whose apartment in the Palace of
Aliaferia a group of soldiers and servants are reclining) commands the armies of the King of Aragon;
while a mysterious troubadour, the Count's rival for
Leonora's affection, fights on the side of Urgel and
his army of rebellion. Ferrando, the Count's faithful retainer, rouses the dozing servants, and they discuss the mysterious troubadour, the Count's jealousy,
and his habit of watching for Leonora underneath
her window. To keep them awake, Ferrando begins
the story of the former Count di Luna and his two
children.

One day the nurse awoke by the cradle she was
supposed to have been watching and discovered an
old gypsy woman staring menacingly upon the child
(No. 1).* Her cries brought help and the sorceress
was driven off; but when the child sickened, the

---

*Thematic Guide, p. 369.

gypsy, held accountable, was retaken and burned at the stake. However, the woman's daughter disappeared with the ailing child. Neither has been seen or heard of since, but before the abduction, a child's charred bones were discovered in the remains of the gypsy's pyre. It was assumed that in revenge for her mother's death, the daughter had burned the child at the same stake.

Upon his deathbed, the old Count committed his surviving son (the present Count di Luna) to continue the search for his lost brother, in whose death he refused to believe. Thus far all efforts have proved vain, and throughout the years the neighborhood is still haunted by the spirit of the old gypsy. In horrified chorus, soldiers and servants attest to having seen her flying over the housetops as a vampire. Further instances of her unearthly transformations are recounted, and the mounting horror is abruptly brought to a close by the sudden sound of a bell striking the midnight hour.

The scene shifts to the gardens of the palace where Leonora, resident in the palace as lady in waiting to the Queen, confides to Inez her love for the mysterious troubadour. Although Inez reminds her that the Queen desires her presence, Leonora must first recount her story of an unknown knight clad in black armor, who appeared at a tournament and overthrew all contestants. She herself awarded him the wreath of honor, but at the outbreak of war he disappeared. One silent night she heard his voice again, calling her name and singing a fervent song of love (No. 2).

Despite Inez' misgivings, Leonora announces her rapturous surrender in a brilliant and vivacious epilogue to her aria (No. 3). As they ascend the palace steps, Inez' voice joins Leonora's, adding to the latter's expression of single-minded devotion the sober wish that it may never be regretted.

Several measures of slow music precede the Count di Luna's appearance. Inflamed by his love for Leonora, he is about to ascend the steps to her apartment when the sound of a harp is heard, followed by the troubadour's voice singing a short and appealing serenade (No. 4). Leonora rushes out and into the arms of the Count di Luna, whom in the dark she mistakes for her lover. But when the troubadour—whose visored face the moon now reveals among the trees—accuses her of treachery, she realizes her error, and throwing herself at his feet, begs his forgiveness.

Upon Luna's demand that he reveal himself, the troubadour raises his visor and announces his name: Manrico. He is one of the rebels, and his audacity in venturing into Luna's territory and in taunting the latter to arrest him provokes the Count into a jealous fury (No. 5).

In the ensuing trio, Manrico's and Leonora's voices are joined, his in defiance, and hers in a plea to the Count for his vengeance to fall upon her (No. 6), while Luna declares that Leonora's passion for Manrico has doomed the troubadour to death. As the two men rush off with swords drawn to settle the issue in single combat, Leonora falls to the ground in a faint.

Il Trovatore

Act 2

(*The Gypsy*)

By a fire within a ruined dwelling in the Biscayan mountains sits Azucena, an old gypsy woman. Near her, on a low couch, lies Manrico, his helmet at his feet, staring at the sword he holds in his hand. Dawn is breaking over the gypsy encampment, but its occupants are already up and about, the men at work at the forge, and the women scattered, some working, some dancing. A short and exotically flavored prelude (Nos. 7-a and 7-b) sets the pace for the virile "Anvil" chorus (Nos. 8-a and 8-b) which the men at the forge accent by striking their hammers on the anvils.

After a pause for refreshment, the men repeat the chorus and the gypsies then gather around Azucena, who narrates in gruesome detail the story of the burning of a gypsy woman (No. 9). While the bystanders comment upon the doleful tale, Azucena turns to Manrico and in an undertone utters the words he has heard since childhood: "Avenge thou me."

One of the gypsies reminds the others that it is daybreak, time for them to be off seeking their daily bread. When the sound of their voices (No. 8-b) has faded in the distance, Manrico asks to hear the conclusion of this strange tale.

It was her mother who was burned, says Azucena, and her stake stood at the very spot where Manrico is now standing. He recoils in horror while she continues to narrate how, with her own infant on her shoulder, she tried to reach her martyred mother (No. 10). But the guards held her off with their spears and, goaded by her mother's agonized cry "Avenge thou me," she stole the Count di Luna's child. A moment of pity for the infant stirred within her as she kindled the fire, but—and this Azucena utters very softly as the "flame" theme (No. 9) flickers feverishly in the orchestra—a cloud darkened her mind, and obsessed by the vision of her mother at the stake screaming to her for vengeance, she threw the child into the flames. When the vision passed and her mind cleared, she discovered that she had committed her own child, not the Count's, to the pyre.

Manrico can stand no more. The lurid story leaves him dumb with horror, while Azucena, in utter exhaustion, whispers slowly, "The remembrance is death; I can no more; I can no more."

While it is clear to the audience that Manrico is the present Count di Luna's long lost brother, he, nevertheless, only imperfectly perceives the significance of the story. Recovering quickly, Azucena brushes his questions aside, assuring him that she is his mother. As for what she may have said a moment ago, her mind was momentarily darkened and deranged by the remembered nightmare of her mother's death. She recalls to him the care she has always lavished upon him; the time, for example, when she rescued him from among those left for dead upon the ramparts of Pelilla and nursed him back to life.

Manrico too, with pride, recalls his courage upon

that occasion when he fell under the onslaught of the cruel Count and his troops. In single combat, however, he has had Luna at his mercy—presumably this refers to the duel which they went off to fight at the close of Act I—but, confesses Manrico, at the moment when he might easily have killed him, he found himself spellbound (No. 11). She urges him, and he promises, never to show Luna such mercy again.

A horn call sounds in the distance and as Manrico answers the signal, Azucena, still absorbed, mutters, "Avenge thou me." The letter from Ruiz (one of Manrico's followers) which a messenger now delivers, informs Manrico that he must leave immediately for the defense of Castellor which has just been taken, and also that Leonora, deceived by false tidings of his death, is about to become a nun. The messenger is promptly dispatched for a horse and, brushing aside Azucena's protests, Manrico dons cloak and helmet and prepares to depart. But calling upon her authority as his mother, she forces him to listen. Quite forcibly he insists that she must not restrain him. Their voices join in a short but powerful duet, and despite her efforts, he tears himself away.

Leonora's resolve to become a nun has brought the Count, attended by Ferrando and several followers, to the courtyard of a convent near Castellor. He tells Ferrando that this new maneuvre will avail Leonora nothing, and testifies to his passion for her in a sumptuous aria (No. 12). When the sound of a bell signals that the ceremony of the taking of the veil is about to begin, Luna's followers disperse, promising *sotto voce* to execute his orders with silence and dispatch.

Once more Luna vows that Leonora will yet be his (No. 13), and while a chorus of nuns (off stage) celebrates the blessings of convent life, he reiterates his vow, heedless of his followers who (hidden behind trees) whisper to him to beware.

As Leonora enters on her way to the chapel with Inez—they are bidding farewell to each other—the Count emerges to confront them. They stand aghast, but when Manrico appears almost immediately after, Leonora falls on his neck, panting her unbelief in broken phrases (No. 14). The exchange of defiances between the two rivals soon builds up into a massive chorus in which everybody on stage (Leonora, Inez, Manrico, the nuns, Luna, Ferrando, and the Count's followers) is involved in an expression of their respective and utterly diverse sentiments. As the scene rises to its climax, Ruiz enters with a band of Manrico's armed followers, who surround and disarm the Count.

Act 3

(*The Gypsy's Son*)

Count di Luna and his army are encamped before
Castellor, whose towers can be seen in the distance.
Soldiers are scattered about in groups, polishing their
armor as they play dice and sing. When Ferrando
informs them of the planned assault on Castellor and
of the rich booty awaiting them there, they respond
with a rousing declaration of their readiness for battle (No. 15). Luna emerges from his tent, glancing
balefully towards Castellor, where he envisions Leonora safe in Manrico's arms. A commotion off stage
brings Ferrando back with news of an old gypsy
woman, just apprehended as a possible spy and now
being led to the Count for questioning.

It is Azucena, dragged in by guards, her hands
bound, and spicing her resistance with alternate pleas
and curses. She is ordered released, and in reply to
the Count's question concerning her destination,
mumbles vaguely that it is the way of the gypsy to
wander from place to place. Another question produces the disconcerting information that she is from
Biscay. The mere mention of the locale of that famous burning startles both Ferrando and the Count,
and they grow visibly uneasy as she continues quite
pathetically to tell them of her son who has left her,
and for whom she is now searching.

His suspicions mounting, Luna asks Azucena
whether she remembers the abduction of a noble-

man's child some fifteen years ago. Before she can collect herself and deny all knowledge of the occurrence, she blurts out the revealing question: "Art thou —canst thou be?" "That child was my brother," grimly replies the Count, and Ferrando, now recognizing her despite her belated denials, urges that vengeance be swiftly executed. In despair she calls upon Manrico, realizing too late that by revealing herself as the troubadour's mother, she has only added fuel to the Count's fury.

The scene now begins to move toward its climax with Azucena turning upon the Count in defiance (No. 16), while he glories in his revenge, and the guard, led on by Ferrando, roars its promise to consign her to an everlasting burning. As this powerful ensemble draws to an end, Azucena is led off under guard while Luna and Ferrando enter the Count's tent.

In a hall adjacent to the chapel in Castellor, Leonora and Manrico are about to solemnize their marriage. An atmosphere of unease pervades what should be a festive occasion. Plainly nervous over the expected assault by Luna's army, Manrico dispatches Ruiz to see to the defenses. He consoles Leonora with the cheerless thought that if he should fall tomorrow in her defense, his soul will wait for hers in Heaven (No. 17).

From within the chapel an organ sounds a summons for them to enter, but their duet, in which they exchange promises of abiding love, is cut short by Ruiz's hasty return. Azucena, he announces, has been captured and the pyre for her already lighted. The news stuns them, Leonora as well an Manrico, since from her lover's frenzied exclamations she learns for the first time that the gypsy is his mother. He collects himself as best he can and, sending Ruiz to marshal his men, breaks into his famous and stirring denunciation of tyrants (No. 18), "Tremble, ye tyrants" *(Di quella pira)*.

The soldiers, who enter as the aria comes to an end, chorus their readiness for battle. Manrico's voice, rising above theirs as he bids farewell to Leonora, exclaims in anguish over his mother's torment and ends by urging his followers to arms. They exit amid the din of arms and the sound of the trumpet calling them to battle.

Act 4

(*The Punishment*)

A slow and forebodingly quiet introduction precedes Leonora's appearance on the darkened stage. Accompanied by Ruiz, she has come to Aliaferia in the hope of saving Manrico, who now lies imprisoned in the palace tower after his raid on Luna's stronghold ended in defeat and capture. Ruiz retires, and Leonora, remarking quietly that the ring on her finger contains her safeguard, turns toward the tower enjoining the breezes of the night to carry her song to her lover (No. 19).

A death bell tolls and a male chorus behind the scenes, intoning the somber "Miserere" (No. 20), rouses Leonora to the terrified realization of Manrico's closeness to death (No. 21). His own voice, coming from the tower, bids her farewell (No. 22); and as the solemn prayer for the departing soul is resumed off stage (No. 20), their voices rise in ecstasy and terror. Vowing that she is forever his, Leonora determines to make one more attempt to save him.

She conceals herself as Luna enters dispatching his attendants to prepare for the beheading of Manrico and the burning of Azucena. If he exceeds his authority, he tells himself, it is because his love for Leonora has driven him to desperation. She comes forward and, in the ensuing duet, pleads for her lover's life while the Count remains bitterly adamant. At last, falling on her knees before him, she offers her life for Manrico's, but this evidence of the futility of his possessing her only goads Luna to expressions of almost unendurable hatred for the troubadour.

As Luna is about to leave, Leonora, clinging to him, forces herself to make the only offer the Count will consider: herself. Finally triumphant, he makes her swear that she will give herself to him and, as he summons a guard to whom he imparts whispered instructions, Leonora takes poison from the ring, murmuring apart: "I shall be thine, but mute, cold, and lifeless." Upon his announcement that Manrico will be freed, her voice rises in a brilliant and joyful burst of song, which the Count turns into a duet, for he can scarcely contain his own jubilation at this stroke of good fortune. They enter the tower together as the curtain falls.

Inside the dimly lit tower, Manrico attempts

to console Azucena. She is prey to all manner of fearful visions; her speech is disjointed and, as the "flame" theme (No. 9) rises in the orchestra, she recalls once more the ever-present scene of her mother at the stake. Finally falling back exhausted in Manrico's arms, she allows him to lead her to a couch, admitting, in a singularly touching little melody, that she must sleep, for her soul is weary (No. 23).

A tender and soothing phrase (No. 24), which he utters in reply, becomes his part in the developing duet, for Azucena, now between sleeping and waking, imagines herself with Manrico at peace for the remainder of their days amid their native mountains (No. 25), "Home to our mountains" *(Ai nostri monti)*.

The door opens while Manrico is still kneeling by his mother's side. Leonora enters telling him that the gate is open and urging him to leave without delay. She admits, however, that she has promised to remain behind; and when, his suspicions aroused, he demands to know the price that was pledged for his liberty, her eloquent silence is answer enough. Amid his angry reproaches for having sold herself to the Count, and her increasing desperation at his refusal to leave, Azucena's voice sounds through, singing pathetically of their return to the mountains (No. 25).

The trio comes to an end as Leonora falls at Manrico's feet, still imploring him to be gone. But he continues to berate her until she slumps forward on her face, gasping that the poison is working more quickly than she had expected. As Manrico begs forgiveness for having doubted her, and Leonora repeats that she would die a thousand deaths rather than live without him, the Count enters and, realizing that he has been deceived, swears that this insult shall not go unavenged.

Leonora dies; Manrico is led away by guards; and Azucena, scarcely awake and calling for her son, is compelled by the Count to watch his execution from the window. Instantly upon Luna's triumphant cry that his rival has perished, Azucena turns upon him with the revelation that Manrico was his brother. A horrified exclamation escapes him, and as Azucena, screaming "Thou art avenged, O mother," falls senseless in front of the window, the curtain falls with Luna crying out, "And yet I live!"

THEMATIC GUIDE

For the Thematic Guide, George Mead has graciously permitted the use, wherever possible, of the translations of texts he prepared for A TREASURY OF GRAND OPERA, published by Simon and Schuster, Inc. The rest of the translations and musical texts are based on vocal scores published by G. Schirmer, Inc., with the exception of the Puccini operas, whose vocal scores are published by G. Ricordi & Co.

AÏDA

1 ANDANTE MOSSO
pp

2 ANDANTE
ppp

3 ANDANTINO
p

Heav'n - ly ___ A - ï - da, ___ Fair as ___ the sun - rise,
Ce - le - ste A - ï - da, ___ for - ma di - vi - na,

pp

Soft as ___ the star - light Touch - ing ___ a flow'r.
mi - sti - co ser - to di lu - ce e fior.

4 ALLEGRO ASSAI MODERATO
p

5 ALLEGRO MAESTOSO
mf

Guard the Nile's re - mot - est ___ reach - es from the
Su! del Ni - lo al sa - cro li - do ac - cor

Aïda

bold in-vad-ing horde!
re - te E - gi - zit e - roi!

ALLEGRO

f Re-turn the con-quer-or!
Ri - tor - na vin - ci - tor!

CANTABILE

pp Gods of my youth, hear me a-gain,
Nu - mi pie - tà del mio sof - frir!

Pi - ty this heart, ach - ing with pain!
Spe - me non v'ha pel mio do - lor!

ANDANTE

mf Most might - y, most might - y Phthà!
Pos - sen - te, pos - sen - te Fthà!

GRAVE

p Great God and great a - veng - ing pow'r,
Nu - me, cus - to - de e vin - di - ce

Guard of this ho - ly coun - try!
di ques - ta sa - cra ter - ra!

MAESTOSO

ff Glo - ry to E - gypt's might - y gods,
Glo - ria al E - git - to ad I - si - de

309

glo - ry for our sal - va - tion!
che il sa - cro suol pro - teg - ge!

11 MAESTOSO

mf

etc.

12 ANDANTE

pp Ah, great King, at the height of your splend-or, Pi - ty
Ma tu, Re, tu si - gno - re pos - sen - te, a co -

us who are forc'd to sur - rend - er.
sto - ro ti vol - gi cle - men - te.

13 ANDANTE CANTABILE

pp O land of a - zure skies with fra - grant warm
O cie - le az - zur - ri, o dol - ci au - re na - ti -

breeze, Land of my child - hood, bright hap - py days of yore.
ve, do - ve, se - re - no il mio mat - tin bril - lò.

14 ANDANTE SOSTENUTO

p Think how thy race, down-trod-den by the con - qu'ror,
Pen - sa che un po - - po - lo vin - to, stra - zia - to,

15 ANDANTINO
dolciss.

There, where the age-old for-est sleeps,
Là tra___ fo-res-te ver-gi-ni,

Where scent-ed flow'rs are grow-ing,
di fio-ri pro-fu-ma-te,

16 ANDANTE
pp

Oh earth, fare-well, fare-well, oh val-ley of
O ter-ra, ad-di-o, ad-di-o val-le di

weep-ing; Oh, dream of joy so soon to fade___ a-way!
pian-ti, sog-no di gau-dio che in do-lor___ sva-ni!

THE BARBER OF SEVILLE

1 ALLEGRO
pp

2 ALLEGRO
p cantabile

3 LARGO

Dawn, with her ro-sy man-tle,
Ec-co ri-den-te in cie-lo

311

4 ALLEGRO VIVACE

5 ANDANTE *mezza voce*

6 ALLEGRO MAESTOSO

7 ALLEGRO

8 ANDANTE

9 ALLEGRO

Stands at the gate of morn — ing;
spun - ta la bel - la au - ro - ra,

I'm the fac - to - tum of all the town, make way!
Lar - go al fac - to - tum del - la cit - tà, lar - go!

Who for - e'er'neath thy win - dow is sigh — ing,
Se il mio no - me sa - per voi bra - ma - te,

'Tis the spring of all in - ven - tion,
Al - l'i - dea di quel me - tal - lo

Love's own en - chant - ment this day shall fire me,
Ah che d'a - mo - re la fiam - ma io sen - to,

There's a voice that I en - shrine In my
U - na vo - ce po - co fa qui nel

heart and none must know;
cor mi ri - suo - nò,

Slan - der's whis - per, when first be - gin - ning,
La ca - lun - nia è un ven - ti - cel - lo,

The Barber of Seville

10 ANDANTE MAESTOSO

To a man of my im - por - tance
A un dot - tor del - la mia sor - te

11 MODERATO

Fare you well,—sir, plea - sant slum - ber, Fare— you—
Buo - na se - ra, mio si - gno - re, Buo - na,—

well, sir, pleas - ant— slum - ber!
se - ra, buo - na— se - ra!

12 ALLEGRO

Ev' - ry grey - beard needs must mar - ry, And the
Il vec - chiot - to cer - ca mo - glie, vuol ma -

maid - en will not tar - ry
ri - to la ra - gaz - za,

13 ALLEGRO

_p_ Let us fly by yon - der win - dow While they
Zit - ti zit - ti, pia - no pia - no, non fac -

en - ter in to stay— us;
cia - mo con - fu - sio - ne;

LA BOHÈME

1 ALLEGRO VIVACE

La-zi-ly rising, See, how the smoke from
Nei cie-li bi-gi guar-do fu-mar dai

thou-sands of chim-neys floats up-ward.
mil-le co-mi-gno-li Pa-ri-gi,

2 ANDANTE MODERATO   UN POCO PIÙ MOSSO

Oh! how stu-pid, how stu-pid, the
Oh! sven-ta-ta, sven-ta-ta! La

key of my poor cham-ber, where can I have left it?
chia-ve del-la stan-za do-ve l'ho la-scia-ta?

3 ANDANTINO

Your ti-ny hand is fro-zen! Let me warm it in-to
Che ge-li-da ma-ni-na, se la la-sci ris-cal

life. Our search is use-less; In dark-ness all is hid-den.
dar. Cer-car che gio-va? Al bu-io non si tro-va.

3a ANDANTE LENTO CON MOLTO ESPRESSIONE

Bright eyes as yours, be-lieve me, steal my price-less
Ta-lor dal mio for-zie-re ru-ban tu-ti i gio-

314

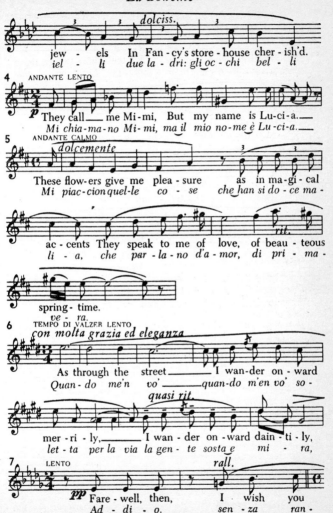

jew - els In Fan - cy's store - house cher - ish'd.
iel - li due la - dri: gli oc - chi bel - li

They call me Mi-mi, But my name is Lu-ci-a.
Mi chia-ma-no Mi-mi, ma il mio no-me è Lu-ci-a.

These flow-ers give me plea-sure as in ma-gi-cal
Mi piac-cion quel-le co - se che han si do - ce ma-

ac - cents They speak to me of love, of beau - teous
li - a, che par-la-no d'a-mor, di pri - ma-

spring - time.
ve - ra.

As through the street I wan-der on - ward
Quan - do me'n vo' quan-do m'en vo' so-

mer - ri - ly, I wan - der on - ward dain - ti - ly,
let - ta per la via la gen - te sosta e mi - ra,

Fare - well, then, I wish you
Ad - di - o. sen - za ran-

ANDANTINO

well! Nay, lis - ten, lis - ten! Those things, those
cor. A - scol ta, a - scol - ta. Le po - che

few old things I've___ left be - hind me
ro - be a : du - na che la - sciai spar - se,

8 ANDANTINO MOSSO

Ah, Mi - mi! false, fick - le
O Mi - mi tu più non

heart - ed! Ah, beaut-eous days de - part - ed!
tor - ni. O gior - ni___ bel - li,

9 MODERATO E TRISTE

Gar - ment ant - ique and rus - ty! A last good-
Vec - chia zi - mar - ra sen - ti, io res - to al

poco rit.   a tempo

bye, fare - well! fad- ed friend so tried and trus - ty__
pian, tu a - scen - de - re il sa - cro monte or de - vi -

10 LARGO SOSTENUTO

fff tutta forza   dim.

CARMEN

1 ALLEGRO GIOCOSO

ff

2 ALLEGRO GIOCOSO

p

3 ANDANTE MODERATO

ff tutta forza

4 ANDANTINO

p

See__ how the smoke light-ly flies, While as-
Dans__ l'air nous sui - vons des yeux La fu-

cend - ing, While as-cend-ing
mé - e La fu - mé - e

5a ALLEGRETTO QUASI ANDANTINO

p Gyp- sy love is a rov- ing
L'a - mour est un oi - seau re -

rap -ture, A wan- ton bird__ that none can tame.
bel - le Que nul ne peut__ ap - pri - voi - ser.

5b ALLEGRETTO QUASI ANDANTINO

p Oh, love is just a gyp-sy
L'a-mour est en-fant de Bo-

lad, He ne-ver could and ne-ver would play fair,
hême, il n'a ja-mais, ja-mais con-nu de loi,

6 ALLEGRO MODERATO

pp I see__ my moth-er's face,__ The hap-py
Ma mè-re je la vois,__ Oui, je re-

home__ I love so well!
vois__ mon vil-la-ge!

7 ALLEGRETTO

pp There's a ca-fé in Se-vil-la,
Près des rem-parts de Sé-vil-le,

Kept by my friend Lil-las Pas-tia.
Chez mon a-mi__ Lil-las Pas-tia.

8 ANDANTINO

p The sounds of sis-trum-bars did greet__ Their
Les trin-gles des sis-tres tin-taient__ A-

ears with dry me-tal-lic ring-ing, To
vec un é-clat mé-tal-li-que, Et

this strange mu-sic soon up - spring - ing The
sur cette é - tran - ge mu - si - - que Les

gyp - sy girls were on their feet.___
Zin - ga - rel - las se le - vaient.___

9 ALLEGRO
p To - ré - a - dor,___ be on___ your___ guard,___
To - ré - a - dor,___ en gar - - - de!___

To - ré - a - dor!___ To - ré - a - dor!___
To - ré - a - dor!___ To - ré - a - dor!___

10 MARCH TIME
Friend or foe? We must know, Son of Al - ca - la!
Hal - te là! Qui va là? Dra - gon d'Al - ca - la!

11 ALLEGRETTO
p La___ la_ la la___ la___ la_ la_ la

12 ANDANTINO *con amore*
p Here is the flow'r you gave so light - ly, The
La fleur que tu m'a - vais je - té - e, Dans

flow'r you wore___ that bloomed so bright - ly.
ma pri - son m'é - tait res - té - e.

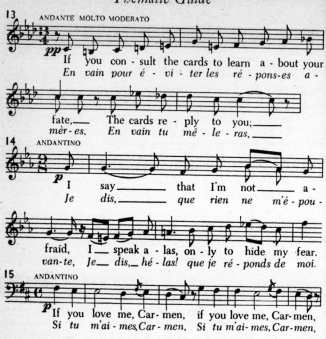

13 ANDANTE MOLTO MODERATO

pp

If you con - sult the cards to learn a - bout your
En vain pour é - vi - ter les ré - pons - es a -

fate,___ The cards re - ply to you;___
mèr - es. En vain tu mê - le - ras,___

14 ANDANTINO

p I say___ that I'm not___ a -
Je dis,___ que rien ne m'é - pou -

fraid, I___ speak a - las, on - ly to hide my fear.
van - te, Je___ dis, hé - las! que je ré - ponds de moi.

15 ANDANTINO

p If you love me, Car - men, if you love me, Car - men,
Si tu m'ai - mes, Car - men, Si tu m'ai - mes, Car - men,

CAVALLERIA RUSTICANA

1 ANDANTE SOSTENUTO

pp

2 ANDANTE

mf O Lo - la, with thy lips like crim - son ber - ries,
O Lo - la bian - ca co - me fior di spi - no,___

320

Cavalleria Rusticana

3 ALLEGRETTO

Proud - ly steps the stur - dy steed,
Il ca - val - lo scal - pi - ta.

Gay - ly ring the mer - ry bells,
i so - na - gli squil - la - no,

4 MODERATO ASSAI

Queen of the Heav - ens, grief is end - ed!
Re - gi - na Coe - li, lae - ta - re

5 MODERATO ASSAI

Let us sing,_____ Christ our Lord's won - drous
In - ne - gia - mo il Si - gnor non è

sto - ry, Let us sing, Christ to - day reigns in glo - ry;
mor - to, in - ne - gia - mo al Si - gno - re ri - sor - to,

6 LARGO ASSAI SOSTENUTO *mestamente con semplicità*

Well do you know, good Mam - ma,
Voi lo sa - pete, o Mam - ma,

ere to the war he de - part - ed,
pri - ma d'an - dar sol - da - to

7 ANDANTE *con forza*

Si - lence, San - tuz - za! Slave will I not be Un - to thy
Ba - da, San - tuz - za! schia - vo non so - no di que - sta

321

foolish, jeal-ous ex-ac-tions!
va na tua ge-lo-si-a!

8 ANDANTE
My king of ros-es!___ Ra-di-ant an-gels
Fior di gia-gio-lo___ gli an-ge-li bel-li

stand in Heav'n in thou-sands,___
stan-no a mil-le in cie-lo___

9 ANDANTE APPASSIONATO
No, no, Tu-rid-du! Re-
No, no, Tu-rid-du ri-

main, oh re-main, Do not leave me!___
ma-ni, ri-ma-ni an-co-ra___

10 ANDANTE APPASSIONATO
con dolore
Lo! here thy San-tuz-za Weep-ing, im-plores thee;
La tu-a San-tuz-za pian-ge e t'im-plo-ra___

11 ANDANTE SOSTENUTO
f raseggiando

12 LARGHETTO
Hail! the red wine rich-ly flow-ing,
Vi-va il vi-no spu-meg-gian-te,

Don Giovanni

molto sentito

ANDANTE CON MOTO

You__must not fal - ter; To San - ta be a moth-er!
Voi_do-vre - te fa - re da ma - dre a San - ta,

DON GIOVANNI

1 MOLTO ALLEGRO

2 MOLTO ALLEGRO

Rest I've none by night or day; Scant - y
Not - te e gior - no fa - ti - car, per chi

fare and doubt - ful pay,
nul - la sa gra - dir;

3 ALLEGRO

When shall I find a to - ken to guide my steps to thee?
Ah! chi mi di - ce ma - i quel bar - ba - ro dov' è?

4 ALLEGRO

Pret - ty la - dy! Here's a list I would show you.
Ma - da - mi - na! Il ca - ta - lo - go è que - sto.

5 ANDANTE

Give me your hand, Zer - li - na; An - swer your lov - er's plea;
Là ci da - rem la ma - no, là mi di - rai di sì;

323

6 ANDANTE

The wretch now thou know-est Who
Or sai, chi l'o-no-re ra-

sought my be-tray-ing,
pi-re a me vol-se,

7 ANDANTE

She is the mea-sure of all my glad-ness,
Dal-la sua pa-ce la mia di-pen-de.

8 PRESTO

Let's have a par-ty, hap-py and heart-y,
Finch' han dal vi-no cal-da la te-sta,

I'm in the mood for laugh-ter and wine!
u-na gran fe-sta fa pre-pa-rar!

9 ANDANTE GRAZIOSO

Beat me, beat me, dear Ma-
Bat-ti, bat-ti, o bel Ma-

set-to, beat your poor, de-spised Zer-li-na;
set-to, la tua po-ve-ra Zer-li-na;

10 TEMPO DI MINUETTO

11 ALLEGRETTO

p I stand be-neath your win-dow To
Deh vie-ni al la fi-ne-stra, o

sing_____ my song to you,
mio_____ te-so-ro,

12 GRAZIOSO

I have a cure for you, cer-tain and sure for you,
Ve-drai, ca-ri-no, se sei buo-ni-no,

13 ANDANTE GRAZIOSO

p To my be-loved, O_____ has-ten,
Il mio te-so-ro in-tan-to

To com-fort, to com-fort_her sad heart!
an-da-te, an-da-te a-con-so-lar!

14 LARGHETTO

Tell me_____ not,_____ Oh thou be-lov'd one.
Non mi_____ dir,_____ bell' i-dol mi-o.

FAUST

I ALLEGRETTO

p Care-less, i-dle maid-en, Where-fore dream-ing still?
Pa-res-seu-se fil-le, Qui som-meille en-cor!

325

2 ALLEGRO

Be mine—the de - light— of Beau - ty's ca - ress - es, Her
A moi les plai - sirs,— Les jeu - nes mai - tres - ses! A

soft— wav - y tress - es, Her smile— beam - ing bright!
moi— leurs ca - res - ses,. A moi— leurs dé - sirs!—

3 ALLEGRETTO

Beer or— bran - dy, Bran - dy or
Vin ou biè - re, Bière ou—

beer We're not par - tic - u - lar, Bring it here!
vin, Que mon— ver - re soit— plein!

4 MODERATO

E - ven brav - est heart may swell
A - vant de quit - ter ces lieux,

In the mo - ment of fare - well.
Sol na - tal de mes a - ïeux.

5 ALLEGRO

Clear the way— for the Calf of
Le veau d'or— est vain - queur des

Gold! On their thrones the Gods de - fy - ing,
dieux! Dans sa gloi - re Dé - ri - soi - re,

6 ALLEGRO MODERATO

'Gainst the pow'rs of e - vil our arms as - sail - ing,
De l'en- fer qui vient é -mous- ser nos ar - mes,

7a TEMPO DI VALZER

7b TEMPO DI VALZER

8 ANDANTINO

Pray, do not think me bold, My fair and gen - tle
Ne per- mett- rez - vous pas, ma bel - le de - moi-

maid - en;
sel - le,

9 ALLEGRO AGITATO

May these flow - ers con - vey What I ___ would say!
Fai - tes - lui mes a - veux, Por - tez___ mes voeux!

10 LARGHETTO

Fair home of hea - ven's fair - est an - gel, Fair
Sa - lut! de-meu - re chaste et pu - re. Sa -

home of heav - en's fair - est an - gel!
lut! de - meu - re chaste et pu - re!

327

light, For - ev - er - more en - fold us!
cieux, les cieux Dans nos deux â - mes!

13c ANDANTE

Marguerite *pp* Take all my love, I lay my heart here be - fore you!
Je veux t'ai - mer et te ché - rir! Parle en - co - re!

14 ANDANTE

p When all was young and pleas - ant May was bloom - ing,
Si le bon - heur à sou - ri - re t'in - vi - te,

15 TEMPO MARZIALE

f Here's to the men who have gone be - fore,
Gloire im - mor - tel - le De nos a - ieux,

He - roes of man - y an an - cient war!
Sois nous fi - dè - le, Mour - ons comme eux!

16 ALLEGRETTO

p Don't pre - tend that you are sleep - ing On your
Vous qui fai - tes l'en - dor - mi - e, N'en - ten -

down - y cot, For I know you're not!
dez - vous pas, N'en - ten - dez - vous pas,

Now your love - ly eyes are peep - ing through the win - dow
O Ca - the - ri - ne, ma mi - e, N'en - ten - dez - vous

slot On this ver - y spot!___
pas Ma voix et mes pas?___

17a MODERATO MAESTOSO

An - gel host, shin - ing in the sky,___ Lift up my
An - ges purs, an - ges ra - di - eux,___ Por - tez mon

soul to God on high!___
âme au sein des cieux!___

LOHENGRIN

1 ADAGIO

2 ALLEGRO

3a ANDANTE

3b ANDANTE

Lohengrin

4 ANDANTE

p Friend-less and all for-sak-en, Bur-dened with
Ein - sam in trü - ben Tag - en, hab' ich zu

grief and care,
Gott ge - fleht,

5 *8va* ANIMATO

p

6 ALLEGRO MODERATO

ff

7 ADAGIO

p Your task is done, my faith-ful swan!
Nun sei be- dankt, mein lie - ber Schwann!

8 LENTO

f Ne'er must thou dare to ask me,
Nie sollst du mich be - frag - en,

9 LARGO

ff Oh Lord and God, be with us now!
Mein Herr und Gott, nun ruf' ich dich!

10 LARGO

p

11 ANDANTE

Oh wind that heard my weep-ing, and waft-ed it a - bove,
Euch Lüf- ten, die mein Kla- gen so trau - rig oft er- füllt,

12 MODERATO

13 LARGO

14 ALLEGRO MOLTO

15 MODERATO

Long may you live, Long may you love,
Treu - lich ge- führt zie - het da - hin,

Long may the bless -ings of heav -en a -bound!
wo euch der Se- gen der Lie- be be- wahr!

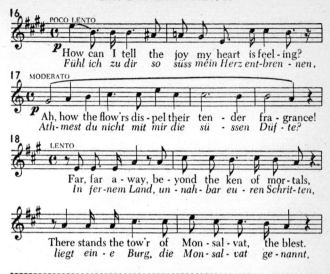

16 POCO LENTO

How can I tell the joy my heart is feel-ing?
Fühl ich zu dir so süss mein Herz ent-bren - nen,

17 MODERATO

Ah, how the flow'rs dis-pel their ten - der fra-grance!
Ath-mest du nicht mit mir die sü - ssen Düf - te?

18 LENTO

Far, far a - way, be - yond the ken of mor-tals,
In fer-nem Land, un - nah-bar eu - ren Schrit-ten,

There stands the tow'r of Mon - sal - vat, the blest.
liegt ein - e Burg, die Mon - sal - vat ge - nannt,

LUCIA DI LAMMERMOOR

1 LARGHETTO

Tor - ments of hate and ven geance,
Cru - da, fu - ne - sta sma - nia

Now in my heart a - wak - en!
tu m'hai sve - glia - to in pet - to!

2 ALLEGRO MODERATO

If thou plead'st for — her, I scorn thee, Cast thee
La pie - ta - de in suo fa - vo - re, Mi - ti

from me, then let me warn thee, thee,
sen - si in - van mi det - ta ta

LARGHETTO

In si - lence all__ lay slum - ber - ing,
Re - gna - va nel__ si - len - zi - o

Dark was the night, and o'er - cloud - ed,
al - ta la not - te e bru - na,

MODERATO

Were he but here, oh, ec - sta - sy,
Quan - do ra - pi - to in e - sta - si

Naught should I know of sor - row,
del più co - cen - te ar - do - re,

LARGHETTO

By the ash - es of my fath - ers, By their
Sul - la tom - ba che rin - ser - a il tra -

tombs, un - wept, un - guard - ed,
di - to ge - ni - to - re,

LARGHETTO

Calm thy an - ger, calm thy an - ger, turn and
Deh! ti pla - ca, deh! ti pla - ca, deh! ti

heed me!
fre - na!

7 MODERATO ASSAI

When twi - light shad - ows low - er, My
Ve - ran - no a te sul - l'a - u - re i

ar - dent pray'rs as - cend - ing,
miei so - spi - ri ar - den - ti,

8 MODERATO

If my cheek is blanch'd with ter - ror, Well thou
Il pal - lor fu - ne - sto or - ren - do, che ri -

know - est my cause of griev - ing;
co - pre il vol - to mi - o,

9 LARGHETTO

In si - lence and sor - row I
Sof - fri - va nel pian - to, lan -

lang - uish'd un - re - pin - ing,
gui - a nel do - lo - re,

10 VIVACE

To my ru - in then con - sent - ing,
Se tra - dir - mi tu po - tra - i,

Cold and si-lent, thou yet dost brave me;
la mia sor-te è già com-pi-ta;

11 CANTABILE

'Tis to suc-cor thy hap-less broth-er That I
Ce-di, ce-di, o più scia-gu-re-ti so-

ask thee, that I ask them to o-bey— me,
vra-stan, ti so-vra-sta-no, in-fe-li-ce.

12 MODERATO MOSSO

Hail to the hap-py brid-al— day
Per te d'im-men-so giu-bi-lo

Hence, ev'-ry thought of sor-row!
tut-to s'av-vi-va in tor-no!

13 LARGHETTO

What from ven-geance yet re-strains me, Words suf-
Chi mi fre-na in tal mo-men-to? chi tron-

fice not to up-braid thee;
cò del-l'i-re il cor-so?

14 VIVACE

f Hence, be-gone, ere our fu-ry as-sails thee,
E-sci,— fug-gi il fu-ror— che m'ac-cen-de

15 VIVACE

Save—him, heav'n, from de-struc-tion and dan-ger,
Dio,— lo sal - va in si fie - ro mo-men-to

16 MODERATO MAESTOSO

From the cham-ber where sad and si-lent, To her
Dal - le stan - ze o - ve Lu-ci - a trat-ta a-

lord I Lu-cy guid-ed,
vea col suo con - sor - te,

17 LARGHETTO

At last I'm thine, love, at last thou'rt mine, love;
Al - fin— son tu - a, al - fin sei mi - o,

18 MODERATO

Cast on my grave a flow-er,
Spar - gi d'a - ma - ro pian - to

But let there be no weep - - ing;
il mio ter - re - stre ve - - lo,

19 LARGHETTO

To earth I bid a last fare-well, The
Fra po - co a me ri - co - ve - ro da-

tomb will soon close o'er— me;—
rà ne - glet-to a - vel - lo,—

20 MODERATO

Thou hast spread thy wings to heav-en, O thou
Tu che a Dio spie-ga-sti l'a-li, o bel-

spir-it, pure and ten-der,
l'al ma in-na-mo-ra-ta,

MADAME BUTTERFLY

1 ALLEGRO

2 ALLEGRO MODERATO

3 ALLEGRO MODERATO

4 ALLEGRO CON SPIRITO

The whole world o-ver, on bus-i-ness and plea-sure,
Do-vun-que al mon-do lo Yan-kee va-ga-bon-do

5 ALLEGRO MODERATO

Is't love or fan-cy, I can-not tell you.
A-mo-re o gril-lo, dir non sa-pre-i.

Madame Butterfly

9 MOLLEMENTE

O Ka - mi! O Ka - mi! Let's drink to the
O Ka - mi! o   Ka - mi! Be - via - mo ai no -

new - ly mar - ried cou - ple.
vis - si - mi le - ga - mi.

339

11 ANDANTINO CALMO
pp

12 ANDANTE SOSTENUTO
pp

13 ANDANTE MOLTO CALMO
pp

One____ fine day we'll no - tice   A

Un ____ bel dì, ve - dre - mo   le -

thread ____ of smoke a - ris - ing

var - si un fil di fu - mo

14 ALLEGRO
ff

15 ANDANTINO
ppp

16 MODERATO

ff

17 ANDANTE

pp

poco rit.   *a tempo*

18 ANDANTINO

p

Shake that cher - ry tree till ev' - ry flow - er
Scuo - ti quel - la fron - da di ci - lie - gio

19 ANDANTE

pp

Fare - well,_____ oh hap - py home, Fare -
Ad - di - o, fio - ri - to a - sil, di le-

well,_____ home of love!
ti - zia e d'a - mor!

20 ANDANTE SOSTENUTO

f My son, sent to me from
O a me, sce - so dal

Heav - en, straight from the throne of glo - ry,
tro - no del - l'al - to Pa - ra - di - so,

THE MARRIAGE OF FIGARO

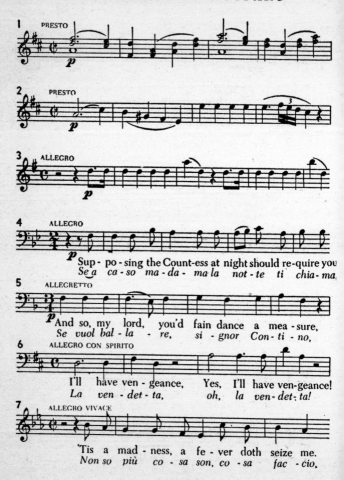

4. Sup - po - sing the Count-ess at night should re-quire you
Se a ca - so ma - da - ma la not - te ti chia - ma,

5. And so, my lord, you'd fain dance a mea - sure,
Se vuol bal - la - re, si - gnor Con - ti - no,

6. I'll have ven - geance, Yes, I'll have ven-geance!
La ven - det - ta, oh, la ven-det - ta!

7. 'Tis a mad - ness, a fe - ver doth seize me.
Non so più co - sa son, co - sa fac - cio,

The Marriage of Figaro

8 ALLEGRO

Now your days of phi-land 'ring are o - ver,
Non più an-drai, far - fal - lo - ne a - mo - ro - so,

9 LARGHETTO

Thou, oh love, thou canst re - store me,
Por - gia a - mor, qual - che ri - sto - ro

10 ANDANTE CON MOTO

Say, ye who bor - row Love's witch - ing_ spell,
Voi, che sa - pe - te che co - sa è a - mor,

11 ANDANTE

My sad heart_ now re - cov - ers,
Mi sen - to dal con - ten - to,

Joy then at last_ is_ mine._
pie - no di gio - ja il cor._

12 ALLEGRO

Shall I in sor - row lang - uish For
Ve - drò mentr' io so - spi - ro, Fe -

bliss her heart de - nies me?
li - ce un ser - vo mi - o!

13 ANDANTINO

Flown for - e - ver love's sun - ny splen - dor,
Do - ve so - no i bei mo - men - ti,

14 ALLEGRETTO

"When the wes-tern breeze is dy-ing,
"Che so a- ve ze- fi- ret- to,

15 MODERATO

Ye men, will no - thing school ye,
A- pri- te un po' quegl' oc- chi,

Shall wo-men e - ver fool ye?
Uo- mi- ni in cau- ti e scioc- chi,

16 ANDANTE

Oh come, my heart's de-light, where love in - vites thee,
Deh vie- ni, non tar- dar, o gio- ja bel- la.

17 ANDANTE

Dear an - gel, for- give me, for - give, I im - plore thee!
Con- tes- sa, per- do- no, per- do- no, per- do- no!

PAGLIACCI

1 VIVACE

f

2 LARGO

p   *stentate*

344

Pagliacci

3 ANDANTE CANTABILE

p

4 MISTERIOSO

p

5 VIVO

Dear la - dies and gen - tle - men, our
Ve - ni - te, o - no - ra - te - ci, si -

show__ will be giv - en
gno - ri e si - gno - re!

6 ADAGIO MOLTO

f Jokes like that one, I'm warn - ing you,__
Un tal gio - co, cre - de - te - mi,__

7 ANDANTINO GRAZIOSO

Ding dong, 'tis the ves - per bell, come girls, come a -
Din, Don, suo - na ve - spe - ro, ra - gaz - ze e gar -

long!__ Ding dong!__
zon,__ Din, don!__

8 VIVACE

On - ward they fly__ to lands be -
Van - no lag - giù__ ver - so un pa -

345

yond   our   know - ing,
e - se   stra - no

ADAGIO

On   with   your   cos - tume   and   your
Ves - ti   la   giu - ba   e   la

grease - paint   and   pow - der.
fac - cia in - fa - ri - na.

ALLEGRETTO

O____ Co - lum - bine, your   faith - ful Har - le - quin is
O____ Co - lum - bi - na, il   te - ne - ro fi - do Ar - lec-

near,   O - pen   and   hear!
chin   è a   te   vi - cin!

CANTABILE ESPRESSIVO

I   hoped,   ah!   I   was   blind - ed   in -
Spe - rai,   tan - to il   de - li - rio ac - ce-

deed   in   my   mad - ness.
ca - to   m'a - ve - a.

RIGOLETTO

1 ANDANTE SOSTENUTO

2 ANDANTE SOSTENUTO
ff

3 ALLEGRO CON BRIO
8va
ff

4 ALLEGRO CON BRIO
8va
mf

5 ALLEGRO CON BRIO
mf

6 ALLEGRETTO *con eleganza*
p

In my heart all_____ are e - qual - ly
Que sta o quel - la_____ per me pa - ri -

cher - ish'd Ev' ry thought of ex - clu - sion____
so - no a quant' al - tre d'in - tor - no,____

347

with - in me I smo - ther.
d'in - tor - no mi ve - do.

7 ANDANTE MOSSO
pp

8 ANDANTE CON ESPRESSIONE
p Ah, why re - call in mi - se - ry?
Deh non par - la - re al mi - se - ro?

9 ANDANTE
Stay, oh say no more, oh say no more! my
Oh quan - to do - lor! quan - to do - lor! che

words have wa - ken'd thy hid - den fount of tears!
spre - me - re si a - ma - ro pian - to puo?

10 MODERATO ASSAI
pp Ah! watch, I pray thee, o'er this flo - wer, In its
Ah! ve - glia don - na, ques - to fio - re che a te

in - no - cence con - fid - ed to thy truth, by heav - en
pu - ro con - fi - da - i, Ve - glia at - ten - ta, e non sia

dim. *pp*

guid - ed Do thou guard it ev - er more.
ma - i che s'of - fu - schi il suo can - dor.

348

11 ANDANTINO CANTABILE

Sun of the soul, a di - vine in - spi - ra - tion,
E il sol dell' a - ni - ma, la vi - ta è a - mo - re,

12 ALLEGRO MODERATO *dolcissimo*

Carv'd u - pon my in - most heart Is that
Ca - ro no - me che il mio cor fes - ti

name for ev - er - more;
pri - mo pal - pi - tar,

13 ADAGIO DOLCE

p CANTABILE

Art thou weep - ing in lone - li - ness?
Par - mi ve - der le la - gri - me

14 ALLEGRO ASSAI MODERATO

We roam'd a - bout, by fall - ing night pro - tect - ed,
Scor - ren - do u - ni - ti re - mo - ta vi - a

15 ALLEGRO

DECISO

Now hope re - newed is glow - ing, with - a
Pos - sen - te a - mor mi chia - ma, vo -

in my heart, o'er - flow - ing;
lar io deg - gio a le - i;

16 ALLEGRO ASSAI MODERATO

p

349

17 ANDANTE MOSSO AGITATO

Race of court-iers, vile rab-ble de-test-ed!
Cor-ti-gia-ni, vil raz-za dan-na-ta!

18 ANDANTINO

On ev'-ry fes-tal morn-ing,
Tut-te le fes-te al tem-pio

near to the ho-ly al-tar,
men-tre pre-ga-va Id-di-o,

19 ALLEGRO VIVO

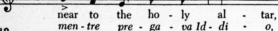

Yes, my__ ven-geance__ fierce hath__ doom'd thee
Si, ven-det-ta,__ tre-men-da__ ven-det-ta

20 ALLEGRETTO CON BRIO

Plume in the sum-mer wind way-ward-ly play-ing,
La don-na è mo-bi-le qual piu-ma al ven-to,

21 ANDANTE

Fair-est daugh-ter of the gra-ces,
Bel-la fi-glia dell' a-mo-re,

22 ANDANTE
Maddalena

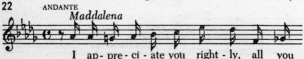

I ap-pre-ci-ate you right-ly, all you
Ah! ah! ri-do ben di co-re, chè tai

350

Gilda

say is just to flat-ter.Ah!___ to___ speak of
ba - je co-stan po-co;Ah!___ co-si___ par-

love thus light-ly!
lar___ d'a - mo-re!

23 ANDANTE

pp From yon-der sky with the blest an-gels fly-ing,
Las-sù, in cie - lo, vi-ci-na al-la ma-dre,

THE VALKYRIE

1 STÜRMISCH

f

2 STÜRMISCH

ff

3 STÜRMISCH

fp *p*

4 ETWAS BELEBT

p

11 LANGSAM

piu f — *f* — *p*

12 MÄSSIG BEWEGT

Win - ter storms have waned in the moon of May,
Win - ter - stür - me wi - chen dem Won-ne-mond,

13 MÄSSIG BEWEGT

O sweet - est en - chant - ment! Wo-man most blest!
O süs - ses - te Won-ne! Se - lig-stes Weib!

14 SEHR SCHNELL

Ho - li - est love's most high-est need
Hei - lig - ster Min - ne höch - ste Noth

15 HEFTIG

ff

16 HEFTIG

Ho - jo - to - ho!__ ho - jo - to - ho!__ hei - a -

ha! — hei - a - ha! —

17 SEHR BEWEGT

ff — *dim.* — *p*

18 LANGSAM

ff *dim.* *p*

19 SEHR FEIRLICH UND GEMESSEN

pp *pp*

20 SEHR FEIRLICH UND GEMESSEN

pp *pp* *lunga*

21 SEHR LEBHAFT UND SCHNELL

p

22 DRANGEND

ff Oh high - - est of won - ders!
O hehr - - stes Wun - der!

23 ETWAS LANGSAM

24 ETWAS LANGSAM

25 LEBHAFT

26 *8va*

MÄSSIG BEWEGT

TANNHÄUSER

Come to these bow — — ers

Naht euch dem Stran — — de!

8 ALLEGRO

Go forth, thou mad-man! There seek thy joy!
Zieh' hin, Be-thör-ter! su-che dein Heil!

9 MODERATO

To Thee, Oh Lord, my steps I bend!
Zu dir wall' ich, mein Herr und Gott!

10 ALLEGRO

Ah, dost thou smile once more up-on me,
Ha, jetzt er-ken-ne ich sie wie-der,

Thou ra-diant world____ that I had lost.
die schö-ne Welt,____ der ich ent-rückt.

11 ALLEGRO

Oh hall of Song,____ I give thee greet-ing!
Dich, theu-re Hal-le, grüss' ich wie-der!

12 ALLEGRO

p

12a ALLEGRO

p

13 ADAGIO

I pray for him, spare him, oh I im-plore ye!
Ich fleh' für ihn, ich fle-he für sein Le-ben!

357

TOSCA

358

4 ALLEGRETTO GRAZIOSO

5 PIU LENTO

Strange har - mo - ny of con - trasts
Re - con - di - ta ar - mo - ni - a,

Thus de - li - cious - ly blend - ing!
di bel - lez - ze di - ver - se!

6 ANDANTE SOSTENUTO

pp dolciss. e con tutta l'espressione

7 ALLEGRO MODERATO

Do you not long for our cot - tage se -
Non la so - spi - ri la no - stra ca -
rit.

clu - ded From which all cares and vex - a - tions
set - ta che tut - ta a - sco - sa nel ver -
a tempo

are ex - clu - ded?
de ci a - spet - ta?

8 ANDANTE MODERATO   ANDANTE MOSSO *Tosca*
Cavaradossi.

Jea - lous   dar - ling! Yes, I   feel that I__ tor-
Mia ge - lo - sa! Si, lo sen - to…ti tor-

ment thee with - out   rea - son!
men - to   sen - za   po - sa.

9 TEMPO DI GAVOTTE

p molto moderato

10 ALLEGRO MODERATO *sensibile*

p

11 ANDANTE SOSTENUTO

Heav'n - ward a - scends our ho - ly__ song__ of praise,
Sa - le a - scen - de l'u - man__ can - ti - co,

12 ANDANTE MODERATO *con galanteria*

Now let us have a friend - ly talk to - ge - ther.
Ed or fra noi par - liam da buo - ni a - mi - ci.

13 ALLEGRO CONCITATO

Thou spi - rit of   ven - geance, a - wake!
L'al - ba   vin - di - ce ap - par

Let ty - rants and myr - mi - dons quake!
che fa   gli em - pi tre - mar!

LA TRAVIATA

4 ALLEGRETTO

p You lov— ers of laugh-ter and life__ and
Li - bia - mo, li - bia - mo ne' lie - ti

love— li - ness, Emp— ty__ your life - giv - ing glass- es!
ca— li - ci, che la - bel - lez - za__ in - fio - ra!

5 ANDANTINO

p The day I met you, O bless- ed day,
Un di fe - li - ce, e - te - re - a

When first you came be - fore_____ me,
mi ba - le - na - ste in - nan - - - te,

6 ANDANTINO

mf Dreamed of a love that would fill__ my life for me, *p*
Di quel - l'a - mor, quel - l'a - mor ch'è pal - pi - to

7 ANDANTINO

p Ah, can it be that this is he
Ah, for - s'è lui che l'a - ni - ma

Of whom my heart fore - told me,
so - lin - ga ne' tu - mul - ti,

of whom my heart fore - warned me.
so - lin - ga ne' tu - mul - ti,

362

8 ALLEGRO BRILLANTE

mf

Ev - er free to take___ my chanc - es in the
Sem - pre li - be - ra___ deg - g'i - o fol - leg-

game of fol - ly and pleas ure!
gia - re di gio - ja in gio - ja!

9 ANDANTE

p

Fe - ver'd and wild my dream of youth,
De' miei bol - len - ti spi - ri - ti

no star on high to guide___ me,
il gio - va - ni - le ar - do - re

10 ALLEGRO MODERATO

I have a daugh - ter dear to me,
Pu - ra sic - co - me un an - ge - lo,

Pure as an an - gel from a - bove,
Id - dio me diè u - na fi - glia;

11 ANDANTINO

Speak to your bless - ed child, Say, when you
Di - te al - la gio - vi - ne si bel - la e

see___ her,
pu - ra

12 ANDANTE

p

In Pro - vence the south - ern sea soft - ly
Di Pro - ven - za il mar, il suol chi dal

cools the sun - lit shore, O the peace - ful
cor ti can - cel - lò? chi dal cor ti

sun - lit shore of Pro - vence be -side the sea!
can - cel - lò di Pro - ven - za il mar, il suol?

13 ALLEGRO

Why, ah, why,___ came I hith - er? For -
Ah, per - chè___ ven - ni in - cau - ta? Pie -

sake me not, Heav - en for - sake me not!
tà, gran Dio, pie - tà, gran Dio di me!

14 LARGO

p

Oh Al - fred, Al - fred, a - las, thou know'st not
Al - fre - do, Al - fre - do, di que - sto co - re

How true and ten - der - ly this heart hath lov'd thee!
non puoi com - pren - de - re tut - to l'a - mo - re!

15 ANDANTE

pp

TRISTAN AND ISOLDE

3 LANGSAM UND SCHMACHTEND

4 LANGSAM UND SCHMACHTEND

5 BELEBEND

6 MÄSSIG LANGSAM

The   west wind wild   blows home - ward now
Frisch weht der Wind   der   Hei - mat zu.

7 LEBHAFT

To lay a   tax on   Cor - nish backs Sir
Herr Mo- rold zog zu   Mee - re— her, in

Mo - rold once was   fer - ried
Korn - wall Zins   zu   ha - ben

8 SEHR MÄSSIG

Then there dawned— in my heart a   ten - der night.
da   er - däm - mer - te mild er - hab'- ner Macht

So might we die as ne'er___ to part

So stür - ben wir, um un - ge - trennt

IL TROVATORE

1. ALLEGRETTO *con mistero*

Swar - thy and threat - en - ing, a___ Gip - sy wo - man
Ab - biet - ta zin - ga - ra, fo - sca ve - gliar - da!

2. ANDANTE

No star shone in the heav'n-ly___ vault, In si - lence all was sleep - ing:
Ta - cea la not - te pla - ci - da e bel - la in ciel se - re - no;

3. ALLEGRO GIUSTO

The love my heart o'er - flow - - - ing
Di ta - le a-mor che dir - - - si

369

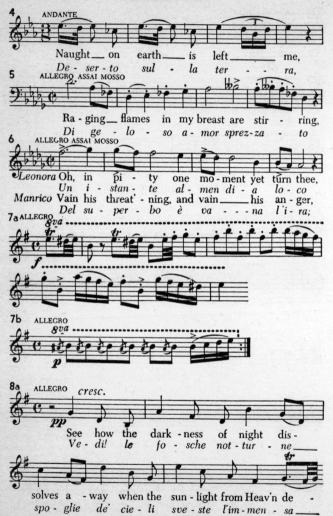

4 ANDANTE

Naught___ on earth___ is left___ me,
De - ser - to sul - la ter - - ra,

5 ALLEGRO ASSAI MOSSO

Ra - ging___ flames in my breast are stir - - ring,
Di ge - lo - so a - mor sprez - za - to

6 ALLEGRO ASSAI MOSSO

Leonora Oh, in pi - ty one mo - ment yet turn thee,
Manrico Vain his threat' - ning, and vain___ his an - ger,
Un i - stan - te al - men di a - lo - co
Del su - per - bo è va - - na l'i - ra;

7a ALLEGRO

7b ALLEGRO

8a ALLEGRO cresc.

See how the dark - ness of night dis -
Ve - di! le fo - sche not - tur - ne___

solves a - way when the sun - light from Heav'n de -
spo - glie de' cie - li sve - ste l'im - men - sa___

scend - eth;
vol - ta:

8b ALLEGRO

f Who cheers the days ___ of the rov - ing ___ Gip-sy?
Chi del gi - ta - no i gior - ni ab-bel-la?

9 ALLEGRETTO

Fierce flames are soar - - - ing,
Stri - de la vam - - - pa!

10 ANDANTE MOSSO

p In chains to her doom they dragg'd her,
Con - dot - ta el - l'e - ra in cep - pi

11 ALLEGRO

I as - sault - ed, he feeb - ly de - fend - ed,
Mal reg - gen - do al - l'a - spro as - sal - to,

12 LARGO CANTABILE

In the light of her sweet glan - ces,
Il ba - len del suo sor - ri - so

13 ALLEGRO ASSAI MOSSO *un poco meno*

The pas - sion that in - spires ___ me
Per me o - ra fa - ta - - le,

14 ANDANTE MOSSO *con tutta forza di sentimento*

Can I ___ be - lieve the vis - ion blest?
E deg - gio e pos - so cre - der - lo? ___

15 ALLEGRO MODERATO MAESTOSO *grandioso*

Cla - rions blow - ing and bu - gles re-sound-ing Call us
Squil - li, e - cheg - gi la trom - ba guer-rie - ra, chiam i al-

forth to the fight and to glo - - ry;
lar - mi, al - la pu - gna, al - l'as - sal - - to:

16 ALLEGRO

Oh! ty - rants, loose these cru - el bonds that
Deh! ral - len - ta - te o bar - ba - ri, le a -

griev - ous - ly con - fine me!
cer - be mie ri - tor - te!

17 ADAGIO CANTABILE *con espressione*

Oh, come let links e - ter - nal bind the
Ah, si, ben mio, coll' - es - se - re io

vows we fond - ly plight - ed;
tuo, tu mia con - sor - te,

18 ALLEGRO

Trem - ble, ye ty - - rants. I will chas - tise___ ye!
Di quel - la pi - ra l'or - ren - do fo - co

19 ADAGIO *con espressione*

Love, fly on ro - sy pin - ions,
D'a - mor sull' a - li ro - se - e

20 ANDANTE

a mezza voce

Mi - se - re - re a - gain the wail of sor - row,
Mi - se - re - re d'un al-ma già vi - ci - na

For him whose eyes shall ne'er be-hold the mor - row!
al - la par - ten-sa che non ha ri - tor - no;

21 ANDANTE *assai sost.*

What voic - es of ter - ror!
Quel suon, quel - le pre - ci

22 ANDANTE *assai sost.*

Ah! send thy beams, Au - ro - ra,
Ah! che la mor-te o-gno - ra

23 ANDANTINO

Yes, I will rest, for my soul is wear - y,
Si la stan-chez-za m'op - pri - me, o fi - glio.

24 ANDANTINO
a mezza voce

Sleep, oh my mo -ther, and may heav -en grant thee
Ri - po-sa, o ma - dre; Id - di - o con - ce - da

25 ANDANTINO

Home to our moun - tains
Ai no - stri mon - ti

ABOUT THE AUTHORS

HENRY W. SIMON received his musical training privately, his literary training at Columbia and Oxford Universities. For twenty years he taught literature and music, the last ten of them at Columbia. He was music critic on the newspaper PM from 1940 to 1945, serving one term as Chairman of the New York Music Critics Circle. At present he is music editor for Simon and Schuster, who published his *A Treasury of Grand Opera*.

ABRAHAM VEINUS, formerly research director for RCA-Victor, received his graduate training in musicology at Cornell and Columbia Universities, holding the Clarence Barker Fellowship at Columbia. He is the author of *The Concerto* (Doubleday) and *The Victor Book of Concertos* (Simon and Schuster) and at present is Associate Professor of Music at Syracuse University.